D0453644

On the Nature of Things

LUCRETIUS

ON THE NATURE
OF THINGS

➼➼❈❈

Translated by
FRANK O. COPLEY

W · W · NORTON & COMPANY

New York · London

For information about special discounts for bulk purchases, please contact
W. W. Norton Special Sales at specialsales@wwnorton.com or 800-233-4830

Manufacturing by: Courier Westford
Production manager: Louise Mattarelliano

Library of Congress Cataloging-in-Publication Data

Lucretius Carus, Titus.
[De rerum natura. English]
On the nature of things / Lucretius ; translated by Frank O. Copley.
p. cm.
Includes bibliographical references.
ISBN 978-0-393-34136-2 (pbk.)
1. Didactic poetry, Latin—Translations into English. 2. Philosophy,
Ancient—Poetry. I. Copley, Frank Olin. II. Title. III. Title: Nature of things.
PA6483.E5C6 2011
187—dc22

2011017650

W. W. Norton & Company, Inc., 500 Fifth Avenue, New York, N.Y. 10110
www.wwnorton.com

W. W. Norton & Company Ltd., Castle House, 75/76 Wells Street, London W1T 3QT

1 2 3 4 5 6 7 8 9 0

Contents

Introduction

Lucretius was a poet, not a philosopher, and it is as the work of a poet that his poem *De Rerum Natura* ("The Nature of Things") must be read. The poem as it stands is clearly unfinished; it contains repeated and obviously misplaced lines and passages; its argument, for lack of the final hand of organization, is frequently unclear and confusing. But its overall proportions are poetically and artistically sound, its imagery superb, and its word choice and word manipulation as sensitive as any displayed by any of the poets of antiquity. And while Vergil was later to depict, with wonderful patience and understanding, the glory and the joy, the pathos and the tragedy that are the life of man, Lucretius saw into the hearts of individual men as they faced the immediacies of their lives. Lucretius' analysis of why men think and act as they do, why they are affected as they are by the experiences of their lives, day by day, is not always entirely accurate or free from preconception; it is easy enough, from the vantage point of modern psychology, to show where Lucretius erred in his analysis of human thought and behavior. But his sympathy and understanding not of man, but of *this* man and *that* man, not of mankind, but of people, was hardly surpassed in antiquity, and perhaps has never been equaled.

Lucretius (Titus Lucretius Carus) was about ten years younger than Cicero and perhaps ten years older than the lyric poet Catullus. With them, he lived through the fascinating but terrifying years that marked the end of the Roman republic; he must have witnessed Cicero's rise to power, the conspiracy of Catiline, and Julius Caesar's ascendancy. He must have observed the moral breakdown that accompanied the dissolution of old ways as Romans struggled to rise from institutions adequate for a small city-state to standards and institutions that they hoped would be adequate for the governing of a world empire. He most certainly must have been in the middle of the intellectual ferment that brought forth, on the one hand, Cicero's meticulous studies of philosophy and rhetoric and, on the other, the lively, unrestrained, and imaginative poetry of the New Poets, chief of whom was Catullus.

What his position was with relation to the New Poets cannot now be determined; traditionally, it has been asserted that he was a "conservative," who by definition would have had little sympathy with the rebellious innovations of Catullus and his friends. The fact remains, however, that Lucretius is no less venturesome than they, for he was bold enough to select as his subject a topic never before attempted in Latin literature, to attempt to mold that subject into an epic with all nature as its heroine, to search the Latin language over and over again for a vocabulary adequate to his needs, and to range all over the world of the visible and the imaginary to find appropriate illustrative material for his poem.

Of Lucretius himself very little is known. The chronicler Jerome reports that he was born in the year 95 and died in 52 B.C., but since he adds that the poet died at the age of forty-four, he has either got the length of the poet's life wrong or has erred in reporting the date of his birth or of his death. It is certain only that he was born somewhere in the mid-nineties B.C., and died some time after the mid-fifties, and was forty, or thereabouts, when he died. Jerome has nothing whatever to say about his family; he reports only that the poet was driven mad by a "love potion," that in the intervals of his insanity he wrote "books" which were later edited by Cicero, and that he eventually committed suicide. He tells us nothing of the poet's station in life, whether he was of the aristocracy, as his illustrious name would suggest, or whether he was a freedman or perhaps the merest slave; nor have we any reliable evidence on these points from any other source. Lucretius dedicates his poem to Memmius, generally identified as Gaius Memmius, praetor in 58 B.C. and governor of Bithynia in 57. This would make him identical with the Memmius who, to the poet Catullus, was the embodiment of all evil, yet Lucretius always speaks of Memmius with respect and affection.

As for Jerome's assertion that Lucretius was driven mad by a love potion, we may accept it or not as we choose. Love potions were common enough in antiquity—supposedly aphrodisiac potions administered, whether openly or secretly, to unresponsive husbands and lovers by their wives or mistresses, or *vice versa*. That such concoctions might have produced digestive upsets or have been downright poisonous is not at all unlikely, since the ancient world had a very sketchy understanding of toxicity and hygiene, but that a potion would drive a man insane seems a bit farfetched.

Far more interesting is Jerome's reference to Cicero's having "edited" the "books" that Lucretius wrote. On the face of it, this is a strange assertion, partly because Cicero himself, who in his *Letters* is quite revelatory of the events of his life, makes no mention of any such activity, and partly because, of all the philosophies of antiquity, Epicureanism—the basis of Lucretius' poem—was the one with which Cicero had the least patience and which he least bothered to understand.

Our puzzlement in the matter is further increased by a reference to Lucretius in one of Cicero's letters; writing to his brother Quintus, he remarks, "The poems [*sic*] of Lucretius are just as you describe them; they show many flashes of genius and yet evince considerable artistic skill." To Cicero, obviously, genius and skill are two quite separate things; genius would presumably create a compelling and intrinsically interesting body of ideas, while skill would shape these ideas artfully and neatly into an esthetically pleasing composition. Obviously a poet might have one or the other of these qualities, or have them in varying degrees; the thing that struck Cicero about Lucretius was that the veritable flood of ideas that he presents might easily have been more than ordinary poetic skill could handle, yet this poet had managed to handle them in an esthetically pleasing way.

As for the "editing" of the "books," the problem remains unsolved to this day. That Cicero had read *a* work by *a* Lucretius is patent; it is also probable that the work was the work of our Lucretius, and was in fact his poem *De Rerum Natura*. We know of no other Lucretius of the period whose "books" Cicero might have read and commented on in this manner, nor do we know of any other work that our Lucretius produced. We do not even know what Jerome meant by "editing" (*emendavit*). That Cicero should have made an annotated edition of the poem seems, on the face of it, quite unlikely; that he might have proofread the manuscript of the poem after the poet's death remains a possibility. The suggestion has been made that the "Cicero" referred to by Jerome was not the famous Marcus but his more obscure brother Quintus; this too remains a possibility, although it would be strange if Jerome, using the single name "Cicero," had meant his readers to think of anyone other than Marcus.

In sum, all of the questions raised by Jerome's account remain, and probably will continue to remain, unsettled. Fortunately for our comprehension and enjoyment of Lucretius's poem, neither Jerome's account nor any other can tell us anything of significance about the poem itself. Like all good poems, it is an independent, self-contained work of art, written for our instruction and delight by one of Rome's most original poetic geniuses.

II

The Philosophy of Epicurus (342–270 B.C.)

It must have been apostolic fervor that led Lucretius to choose Epicureanism as the subject for his poem; only an immeasurable enthusiasm and a profound conviction that in this philosophy lay the salvation of man could have led a poet to attempt to embody in verse so unlikely and intractable a subject. Epicureanism was a philosophy that brought peace and quiet rather than inspiration and exhilaration; based on a theory of the exclusive validity of sense perception and on an ethical doctrine that pleasure was the criterion of the good, it lent

itself not only to a dull and flat dialectic but also to gross misinterpreta-
tion. Although, in the Hellenistic period and later in the Roman, it
was the second of the two great philosophies (the first was Stoicism),
yet it trailed far behind its rival and gained relatively few adherents,
these chiefly among poets, philosophers, and others of a contempla-
tive rather than an active disposition.

Starting with the question "How do we get our knowledge?"
Epicurus concludes that we get it through the senses; sensation, he
declared, is the only reliable source of knowledge, and consequently
the only source of truth. From this starting point, the philosophy
proceeds with very nearly relentless logic to explain every phe-
nomenon—and the correct word is "every"—of which the ancient
world was aware. In every instance in which sensation gives us direct
evidence, we are required to accept that evidence as truth; in instances
in which sensation proves unable to give direct evidence, because our
senses are too limited to encompass them, we are required to accept as
valid only those theories that do not contradict such evidence as the
senses can and do give us. And in declaring true every theory that does
not contravene the evidence of the senses, Epicurus does not blink the
fact that the philosopher may arrive at more than one explanation for
a given phenomenon—in some cases, even at explanations that are
mutually exclusive or contradictory. They must all be accepted as
true. One of them must apply in this world of ours; it does not much
matter which one. The others will find application in some other
world out in the endless reaches of an infinitely varied universe. Nor
did Epicurus shrink from the fact that our senses at times seem to give
us false information; patently, we may misjudge the size or color or
shape of a given object, especially if we should view it from a distance.
But, says Epicurus, in these cases it is not the senses that are at fault.
The data they transmit to the mind are correct; it is the mind that is in
error, for it has misjudged the information correctly supplied to it by
the senses.

Our senses show us a material world, and therefore we conclude
that matter is the sole reality; all being is material being. Our senses
also show us that matter moves, but nothing can move unless it has
space in which to move. The second reality, therefore, that our senses
demonstrate to us is the existence of empty space, or void. If our
universe were completely full of matter, nothing could move, for
everything that attempted to move would find its movement instantly
stopped by some other thing. Movement is conceivable only if some-
where in the system there is empty space into which, so to speak, some
bits of matter may be pushed aside to enable other bits of matter to
move.

Granted the validity of this basic statement of the nature of being,
that it includes two mutually exclusive opposites, matter and void,
how are we to describe matter itself? The direct evidence of the senses

shows us an infinite variety of forms of matter, but also shows us that every one of these forms, however hard and durable it may appear to be, sooner or later suffers change and destruction. We conclude, therefore, that these sensible forms of matter cannot be ultimate or basic, for if they were, all being would long since have crumbled into nothing.

Here we must depart from the immediate evidence of the senses and resort to theory. What form must matter have if it is to account, not only for all the sensible forms, but also for their movement and their continuing existence? Epicurus found his answer to this question in the theories of Democritus (*c.* 460–*c.* 370 B.C.), who had declared that the basic form of matter was the atom, an indivisible, indestructible, uncreatable particle having no specific properties other than size, shape, and weight. Atoms are far too small in themselves to be apprehended by the senses, but they are the only form of matter that can adequately account for all the forms that the senses can apprehend.

Everything that we see can be adequately explained as an aggregate or combination of atoms, provided only that we posit two further things about them; first, that there are many different kinds of atoms, that is to say, they are not all of the same size or shape; and second, that they are infinite in number, for if they were not, they would long since have piled up in some corner of the universe, and our world would not be as we see it is. As a corollary, it must be asserted that the number of kinds of atoms is limited, for obviously, if it were not, some atoms would be big enough for the senses to apprehend, but we see that this is not the case. There is therefore a finite number of *kinds* of atoms, but of each kind there is an infinite number. No atom is large enough to be seen; conversely, no atom is so small as to have no dimensions at all. Of every size and shape of atom, from those with "least dimensions" to those lying just beyond the reach of the senses, there is an infinite number.

If the number of atoms is infinite, it follows that void, empty space, must be infinite in extent, for if space were finite, the infinite atoms would long since have filled it up.

The primary characteristic of the atom is that it is indivisible; this is, in fact, precisely what its Greek name *atomos* means. But if it is indivisible, it is also indestructible, for destruction is merely the logical extension of division. But if the atom cannot be destroyed, it follows that it also cannot be created, for it has no parts out of which it might be put together. From this it follows that time, like matter and void, is infinite; the universe, in all its aspects and ramifications, has always existed; there was no beginning, and there will be no end.

The persistent problem that had disturbed the atomists prior to Epicurus was that of the way in which atoms might join to create the things which our senses apprehend. It was not difficult to see how various kinds of things could be built of various shapes and sizes of atoms, combined in different patterns and clinging together in those patterns until some force stronger than the bonds that held them together broke up the compounds and sent the individual atoms once more out into the void. The problem was to determine the mechanism by which in the first instance atoms came together to build things. That, once joined, they would cling together by inherent powers of cohesion was patent from the observable fact that such combinations do indeed exist. The problem was to determine how atoms came close enough together so that inherent cohesive forces might attract and bind them into stable, although not permanent, compounds.

Democritus had taught that the natural motion of the atom is "downward." But if all atoms move only in downward paths paralleling each other, how could they meet to form the compounds that make up sensible things? Epicurus' answer to this problem was perhaps his one great stroke of genius; he theorized that, at times not predictable and for no assignable reason, the atom must swerve from its downward path. But no sooner has it swerved than it strikes its neighbor atom and drives it also from its downward path; this strikes another, and another, and another, and so on, until the universe, instead of being a kind of "rainfall" of atoms, comes more closely to resemble an atomic whirlwind, with atoms striking against each other and clinging or springing back, moving now one way, now another, driven partly by their own weight, partly by the impulses given them by other atoms—a vast confusion, in which only the law of chance governs the formation of specific atomic compounds.

Thus, the inherent power of the atom to move by its own weight plus its equally inherent power to swerve from its normal path, plus its power to cling together with other atoms both like and unlike itself, plus the law of chance, can and do account, of and by themselves, without the intervention of any outside force or guiding intelligence, for every form of being that can be observed by one or another of our senses. The disciplined observation of the sensible world will reveal to us with accuracy and truth the nature of every pehnomenon that occurs or may occur anywhere in the universe.

What then of the being that we like to think of as nonmaterial, spiritual, and the like? What of that mysterious something we call the soul? To Epicurus, nonmaterial being and the spiritual were merely delusions; we only deceive ourselves if we imagine that there is any kind of being other than material. As for the soul, Epicurus cheerfully admitted its existence, but asserted that since it did exist, it must be material. It too is made up of atoms, infinitesimally small, delicate, and highly mobile, but atoms nonetheless. In other words, the soul is a *thing* like every other *thing*; it is contained within the body as within a vessel. It guides and directs the activities of the body and of itself; it receives and interprets sense impressions and, in sum, is the one atomic compound that gives the power of life. Intimately connected with the body, as it must be if it is to carry out its various functions, delicate and tenuous, it cannot exist outside the body, and when the body dies, the soul of necessity dies with it.

Death dissolves the atomic compounds that make up the body, and disperses its component atoms; in like fashion death also dissolves the compound that is the soul, and its atoms too are dispersed in exactly similar fashion. The soul then is not immortal; its existence terminates with the termination of the body, and it does not live on in any form, either to enjoy eternal happiness or to face punishment for the sins of which it has been guilty during its connection with the body. Death is nonexistence, nothing, a total blank. Lucretius likes to compare it with the state of our "selves" before we were born: that is for us a total blank; so will it be for us after death. The atoms of body and soul, being indestructible, of course continue to exist, but the compound they had formed, which was "you" and "I," has been forever dissolved. To fear death, then, is foolish, since death is the final and complete annihilation of personal identity, the ultimate release from anxiety and pain.

To Epicurus, the physical system was only of secondary interest; far more interesting to him was the ethical system which was based on the physics. As with the physics, Epicurus begins his search for a valid ethical system by relying on observation. As we examine the behavior of all forms of living creatures, we observe that they seek out what is pleasant and avoid what is painful. Since this is natural, instinctive behavior, and does not require to be taught, it must be derived from the atomic nature of being itself; living creatures behave this way because their structure, in and of itself, compels them to do so.

From this theory Epicurus derived the principle that pleasure is the criterion of good, and pain of evil. Pleasure, moreover, is the natural and normal state of being, the product of properly balanced and integrated atomic structure; pain results from loss of balance and structural harmony. From this it is clear that pleasure is properly defined as the absence of pain and, as a negative and hence an absolute, admits of no degrees. Pleasure demands from us not so much positive as negative acts: we need only avoid pain; we do not have deliberately to seek out pleasure. The symbol of Epicurean pleasure is the "picnic," a group of relaxed, untroubled people, sitting on the soft grass in the shade of a tree near a running stream, enjoying the mere aspect of nature, and caring for their creature needs with the simplest of food and drink.

It should be noted, however, that Epicurus is entirely consistent in his doctrine of pleasure. *All* that is pleasant is good, and this includes the often suspect "pleasures of the flesh": food, drink, and sex. It was probably at this point that the ancient world, and particularly the

Roman, with its stern moral code, began to view Epicureanism with uneasiness and suspicion. To a people whose moral code demanded nothing so much as the control of the appetites, the doctrine that indulgence of those appetites was good sounded suspiciously like an invitation to loose living. They were wrong, of course, for they rarely troubled to follow Epicurus' argument to its end. If they had, they would have noticed that pleasure, being an absolute, will be destroyed if it is accompanied or followed by pain, even in the smallest degree. Pleasure, which is a good, is turned to evil on the instant that the pleasurable activity ceases to be such and becomes painful. Nothing is quite so susceptible of this error as the pleasures of the flesh; good in themselves, if they go beyond the proper limit, they invariably lead to pain, physical or psychological. While, then, they are not to be avoided, they are to be kept under the strictest of controls.

In point of fact, Epicurus thought it wiser to eschew physical pleasures, simply because they were so susceptible of passing over into the realm of pain, and thus of becoming evil. Searching for undeniably pleasurable activities not susceptible to such transmogrification, Epicurus concluded that the intellectual pleasures were to be preferred, and that the life was most likely to be pleasant, and therefore good, which kept all the appetites under strict control. The Epicureans, in fact, far from being the band of pleasure-seekers that both ancient and modern popular thought have made of them, were quietists, who preferred above all things to be allowed to withdraw into the life of study and companionship.

By the proponents of any such doctrine of pleasure and pain, of good and evil, the stress and strain of public activity, the life of the soldier and of the statesman, were bound to be viewed with distrust. While pleasure could be derived from these activities, there were scarcely any so susceptible of turning into pain. Disillusionment, thwarted ambition, treachery, the fickleness of popular favor—all these could turn the happy politician (if ever there were such) into a sick and embittered individual, full of guilt, rancor, and ill will. Epicurus recognized the necessity of government and its activities, and the need for participation in them on the part of loyal citizens; it was his recommendation, however, that this participation be kept to a minimum, and that wherever possible the Epicurean leave it to others and himself retire into the peace and quiet of his garden. In sum, Epicurus recommended as ideal the simple, not to say austere life, with the appetites disciplined to accept only that degree of carnal pleasure that would lead to the harmony and comfort of physical being; he encouraged his followers to withdraw from the dangerous confusion of public affairs into a life that resembles nothing so much as that of the monastery. It is scarcely strange that a world as given to flamboyant activity as the Roman should have found little to attract it in the philosophy of Epicurus.

This is far from being the whole of the Epicurean philosophy, which was an immensely prolix system. Epicurus himself is said to have written three hundred volumes, and his followers countless more. His disciples studied the works of the Master as if they were a veritable Gospel; they memorized his "Golden Sayings" (κύριαι δόξαι) and devoted themselves almost exclusively to pondering and interpreting his endless treatises. Compared to Stoicism, with its grandiose concept of the Universal Soul, its seemingly noble doctrine of the primacy of virtue, its advocacy of public activity and the life of the statesman and soldier, and its doctrine of self-abnegation and self-control, the quietism and near-asceticism of the Epicureans seemed distinctly unappealing.

Furthermore, the system had serious weaknesses from the point of view of the "orthodox" Roman. Although it was not atheistic, it denied the power and influence of the gods on human life. If the world is the product of nothing but natural forces and natural law, divine intervention is impossible. Epicurus' gods did nothing but exist; if they had any function at all, it was simply to stand as symbols for the perfect peace of Epicurean life. Such a theology was unlikely to attract a people used to the sonorous prayers of priests at the altars of splendid temples, the magnificence of religious processions and ceremonies, and the habit, ingrained from childhood, of viewing the world as subject to the whims of unpredictable, often irresponsible and downright dangerous deities.

Another apparent weakness lay in the ethics itself. Epicurus appeared to have set up a purely mechanistic system, since all activity of every sort seemed to be the automatic result of a given type of atomic structure; a man behaved as he did because he was what he was, and not from choice. But if there were no choice, no free will, what was the sense of having an ethical system at all?

Once again, the critics of Epicurus failed to look far enough, for in spite of all appearances, his system was not mechanistic. Humanity, at any rate, does have free will, and in a most ingenious way Epicurus derived free will from the doctrine of the swerve of the atom, saying in effect that the power to make a deliberate choice of action was inherent in the atom itself, which demonstrated that power by unaccountably swerving from its "normal" path. People then do have free will; they could choose the pleasant as against the painful, the good as against the evil; of their own volition they could choose the path that would lead them to the good and happy life. The Epicureans were neither determinists nor atheists, although they were commonly accused of being both, but to the average ancient their theology was flat, stale, and unprofitable, and their doctrine of free will was too subtle for the Roman taste.

III

Lucretius and Epicurus

This, in very general terms, was the philosophy that Lucretius chose to embody in his poem *De Rerum Natura* ("The Nature of Things"); a strictly orthodox Epicurean, he does not deviate in any appreciable way from the teachings of the Master. Here and there, the emphases appear to be different; Lucretius makes much of the fear of death, in fact attributes most human ills to it. Epicurus laid far less stress on this human phenomenon and its consequences. Lucretius is violent and bitter in his hatred of religion—by which, of course, he meant the standard state cult of his day. He saw it as an ignorant, perverted, and vicious distortion of the world and of man's relation to it; in the end, it was only a source of fear and terror, and as such an evil thing. Epicurus himself took a more tolerant view of the standard cult, and even recommended that his followers go to the temples, say the prayers, and attend the religious ceremonies, not because of any practical benefit to be derived from such activity, but only because he thought it good to contemplate the perfect serenity of deity and to attempt to emulate it in his own life. Finally, Lucretius takes far greater interest, and expends far greater space, on an exposition of the physical system of Epicurus, and spends relatively little time on the ethics; with Epicurus himself, the opposite seems to have been true. In effect, to him, the physics was merely a base for the ethics; with Lucretius, the ethics appears to be scarcely more than an adjunct to the physics.

Lucretius begins his poem with an invocation to the goddess Venus, asking for her aid in the writing of the poem he is composing "for my friend, Memmius." He has often been taken to task by scholarly critics for invoking a goddess and asking for her help when patently, by the Epicurean system, she would have been utterly unable to help him even if she had wanted to. But if Milton, at the beginning of *Paradise Lost,* can invoke the Muse and ask for her aid "to my adventurous song," then Lucretius may be pardoned the impulse of poetic imagination that allowed him to see in Venus, as Milton saw in the Muse, an embodiment of poetic power.

Furthermore, Venus was for Lucretius a symbol. She stands for dynamic and creative nature and also represents the Epicurean ideal of peace, quiet, and contentment. As if to drive this point home, Lucretius opposes Venus to the god Mars, who represents discord, strife, and disharmony. In symbolic fashion, the poet prays that Mars may be overcome by Venus' beauty, and at least for the moment cease "the savage acts of war."

Following this comes Lucretius' tirade against religion, ending with his account of the ugly death of Iphigenia at Aulis; Agamemnon's slaughter of his own child stands as a symbol of the evil that religion prompts. For true knowledge, humanity should turn away from the perversions and distortions of religion to the actuality of the world, its outer appearance and its inward laws.

The rest of Book I is devoted to the basic theory of the atoms. Three principles are enunciated: first, that matter cannot be created out of nothing; second, that matter cannot be destroyed or dissolved into nothing; and finally, that change is death. After this the poet attacks rival theories of the nature of being, disposing of each of them by showing that they all posit a "basic" substance that is not basic because it is subject to change.

Book II begins with a prologue on the blessings of philosophy and an appeal to humanity to free itself from blindness and to realize that only pleasure—that is, peace and harmony of mind and body—is good and worth seeking.

The largest part of the book is concerned with the atom and its nature, which are investigated in detail and explained in terms of Epicurean theory. Similarly, the void and the concept of time are explained in Epicurean terms. Certain necessary distinctions are made, such as the difference between a "property" and an "accident." The doctrine that sensation is the only source of knowledge and truth is reiterated again and again.

The universe knows no limitation of time or space, contains an infinite number of worlds, and as a total entity is never diminished or destroyed. Within it lie individual worlds, each an aggregation of atoms and void, and subject to constant change, whether of growth, diminution, or ultimate destruction. Our world, too, is a compound of atoms and void, limited in the number of atoms it may at any time possess. The atoms in it must be used over and over again; thus the death of one thing becomes necessary for the birth of another. Some few atoms flying in from outer space are added to earth's total; they impinge upon the earth and cling there. However, a far larger number is constantly escaping from the earth and flying out into the void; the net result of atomic activity in the earth is a loss.

Book III opens with praise of Epicurus and a description of the effects of the fear of death. After the prologue, the whole of the book is devoted to dispelling this fear, which to Lucretius is the source of virtually all human ills. Since the soul ceases to exist at death, after death it cannot possibly be subject to suffering in any form; fear of punishment after death is therefore needless and pointless. He shows that the soul is corporeal—that, like the body, it is composed of atoms which differ from those of the body chiefly in being much smaller, smoother, finer, and more mobile. It is divided into two parts; one diffused throughout the body, the other concentrated in the breast. The diffused part receives sense impressions and transmits them to the central mass in the breast, which interprets the nature of the message and determines what the reaction of the individual will be. Lucretius understood that these sense impressions are tactile, caused by the impact upon the soul of material particles.

This soul, Lucretius says, can maintain its identity only so long as it is contained within its vessel, the body. When, at death, the bonds that hold the atoms of the body together are weakened, and the body-atoms begin to fall away from each other, countless channels are opened up through which the soul-atoms make their way out of the body and are dissipated into space. The ultimate result is total dissolution, i.e., death of both soul and body. There is no afterlife.

After a series of proofs of the mortality of the soul Lucretius urges humanity to accept the mortality of the soul as a fact and to realize with the poet himself that the only hell in all the universe is the one that fools create for themselves in this world.

Book IV is concerned with the operation of the mind, the nature of sensation, the mechanics of seeing, hearing, tasting, smelling, and touching. Lucretius shows that in every instance sense-perception is the result of the impact of atoms of the causative agent upon atoms of the mind, and demonstrates that in the end all sensation is a variation of touch, for only by touch (i.e., physical contact) can one material thing make an impact upon another. There is scarcely an imaginable aspect of the mechanics of sensation to which the poet does not turn his attention and for which he fails to find an atomic explanation.

Lucretius now turns to the far more difficult problem of thought. This too must be given an atomic explanation. Thought exists; therefore by Epicurean doctrine it must be atomic. Here he has recourse to the nature of the soul as he had described it in Book III; made of infinitesimally small, highly mobile atoms, it is susceptible of being directly touched and affected by fine films of atoms far too delicate to be apprehended by the coarser senses, and from their impact arise ideas, pictures, concepts, and even invention. For the soul has a latent power not only to receive and interpret impressions but to combine and even to alter them and thus to produce some previously nonexistent concept. Here again, the system gives proof of Epicurus' sagacity, for without this power of the mind to create new concepts (Latin *anticipatio*; Epicurus himself called it πρόληψις —prolepsis, "the forward reach") his system would have had no room for invention or imagination, and humanity would have been left unable to think of anything that had not been thought of before.

These fine films of atoms also account for dreams and visions; in fact, when the mind is at rest and its guard down, so to speak, it is particularly receptive to these ever-present, ever-moving films of atoms. It is thus that we dream of weird, abnormal, impossibly ugly or impossibly beautiful things which, in our waking hours, the "guardian" of the mind would have refused entrance to conscious thought.

The subject of dreams leads Lucretius to think of one of their particular forms, the sexual dream, which causes the boy reaching puberty to ejaculate semen during sleep; he then goes on to discuss at length the whole phenomenon of sex and sexual behavior. The passage is brilliantly written and, considering the level of physiological and psychological knowledge of the poet's day, amazingly accurate.

Book V is concerned with our world—that is to say, with the earth, the sun, the moon, and the other visible celestial phenomena. Lucretius' astronomy must strike us now as fanciful and even amusing. His great lack here was mathematics. His disregard even of the mathematics of his own day—to say nothing of his ignorance of more modern mathematical developments—renders him incapable of understanding even so simple a phenomenon as perspective; and of the size and speed of movement of heavenly bodies he has conceptions scarcely less childish than those of his more orthodox contemporaries.

It is when Lucretius turns to the earth itself, and to a consideration of life in its many forms, that he comes closest to scientific truth. He sees correctly that all living creatures are composed of materials drawn from the earth. He theorizes accurately that plant life preceded animal life but makes the mistake of denying that life on land could have come out of the sea. As for the origin of living organisms themselves, Lucretius reasons back from the ancient theory of spontaneous generation; this he ties in with the endless combining, recombining, and decombining of the atoms in patterns dictated solely by the properties of the atom itself and by the laws of chance, and concludes that life must have begun when the "right" atoms, in the "right" combinations, happened by sheer chance to be present at the "right" time and under the "right" circumstances. These same laws of atomic behavior account for the immense variation in the kinds of life we observe on earth; these too have resulted from the chance combination of atoms in forms and at times and under conditions that favored their creation, arrival, and subsequent development. Man, for example, has developed from a great, shaggy, solitary wanderer in field and forest to the relatively delicate, refined, efficient, and well-organized man of the poet's own day. Lucretius also imagines a time when enormous animals might have wandered the earth, creatures far greater than any to be seen in his own day. It is doubtful that he ever saw the fossil bones of a dinosaur; if he had, he would have found in them only confirmation of his theories.

Lucretius next develops a theory of the rise of human institutions, which he explains always in terms of the properties of the atom itself or, in other words, "naturally." Imagining the conditions of life of the primitive man he had described, and with an understanding not frequently to be found in ancient literature, he thinks of the child, of the tender affection which the baby awakes in his parents, as the first civilizing force. Next came family, then the tribe; further development changed the tribe into the nation, and tribal law into formal government.

From here on, the history of man follows rather closely the history of human governments as it was generally understood in antiquity. The first form of government was monarchy, to be succeeded by the rule of the wealthy, in turn followed by a government of law and magistrates. With government came law; with law, punishment; and, with punishment, the fear of punishment. From the fear of punishment by human agencies arose the fear of punishment by agencies greater than human, and from this phobia arose religion, the fear of the gods and of the punishments that they might inflict upon us.

In addition to these major aspects of human life, Lucretius takes up a long list of the institutions and discoveries of man, and shows how they came about through purely natural causes. Language, for example, arose because man had the organs of speech and found it convenient to use them as a means of communication. Man's knowledge of fire came about from forest fires set by lightning, or by the friction of one branch of a tree against another during a windstorm. Everything else—metallurgy, the taming and training of domestic animals, weaving, agriculture, music, and the dance—men learned by natural processes. All these discoveries were made simply because man and the world are what they are, and not by any special creation or dispensation.

Book VI is a kind of catch-all, and has the manifest defects of any such miscellany. Lucretius takes up various phenomena, such as thunder, magnetism, earthquakes, and waterspouts, and explains each of these on an atomic basis. In a good many instances his explanations seem labored and unnecessarily elaborate; it may be that final revision would have simplified a good deal of this part of the poem. It may be too that these elaborate disquisitions were intended to meet possible objections from opponents of Epicureanism, and to give its proponents as many possible explanaitons as the poet could think of, so that if one were refuted, they might have recourse to another.

The long series of miscellaneous phenomena leads Lucretius in the end to a theory of disease, which he attributes, as the ancient world in general did, to the influence of air masses. In this respect, Lucretius is not too far ahead of his contemporaries. He concludes his account with a description of the great plague at Athens (430–429 B.C.) borrowed whole-cloth from Thucydides (2.47–52) and of interest chiefly for the ingeniousness with which Lucretius Latinizes the Greek historian's brilliant account. Book VI comes to an abrupt end; the poem simply stops, and in so doing tends to substantiate the argument that the work is unfinished.

A Note on This Translation

As in my translation of Vergil's *Aeneid* (Bobbs-Merrill, 1975) I have attempted to create a line-for-line version of Lucretius' poem since any translation that varies from the line-for-line plan is bound to destroy all semblance of the architecture of the original.

For the meter, again as with the *Aeneid*, I chose a somewhat loosened form of the English iambic pentameter, as the only form of English verse that adequately represents the dignity of movement and disciplined variation of the Latin hexameter. The problem of getting six Latin feet into five English feet remained a vexing one, and again as in the case of the *Aeneid*, at times resulted in the loss of words or ideas. But I attempted as before to restrict such losses to relatively unimportant elements. The text, except as indicated in the notes, is that of Cyril Bailey (Oxford Classical Texts, 1962).

The Nature of Things

Book I

Mother of Romans, joy of gods and men,
Venus,[1] life-giver, who under planet and star
visits the ship-clad sea, the grain-clothed land
always, for through you all that's born and breathes
is gotten, created, brought forth to see the sun, 5
Lady, the storms and clouds of heaven shun you,
You and your advent; Earth, sweet magic-maker,
sends up her flowers for you, broad Ocean smiles,
and peace glows in the light that fills the sky.
For soon as the year has bared her springtime face, 10
and bars are down for the breeze of growth and birth,
in heaven the birds first mark your passage, Lady,
and you; your power pulses in their hearts.
Then wild beasts, too, leap over rich, lush lands
and swim swift streams; so prisoned by your charms 15
they follow lustily where you lead them on.
Last, over sea and hill and greedy river,
through leaf-clad homes of birds, through fresh green fields,
in every creature you sink love's tingling dart,
luring them lustily to create their kind. 20
Since you, and you only, rule the world of nature,
and nothing, without you, comes forth to the coasts
of holy light, or makes for joy and love,
I pray you be with me as I write these verses
that I compose about the world of nature 25
for my friend Memmius,[2] whom, in every hour,
Lady, you wish in all things blessed and great.
Grant then to my words, Lady, a deathless charm.
Cause meanwhile that all savage works of war
by land and sea drop off to sleep and rest. 30
For you alone can bless our mortal race
with peace and calm: though Mars[3] the War Lord rules
war's savage works, yet often he throws himself
into your arms, faint with love's deathless wound,
and there, with arching neck bent back, looks up 35
and sighs, and feeds a lustful eye on you
and, pillowed, dangles his life's breath from your lips.
Then, as he falls back on your sacred body,

1. The goddess is a poetic symbol, representing creative nature; she also stands for the Epicurean ideal of peace, order, and harmony.
2. Gaius Memmius, praetor, 58 B.C., governor of Bithynia, 57 B.C.; the lyric poet Catullus was a member of his staff. Lucretius loved him; Catullus hated him.
3. The war god, symbol of discord, of the destructive forces in nature, as opposed to Venus, symbol of creation, order, and peace.

Lady, lean over and let sweet utterance pour
from your holy lips—a plea of peace for Rome.   40
For in my country's hour of trial I cannot
sit calmly writing, nor can Lord Memmius
in such a season fail the common weal.[4]

* * *

Now turn attentive ears and thoughtful mind,   50
by trouble undistraught, to truth and reason;
my gifts displayed for you in loyal love
you must not scorn before you grasp their meaning.
For I shall tell you of the highest law
of heaven and god, and show you basic substance,   55
whence nature creates all things and gives them growth,
and whither again dissolves them at their death.
"Matter," I call it, and "creative bodies,"
and "seeds of things"—such terms I'll often use
in my discourse, and sometimes call the same   60
"prime bodies," for with them everything beings.[5]
　　When human life lay foul before men's eyes,
crushed to the dust beneath religion's weight
(from the high realm of heaven she showed her face
in hideous grimace of terror to mortal men)   65
a man of Greece[6] first dared to raise the eye
of mortal against her, first stood ground against her.
Not all god's glory, his lightning, heaven's rumble
and rage, could stop him; rather they rasped his heart
to keener courage, and made him a pioneer   70
eager to burst the bolts on nature's door.
His quick and cunning intellect won him paths
to freedom beyond the world's far-flaming walls;
in mind and thought he marched the boundless Whole
and then, victorious, taught us what can be   75
and what cannot; yes, and what law defines
the power of things, what firm-set boundary stone.
And now religion in turn beneath our feet
is trampled; the victory makes us match for heaven.
　　This troubles me: that you may think yourself   80
beginning to study blasphemy—"that first step
to a life of crime." Why, no! More commonly

---

4. Editors commonly indicate the loss of an unknown number of lines here.
5. Here Lucretius invents a number of Latin synonyms for the Greek *atomos* ("atom"). Why he did not simply transliterate the Greek word is hard to see; his readers certainly knew Greek, and would have had no trouble with the word.

Perhaps he was determined to exclude as many non-Latin words as he could, in spite of the difficulties this posed for him: cf. 1.136–145. In my translation I have not hesitated to use the word "atom" whenever this seemed conducive to clarity.
6. Epicurus. See Introduction, p. ix ff.

religion has prompted vile and vicious acts.
Remember Aulis?[7] How Diana's altar
was shamed and fouled by Iphianassa's blood   85
spilled by the Lords of Greece—great heroes, they!
They coiffed the poor girl for her wedding day;
a ribbon, long braids to hang each side of her face.
But there by the altar she saw her father standing
grief-stricken, and near him acolytes hiding knives,   90
and people staring at her with tear-stained faces.
Voiceless with terror she crumpled to her knees.
Poor thing, no help to her in such an hour
that she'd been first to call the king "my father."
Men led her to the altar, raised her up   95
all trembling, not to say their sacred office
and carry her home with nuptial shout and song,
but that her innocence at the bridal hour
fall criminal victim by a father's blow,
that ships might have clear sailing and fair winds.   100
So much of evil could religion prompt.
    And you, at any moment now, in fear
of hierophantic threats, will seek to leave me.
For think of the endless fantasies your priests
devise, that can subvert all reasoned thought   105
and turn your life to terror and confusion!
Of course! For if men saw that all their troubles
must one day end, somehow they'd find the strength
to stand against the hierophant and his threats.
But now they can't stand ground nor make reply   110
for fear of eternal torment after death.
They do not know the nature of the soul—
if it is born or at birth slipped into us;
whether, destroyed by death, it dies with us,
or goes to see hell's broad and lightless pools,   115
or by some miracle passes to other creatures,
as our loved Ennius[8] sang, who first brought down
from lovely Helicon garlands ever green
to grow in fame wherever Italians live.
Yet Ennius also claimed the underworld   120
exists, and told his tale in deathless verse,
a place where neither soul nor flesh lives on
but a sort of "images"—pale and eerie things.

7. Agamemnon, commander-in-chief of the Greek expedition against Troy, was ordered by an oracle to sacrifice his daughter, Iphigenia (here called "Iphianassa"), to the goddess Diana (Artemis) at her temple at Aulis, in Boeotia, in order that a favorable wind might enable the Greeks to sail for Troy. The story is told by Euripides in his play *Iphigenia at Aulis*.
8. Lived 239–169 B.C., the "father of Latin poetry." He wrote an epic, the *Annals*, now extant only in fragments.

From there the likeness of Homer[9] the Ever-young
appeared to him (he says), and shedding floods   125
of salty tears brought word of the world of nature.
And so we must think with accuracy and care
about the world above—of sun and moon
and how they move, how everything on earth
takes place; but first with all our reasoning power   130
we must inspect the nature of soul and mind,
and things that come to fill our hearts with fear
when we lie ill and awake, or tombed in sleep,
making us think we see and hear right there
men who have died, whose bones the earth embraces.   135

    And well do I know Greek science is obscure
and difficult to explain in Latin verse,
above all when I must work with coined words
where Latin is lacking and the concept new.
But your great goodness and the hoped-for joy   140
of your sweet friendship bid me bear all toil,
and keep me awake at work through cloudless nights
seeking not only words but verses, too,
to be bright shining lights before your mind,
that you may see deep into hidden truth.   145

    This fright, this night of the mind, must be dispelled
not by the rays of the sun, nor day's bright spears,
but by the face of nature and her laws.
And this is her first, from which we take our start:
nothing was ever by miracle made from nothing.[1]   150
You see, all mortal men are gripped by fear
because they see so many things on earth
and in the sky, yet can't discern their causes
and hence believe that they are acts of god.
But in all this, when we have learned that nothing   155
can come from nothing, then we shall see straight through
to what we seek: whence each thing is created
and in what manner made, without god's help.

    If things were made from nothing, then all kinds
could spring from any source: they'd need no seed.   160
Man could have burst from ocean, from dry land
the bearers of scales,[2] and from thin air the birds;
cows, horses, sheep, and the rest, and all wild beasts

9. The poet of the *Iliad* and *Odyssey*. Ennius once claimed to be "Homer reborn."
1. This is the first of the basic principles on which the Epicurean system rests. All Being is material, and is created only out of matter; it cannot be created out of nothing. Its creation is brought about solely by natural law. There is no such thing as divine intervention or miracle. The logical argument is this: if anything could be created out of nothing, then anything could be created out of anything, and birth and growth would be quite random. But this, we see, is not the case.
2. I.e., fish. For some odd reason, Lucretius tries to avoid the word for "fish" (*piscis*), substituting one or another euphuism for it, e.g., "scaly shiners" (1.372).

would breed untrue, infesting farm and forest.
Nor would one tree produce one kind of fruit;   165
no, they would change, and all could bear all kinds.
For if there were no factors governing birth,
how could we tell who anyone's mother was?
But things are formed, now, from specific seeds,
hence each at birth comes to the coasts of light   170
from a thing possessed of its essential atoms.
Thus everything cannot spring from anything,
for things are unique: their traits are theirs alone.
And why in spring do we see roses, grain
in summer, vines produce at autumn's call,   175
if not because right atoms in right season
have streamed together to build each thing we see,
while weather favors and life-giving earth
brings delicate seedlings safe to land and light?
But if they came from nothing, they'd spring up   180
all helter-skelter in seasons not their own;
for there would be no atoms to be kept
from fertile union at untimely hours.
Nor would things when they grow have need of time
for seeds to combine, if they could grow from nothing.   185
Why! Babes in arms would turn into men forthwith,
and forests would leap from sprouts new-sprung of earth.
Yet clearly such things never occur: all growth
is gradual, regular, from specific seed,
and with identity kept. Hence learn that things   190
can grow only when proper substance feeds them.
To this we add: without her seasonal rains
Earth could not send up offspring rich in joy,
nor, further, could living creatures without food
beget their kind or keep their hold on life.   195
Better conceive of many atoms shared
by many things, as letters are by words,
than of a single thing not made of atoms.
To continue: why could nature not produce
men of such size that they could cross the seas   200
on foot, and with bare hands pull hills apart,
and live the lifetime of ten thousand men,
if not because each thing has but one substance
marked and designed to bring it into being?
Admit then: nothing can be made of nothing   205
since things that are created must have seed
from which to come forth to the gentle breezes.
Finally, since we see tilled fields excel
untilled, and pay more profit on our toil

surely prime bodies must exist in soil.   210
Plowing the fertile furrow, turning up
the earth, we bring these bodies to the surface.
But if there were none such, everything would grow
spontaneously, and better, without our labors.
And now add this: nature breaks up all things   215
into their atoms; no thing dies off to nothing.[3]
For if a thing were mortal in all its parts,
it would be whisked away, just drop from sight,
since there would be no need of force to wrench
one part from another, or to dissolve their bonds.   220
But things are made of atoms; they are stable.
Until some force comes, hits them hard, and splits them,
or seeps to their inner parts and makes them burst,
nature brings no destruction to our sight.
Besides, take things that time removes through aging: 225
if when they died their matter were all consumed,
whence does Venus bring animals forth to life
kind after kind, and earth, the magic-maker,
nourish, increase, and feed them, kind by kind?
Whence could native fountains and far-flung rivers   230
supply the sea? Whence ether[4] feed the stars?
For everything of mortal mass long since
had been used up as boundless time passed by.
But if the stuff of which this sum of things
is built has lasted down through empty ages,   235
surely it is endowed with deathless nature;
no thing, therefore, can be reduced to nothing.
   Lastly, one given cause could commonly
destroy all things, if they were not held firm
by deathless matter, bonded and intertwined.   240
For death's mere touch would be sufficient cause
for things not built of everlasting atoms
whose fabric must be broken up by force.
But now, because the bonds between the atoms
are ever unlike, and matter is eternal,   245
things will retain their form and mass intact
until they meet a force to match their fabric.
And so no thing reverts to nothing: all
are sundered into particles of matter.
Finally, rains are lost when Father Heaven   250
has dropped them into the lap of Mother Earth.

3. The second basic principle of Epicu-
reanism: as nothing can be created from noth-
ing, so nothing can be reduced to nothing; the
atoms out of which all Being is constituted are
indestructible.

4. Often identified with fire, it is the lightest
form of matter, and is thought of as surrounding
our world like a roughly spherical envelope.

But shining grainfields sprout, and twigs grow green
on trees; the trees grow, too, and bear their fruits;
hence our kind and the animal kind are fed,
hence we see happy cities bloom with children   255
and leafy woods all filled with young bird-song;
hence flocks wearied with fat lay themselves down
out in the fertile fields, and bright white liquor
leaks from their swollen teats; hence newborn lambs
gambol on wobbly legs through tender grass,   260
their baby hearts tipsy with winy milk.
Things seem to perish, then, but they do not:
nature builds one from another, and lets no thing
be born unless another helps by dying.[5]
   Come, now: I've shown that things cannot be made   265
from nothing nor, once made, be brought to nothing.
Still, lest you happen to mistrust my words
because the eye cannot perceive prime bodies,
hear now of particles you must admit
exist in the world and yet cannot be seen.   270
To begin: the whistling wind whips up the sea,
makes great ships founder, and whisks off the clouds;
again, wheeling and funneling over the fields
it strews them with giant boles, and with its blasts
tree-cracking, tears at the hilltops—raging, screaming,   275
howling its threats, the savage tempest roars.
There are, then, unseen particles of wind
that sweep the sea, the land, yes, and the clouds
of heaven, tearing and whipping and whirling them off.
They flow and spread disaster in no way   280
other than water, when that gentle flow
rises in flash flood, fed by cloudbursts high
in the mountains: down the walls of water race,
tossing debris of forests and whole plantations;
strong bridges cannot brook the sudden crush   285
of rushing water: muddy, swollen with rain,
the stream runs at their piers with massive power.
It roars and wrecks, and rolls beneath its waves
huge blocks of stone—whatever dams its path.[6]
So too the blasts of wind must form and move: 290
when like a powerful flash flood they sweep down,
wherever they turn they tumble and topple the world
with drumbeat blows; again, with a twist and whirl

5. Throughout Lucretius' poem, it is important to keep in mind the distinction he draws—not always too clearly—between our world and the universe (the "sum of things"). The former is a "thing" consisting of a strictly limited number of atoms and, like all other "things," subject to ultimate dissolution. The latter is infinite in extent and contains an infinite number of atoms; it can never be destroyed.
6. This is my interpretation of a doubtful piece of Latin.

and a spinning funnel they suck things up and away.
Yes, there are unseen particles of wind,   295
since in their acts and ways they are discerned
to rival rivers, whose substance can be seen.
Now to go on: we sense earth's many odors
yet never see them coming toward the nose;
we cannot see the heat, nor with the eye   300
capture the cold, nor see the sounds of speech;
yet these must all consist of particles
of matter, for they make impact on our senses,
and nothing can touch or be touched other than matter.[7]
To continue, clothing hung where breakers crash   305
grows damp, then dries when spread out in the sun.
And yet, how water-moisture settled there,
cannot be seen, nor how heat drove it off.
Into small parts, then, water is dispersed,
parts that the eye in no way can perceive.   310
Still more: as years and years of sun roll round,
the inner side of a ring is thinned by wearing;
water-drip hollows rock, the iron plow
grows imperceptibly smaller in the field,
and paving stones we see worn down by feet   315
of people passing; then, near city-gates,
bronze statues show their right hands worn away
by touch of the many who greet them and pass by.
Once they're worn down, we see these things are smaller,
but how many particles leave at given times,   320
a niggard nature has blocked our power to see.
Finally, keenest eye cannot detect
the gradual additions made by nature
and time to things, to keep the rule of growth,
nor see how years make them grow old and weak;   325
seaside cliffs are eaten away by brine,
yet one cannot see each moment what is lost.
Invisible particles, then, do nature's work.

   Yet still the whole world is not gripped and packed
solid with matter for there is void[8] in things.   330
Know this, for it will help in many ways,
and will not let you waver, doubt, and question
the law of nature, and mistrust my words.
Thus there is void, intactile, empty space:
If there were not, then there would be no way   335
for things to move. It is the part of matter

---

7. This principle, like those enunciated in 150
and 215–16, is basic to Epicurean thought: all
sensation is caused by physical impact of one
body on another.

8. This is empty space, a postulate without
which, Lucretius says, it is impossible to ex-
plain movement.

to block and stop, and this would always happen
to everything; nothing then could move ahead,
since nothing would ever let anything start to move.
But now on sea and land and in high heaven   340
before our eyes we see things moving, here,
there, everywhere, but if there were no void,
they'd not so much be lacking speed and movement
as never, in reason, have come to be at all
in a world of matter tight-packed and motionless.   345
Further, though we may think that things are solid,
here are signs that their atoms are widely spaced:
in caves and caverns water trickles through
clear-flowing; tear-like drops hang everywhere.
The food of animals spreads throughout their bodies.   350
Trees grow and in due season drop their fruits
because food flows all through them, from their roots
up through their trunks and out through every branch.
Words pass through walls and slip past lock and key,
and numbing cold seeps to our very bones.   355
This you would not see happen, were there not
spaces through which bodies like these might pass.
To continue, why do we see one thing surpass
another in weight, though of no larger size?
For if in a ball of wool there were as much   360
matter as in lead they would weigh the same,
since it's the function of matter to push things down,
and void must be, by contrast, without weight.
Thus what is just as large but has less weight,
declares, you see, that it has more of void;   365
by contrast, the heavier tells us it has more
matter within it, and much less empty space.
Thus, what we've sought, you see, to trace by sense
and reason, is mixed in things: we call it "void."
    Now here is something that may lead you off   370
from truth, and this I must anticipate.
Men say that water yields to scaly shiners
and opens paths for them, because the fish
leave space behind, where waves may flow together;
other things, too, thus move reciprocally   375
and exchange places, though all the world is full.
But see: this whole idea is falsely reasoned.
For where could our fish move to, after all,
if water did not make room? And where could waves
move to, then, since fishes could not stir?   380
Hence we must either deprive all matter of motion
or say that there is void mixed into things,

through which they singly make their start toward movement.
Finally, if from contact two flat plates
leap quickly apart, surely the air must fill   385
the entire void created between those plates.
Further, no matter how fast the streams of air
should flow, the total space could not be filled
at once: the air would occupy the void
by steps, successively, till the whole was filled.   390
But if, when plates have leaped apart, someone
should think this happens when air is self-compressed,
he's wrong, for this makes void what was not void,
and makes fullness of what was void before.
Now air cannot compress itself this way—   395
or, if it could, not without void, I think,
could it pull itself in and draw its parts together.[9]
   Therefore, despite your hesitance and evasions,
you must admit that there is void in things.
And I can give you proof on top of proof   400
to bolster up your faith in what I say.
But, for a man of intellect, these small signs
suffice: through them you'll learn the rest yourself.
For as hill-wandering hounds time after time
sniff out the wild beast's lair, though roofed with leaves,   405
once they have caught the clear scent of his trail,
so you yourself, in things like these, will spy
one thing from another and will work your way
into dark coverts and drag out the truth.
But if you are lazy or a bit reluctant,   410
this promise I can make you, Memmius, flatly:
so vast are the founts, so generous the drafts
that honeyed speech will pour from my heart's hoard,
I fear that old age sooner may creep in
to cripple our limbs and loose our hold on life   415
before, on just one point, my verse can bring
the whole array of argument to your ears.
   But now to resume the weaving of my words:
Nature—unqualified Being—has two forms
that make it up: the atoms, and the void   420
where atoms are placed and travel their varied paths.
That matter exists, we learn, as do all men,

9. The point of this somewhat tortured argu-
ment seems to be this: air is made up of atoms,
but atoms cannot "compress" into each other
(392, 395–97); when the two plates are pulled
apart, they create void between them (393), and
it is into this void that the atoms of air move, bit
by bit, as the plates are pulled farther and farther
apart (384–90.) Concomitantly, as the plates

move apart, they push the atoms of air outside
them into the empty spaces ("void") that lie
between the atoms of air, thus compressing the
air into a "fullness" (394) that was not there
before. The point is that compression and
rarefaction are forms of movement, and no
movement is possible in the absence of empty
space, "void."

by the senses: these we trust, first, last, and always;
else we shall have no point of reference
for reasoned proof of the nature of things unseen.[1]   425
And then, for "place" and "space," which we call "void":
without it, atoms would have nowhere to be,
nor anywhere to pursue their varied paths;
this I've already shown you, just above.
Furthermore, there is nothing one could call   430
discrete from matter and distinct from void,
something revealed as a third form of Being.
No matter what it will be, it must be *something*;
if it has touch, however unsubstantial,
then it will add its increase, great or small,   435
to the ranks of matter, and join Totality;
but if intactile, helpless at any point
to prevent the movement of a body through it,
then it will be the thing that we call "void."
Further, whatever exists must either act   440
or be acted upon by other things in action,
or else have things located or done within it.
But: nothing can act or be acted on but matter,
and (further) nothing make room but empty void.
And so, except for matter and void, no third   445
nature remains within the class of Being,
nothing ever subject to sense perception,
nothing the reasoning mind could ever grasp.
   Name anything else: you'll find it a property
joined to these two, or else an accident of them.   450
A *property* is what never can be cut off
and sundered: its disjuncture spells destruction,
as *weight* to stone, to fire, *heat*, as *liquid*
to water, *touch* to matter, *non-touch* to void.
Contrariwise, slavery, wealth, and poverty,   455
liberty, war, and peace, and all the rest
which, present or absent, make no change in essence—
these we correctly designate *accidents*.
Time doesn't exist as such,[2] but from events
our senses gather what happened in the past,   460
what things are with us, and what are going to be.
No man may assert he senses time as such,
discrete from things in motion and things at rest.

1. Another important basic principle of Epicureanism: sense perception is true, and only by sense perception do we learn truth. As all Being is material—i.e., atomic,—so all knowledge is gained by physical contact with the material—i.e., by sense perception. Cf. 302–4 and note.

2. *Time* is not a thing, but only a relation between things. *Events* in time are not *things*, either; they are not material ("atomic"), therefore they have no existence of their own. They are accidents of the places where they occurred, and we learn of them by learning of those places.

To continue: when men say the "rape of Helen"
and "the defeat of Troy" *exist*, take care   465
we arc not forced to admit thcy arc *as such*
because the men to whom these things once happened
are long since lost in time beyond recall.
No, these events may be called accidents,
some of the world, some of those special regions.   470
Lastly, if there had been no matter at all,
nor place nor space, in which events occur,
the beauty of Helen never had fed the fire
of love that licked at Paris' Phrygian heart,
and kindled bright the flames of savage war;   475
nor had that wooden horse slipped into Troy
by night, to bear her Greeks and burn the city.
Thus you may see: historical events
do not, like matter, exist in their own right;
nor may we describe them as we do the void,   480
but rather, and properly, call them accidents
of matter and of the places where they happen.
   Now further: physical things are partly atoms
and partly atoms joined in combinations.
Those that are atoms no force can overcome;   485
their solid matter must finally prevail.
And yet it is hard to believe that anything
in nature could stand revealed as solid matter.
The lightning of heaven goes through the walls of houses,
like shouts and speech; iron glows white in fire;   490
red-hot rocks are shattered by savage steam;
hard gold is softened and melted down by heat;
chilly brass, defeated by flame, turns liquid;
heat seeps through silver, so does piercing cold;
by custom raising the cup, we feel them both   495
as water is poured in, drop by drop, above.
To such degree is nothing in nature solid.
But since true reason and the world of nature
insist, please hear me while I briefly show
that solid, eternal matter does exist—   500
the seeds, the start of things, as I shall prove,
whence the whole Sum of Things now stands created.
   To begin: since nature is shown to be twofold,
consisting, in fact, of two far different things,
matter, and space in which events occur,   505
each must be single, absolute, and pure.
For where there's empty space (what we call "void")
there, matter is *not*; further, where matter *is*,

there, in no possible way, can there be void.
Prime bodies are solid, then, and without void.   510
Now since there *is* void in created things
it must be solid matter that hems it in.
Nor can true reason prove that anything
holds void concealed within, unless you grant
that what contains it is pure solid matter.   515
Further, it could be nothing but a meeting
of matter that could contain the void in things
Thus matter, which consists of solid body,
can last forever, though all else is destroyed.
Then further, if there were no empty void,   520
all would be solid; but if there were no atoms
to fill whatever space they occupied,
then All-that-Is would be mere space and void.
There are two things, then, separate and distinct:
atoms and void; the world is not simply full,   525
nor empty, either. No, atoms do exist,
that show where "empty" ends and "full" begins.
They cannot be shattered when struck by outside blows;
they cannot be pierced and raveled from within,
nor weakened or damaged in any other way.   530
This I've already shown you, just above.
For it is clear that nothing can be crushed
without void, nor broken, nor split in two by cutting,
nor take up water nor likewise seeping cold
nor fire that, once inside, destroys all things.   535
The more of void each thing contains within,
the more it totters when such things strike its heart.
So, if prime bodies are solid and without void,
as I have proved, then they must be eternal.
And further, if matter had not been eternal,   540
all things long since had been reduced to nothing,
and all we see had been reborn from nothing.
But since I've shown that nothing can be created
from nothing, nor, once in being, brought to nothing,
there must be atoms made of deathless stuff   545
to which all things may finally be reduced
that matter may be on hand to build new things.
Atoms, then, are of solid single substance;
no other way would they have been preserved
till now, through endless time, to build new things.   550
    To continue: if Nature had set no boundary
to breaking things, the particles of matter
had been so cracked and riven by time gone by

that at no given moment could anything
begin with them and fill out a full life-span.   555
For we see that things are broken up more quickly
than put together; and hence what all the span
of the long years of infinite time gone by
till now had broken—disordering, pulling apart—
could never be mended in the time that's left.   560
But now, of course, fixed limits have been set
to break-up, for we see things made anew,
and see that, kind by kind, the span of time
is fixed wherein they reach the bloom of life.
And now add this: although the atoms of matter   565
are purely solid, yet from them can be made
things that are soft: air, water, earth, and heat.
How is this done, and by what power accomplished?
Grant once and for all that void is mixed in things!
Contrariwise, if our basic stuff were soft,   570
how could hard flint and iron be produced?
No logic could tell us how, for then all Being
would utterly lack a base on (which to rest.
There are then particles, solid, single, strong;
when any are gathered in tighter concentration,   575
compressed and close-knit, then they show their strength.
And further, if for breaking of particles
no limit were set, still through eternal time
some basic bodies would have to last till now
that as yet had not been damaged by attack.   580
But since they'd clearly be of fragile substance,
they could not, in logic, last since time began,
buffeted down the years by countless blows.
Further: since, kind by kind, limits are set
to the growth of things and to their hold on life,   585
and since what each thing can and cannot do
has been laid down by nature's law, and sanctioned,
and is not changed, but everywhere holds true
(to such degree that all the different birds
show in their plumage the markings of their species)   590
it follows, you see, that things must have a stock
of changeless matter. For if the basic stuff
could be subdued and changed in any way
then we would be uncertain what can be
and what cannot; yes, and what law defines   595
the power of things, what firm-set boundary stone;
and species could not repeat, age after age,
their parents' nature, habits, food, and movement.

And further, since there's always least dimension[3]

* * *

for that particle which our human senses   600
cannot perceive, and this can have no parts,
is the smallest form of being, and has not been
cut off by itself, nor can it ever be,
since it is part of its neighbor, just "Part One"
and then in order come other parts alike.   605
In close-set column they make up the atom's mass;
and since they cannot exist alone, they must
cling whence they can in no wise be pulled off.
Atoms, then, are of solid, single substance,
made of close-clinging, tightly packed least parts,   610
not by their coming-together put together,
but strong through eternal singularity.
From atoms, nature lets nothing be plucked off
or lessened, but keeps them safe as seeds for things.
Further, without some "least," each smallest bit   615
in turn will consist of infinite particles;
the half of a half, you see, will always have
its half, and nothing will ever mark the end.
What difference, then, twixt "universe" and "least"?
No difference at all! For though the Sum   620
be utterly infinite, still those smallest bits
will consist likewise of just as infinite parts.[4]
But since reason rejects this, and declares
none can believe it, you are constrained to grant
that there are things owning no parts at all,   625
and proven to have least nature. They exist,
hence you must know them solid and eternal.
Last, if creative nature had compelled
all things to be dissolved to their least parts,
she could not now rebuild them from those parts   630
because no particle not endowed with parts
could have the features all creative matter
must have: the bonds, the weight, the striking power,
the meetings, the movements, through which events take place.

3. After this line at least two lines have been lost. The sense of the missing lines must have been to the effect that since things we *can* see have "least dimension" (i.e., exist in forms so small that, if they were any smaller, they would be invisible), then things we *can't* see must also have such "least dimensions" (i.e., exist in forms so small that, if they were any smaller, they would not exist at all).

4. The point is this: *infinity* is an absolute; it admits of no degrees. Therefore, the infinitely *small* is exactly equivalent to the infinitely *large*. Thus the atom is limited in size at the small end of the scale just as it is at the large end: it cannot be so small as to have *no* dimensions nor so large as to be perceptible by our senses.

Thus, men who think that elemental matter   635
is fire, that fire alone makes up the Whole,
have slipped far off, I think, from truth and reason.
Of these Heraclitus[5] leads into the lists,
famed for his cloudy speech more among fools
than among earnest Greeks who seek the truth.   640
For fools, you see, admire and love all things
that they spy lurking under twisted words,
and they call true all that can deftly touch
the ear and is distempered with sweet sound.

For I ask: how can things be so various   645
if they are created of fire, alone and pure?
For if hot fire's compressed or rarified,
what gain, if the particles of fire still have
the same nature the whole fire had to start with?
Condense the particles: heat is more intense;   650
disperse and strew them about: heat then is feebler.
Beyond this, nothing can happen in such event
(as well you know) let alone this manifold world
could be just fire, compressed or rarified.
And more: if they granted void mixed into things,   655
their fire could be compressed or rarified.
But since so often they see their theory blocked,
and run from granting that there is void in things,
for fear of the steep they lose the truthful path,
and don't see that with void removed from things   660
all matter would be condensed, and made one mass
which from itself could cast no particle free,
as fire, heat-bearer, throws off light and warmth,
showing us that its parts are not close-packed.
But if they think that in some other way   665
fire can combine, be quenched, and change its form—
well! If they fail to stop this at some point,
their blaze, of course, will all die down to nothing
and what is created will be made from nothing.
For whatever changes and leaves its natural bounds   670
is instant death of that which was before.[6]
They must have something that survives intact,

5. *Heraclitus,* of Ephesus (c. 500 B.C.) search-
ing for a single element out of which all matter
could be created, found it in fire. He was fam-
ous for his cryptic remarks, for which he be-
came known as "the Murky".

   Throughout this passage (635–920) in which
Lucretius attempts to refute rival theories of
Being, he bases his argument on a single prem-
ise: all theories other than the Epicurean posit a
primal matter which is not primal, since it
would have to suffer change in order to produce
the forms of matter which our senses show us do
exist. But change is destruction (see 1.670–71
and note 6), and primal matter cannot be de-
stroyed (see 1.215–16 and note 3).
6. Another basic Epicurean principle. It is
based on the logical proposition that $x + y$ is not
just x with something added to it, nor is $x - y$
just x with something subtracted from it; rather,
in both cases, it is an entirely different thing, the
creation of which has destroyed the original
"x." In simpler terms, neither $x + y$ nor $x - y$ can
ever $= x$.

lest everything in the world revert to nothing,
and all things spring to life again from nothing.
Now then, since particles, perfectly specific   675
and keeping a changeless nature, do exist,
whose coming or going and changed arrangement change
the nature of things, converting one to another,
you may be sure these particles are not fire.
It would not matter that some might come, might go,   680
or some be added, and others change position,
if they all preserved the attributes of fire,
for all they created would be simply fire.
But no, I think it's this way: there are bodies
whose joinings, movements, position, pattern, shapes,   685
make fire, but with arrangement changed they change
their substance, and resemble neither fire
nor anything further that can cast off bodies
to the senses, and by their impact touch our touch.

    To say, then, "All is fire; there is no real   690
substance among all substances but fire,"
as this man does, is patently absurd.
For he uses the senses to impugn the senses
and batters the base on which all credence rests,
the very power by which he knows his "fire."   695
He believes the senses rightly judge of fire,
but not of the rest, though no less obvious.
This seems to me illogical—yes, insane.
For what is to be our base? What can we have
more sure than sense to tell us false from true?   700
Further, why would one rather cancel out
all else, and allow the substance fire, alone,
than exclude fire and posit some other thing?
Both statements, I think, are equally absurd.

    Therefore those who imagine that basic substance   705
is fire, and that the Whole is made of fire,
and those who decree that everything begins
with air, or think that water of itself
gives things their being, or that earth creates
all things and is converted to all natures,[7]   710
seem to have wandered far away from truth.
Add those as well who double their basic stuff,
pairing up air with fire, and earth with water,[8]
and those who think the world made of four things,

7. Anaximenes (c. 546 B.C.) held that air was the primal matter; Thales (c. 590 B.C.), that it was water. That it was earth seems to have been a kind of popular belief. It is sometimes ascribed to Pherecydes (c. 550 B.C.)

8. The origin of the air and fire theory is unknown; it is sometimes ascribed to Parmenides (c. 500 B.C.). Xenophanes (c. 500 B.C.) was responsible for the earth and water theory.

compounded of fire and earth and air and rain.   715
Chief in their ranks, Empedocles Agrigentine,[9]
son of the island of the threefold shores.
Around it the breakers of the Ionian Gulf
crash, and splash it with brine from cold, gray waves;
and pouring through narrow straits, the sea divides   720
the lands and shores of Italy from its bounds.
Vast Charybdis[1] is here; here Aetna growls
and threatens, with angry flames once more amassed,
to vomit again the fireball from her throat
and once more fling her flashing flame toward heaven;   725
a great land, worthy of wonder a thousand ways,
a place, they say, that every man should see,
wealthy, fertile, and vigorous, filled with people,
yet it had nothing to outshine this man,
nothing more saintly, wonderful, beloved.   730
Yes, more: the writings of his godlike mind
declare and propound his brilliant theories,
so that we scarce believe him born of man.
    Still he, and the others we mentioned—lesser men
in a thousand signal ways, inferior far—   735
for all their discoveries, countless, sound, inspired,
and answers uttered as from templed hearts
more awesomely and with far firmer logic
than all that Phoebus' tree and tripod say,[2]
in basic doctrine they came crashing down   740
(great men they were, and great was the fall thereof!):
they posit motion, but remove the void
from things; they leave their matter soft and porous—
air, sun, and fire, earth, animals, and plants—
yet never admit void to their substances.   745
Then, of the cutting of things they make no end
whatever, nor any stopping place for breakage
nor any fixed "least size" in all the world,
although we observe things have their "least dimensions"—
that smallest that our senses can perceive—   750
and hence conclude that things we cannot see
also have "leasts": those final, smallest parts.
Add likewise: since they posit their basic stuffs
soft—substances we see to be the world's
mere offspring, utterly mortal matter—then   755

9. Empedocles, of Agrigentum (c. 492 B.C.) taught that all matter sprang from the interaction of four elements—earth, air, fire, and water. He was a poet as well as a philosopher; his great poem "On Nature" was probably Lucretius' model for his own work. The "island of the threefold shores" is Sicily.

1. A whirlpool that seems to have existed in the narrow strait between Sicily and Italy. There is no such whirlpool there now. Aetna: the well-known Sicilian volcano, still active.
2. The reference is to the oracle of Apollo at Delphi. The "tree" is the sacred laurel, the "tripod" the stool on which the priestess sat.

their "universe" must soon revert to nothing
and all their "world" be born and grow from nothing.
How far both statements are from truth, you'll know.
Their stuffs are largely incompatible, too—
sheer mutual poisons: join them and they'll die   760
or scatter and run just as, when storm clouds gather,
we see the lightning scatter, and winds and rains.
   To continue: if four things make up the Whole
and into those four all things break up again,
how can the four be called the stuff of things   765
rather than the reverse: the things, of them?
For one begets the other; they trade off colors
and whole identities, every passing hour.[3]
But if perhaps you think that fire and earth   770
combine, and heaven's breeze with water's dew,
without some change of nature at their meeting,
from these, no single thing can be created
with soul, or living, but soulless, like a tree.
Why, of course! Each substance in this jumbled heap   775
will show itself; we'll see air side by side
with earth, and heat with dew—each one unchanged.
But for creating things, atoms must keep
a nature invisible, covert, and concealed,
with nothing protruding to resist and hinder   780
the thing created from being its proper self.
   Still more: they start with heaven and its fires,
and first make fire turn into breezy air;
from this rain is begotten, and from rain,
earth. Then turn all backwards: start with earth,   785
to water first, next air, then on to fire,
with never a stop to the series and the travel
from heaven to earth, from earth to starry sky.
This in no fashion can the atoms do,
for something ever unchanging must survive,   790
lest all the world be broken down to nothing.
For whatever changes and leaves its natural bounds
is instant death of that which was before.
Now therefore, since those elements I just mentioned
do go through changes, they must be composed   795
of others which can nowhere suffer change,
else all the world will be reduced to nothing.
Think rather that the particles endowed
with such a nature, if they should make fire,
could also—add a few, remove a few,   800
change arrangement and speed—make airy breezes,

3. Line 769 = 762, and is therefore omitted.

and thus all things are changed, one for another.
   "But the facts are obvious," you say; "all things
are nourished and grow from earth up into air.
Unless the weather in good season favors   805
with rains, so that the cloud-wrack shakes the trees,
and the sun is kind and grants his share of warmth,
nothing could grow—not animals, grain, or trees."
Of course! And unless dry food and gentle water
sustained us, we'd lose flesh, and life would be   810
dissolved from every muscle, every bone.
For doubtless we are sustained and nourished, too,
by the proper things, and other life likewise.
Why? Because atoms of many kinds, combined
in many ways, are present in many things.   815
Thus things are nourished by things unlike themselves.
It often matters much how given atoms
combine, in what arrangement, with what others,
what impulse they receive, and what impart.
The same ones make up earth, sky, sea, and stream;   820
the same the sun, the animals, grain, and trees,
but mingling and moving in ever different ways.
Why, yes! In the very verse I write, you see
dozens of letters shared by dozens of words,
and yet you must admit that words and verses   825
differ one from another in sound and meaning.
Such power have letters when order alone is changed.
But atoms, our basic stuff, can claim more patterns
of change whence countless things may be created.
   Now view Anaxagoras[4]—his *homoeomeria*;   830
so the Greeks call it: the language of our fathers
(sad, feckless tongue) yields us no word for it,
but a line or two will make the theory clear.
To begin, this thing he calls "homoeomeria"—
take bones: you see, they're made of little bones,   835
wee, tiny ones; and from wee, tiny guts,
guts are created; and blood comes into being
when lots of little drops of blood foregather.
And gold, he thinks, can be made out of grains
of gold, and earth coalesce from baby earths,   840
and fire from fires, and water can come from waters,
and all else likewise: so he theorizes.
But nowhere in all his world does he allow
for void, or for an end to cutting things.
Therefore, in both these matters, he's as wrong,   845

4. Lived c. 450 B.C. His theory of Being, *homoeomeria*, ("made up of like parts") is here adequately, if somewhat irreverently, expounded by Lucretius.

I think, as the men I mentioned just before.
Add that he makes his basic stuffs too weak—
if basic they are, endowed with just such nature
as things themselves, subject like them to death
and damage, with nothing to curb them from disaster.   850
For, when the press is strong, which one will last
to escape from death, under the fangs of doom?
Fire, or water, or air—which? Blood or bones?
None, as I think, for basically each will be
as mortal as anything that we clearly see   855
by some force beaten and banished from our sight.
But nothing drops off to nothing; nothing grows
from nothing: witness the facts I proved before.
  Further, since food augments and feeds the flesh
we may be sure that veins and blood and bones[5]   860

* * *

or if they say all foods are of mixed substance
and have in themselves small particles of sinew
and bone, blood vessels, too, and gouts of gore,
then they must think all foods, liquid and dry,
consist perforce of things unlike themselves,   865
of bone and sinew mixed with blood and gore.
Further, if all the things that grow from earth
exist in earth, then earth must be composed
of the things unlike itself that spring from it.
Change terms, and you may say as much again.   870
If within wood hide flame and smoke and ash
then wood consists of things unlike itself.
Further, all bodies, earth augments and feeds[6]

* * *

of things unlike themselves that spring from wood.
  Here there is left a tenuous subterfuge,   875
which Anaxagoras seizes: think of things
as mixtures of everything, all concealed but one
that shows—the one that's mixed in largest measure
and close to the surface and placed right at the top.
But this we reject: it's far, far from the truth.   880
For then grain, too, on occasion, when it's crushed
by the menacing might of stone, should show some sign

5. At least one line is missing. It probably stated that other parts of the body, too, were made up from substances unlike the parts themselves.
6. One or more lines are missing here. They probably contained an extension of the idea that things tend to be made up out of things unlike themselves.

of blood, or when with mortar and pestle we grind
food for the body, some blood should be pressed out.
And in like fashion, grain, and water too,   885
should emit sweet drops tasting, of course, the same
as milk that comes rich from the woolly sheep.
Again, sometimes, when crumbling clods of earth,
we should see grass and cereal grains and leaves—
miniatures—sprinkled and lurking in the dirt;   890
lastly, when breaking firewood we should see
smoke, ash, and flame trapped there in miniature.
That this never happens, the simple facts make clear,
and thus we know things are not mixed in things.
Rather, there must be seeds, unseen, combined   895
in many ways and common to many things.
    "But often high in the hills," you say, "it happens
that the very tops of neighboring trees are rubbed
together as happens perforce when winds blow strong,
until they flash and burst in a bloom of flame."   900
Of course! Still, there's no native fire in wood,
but there are many seeds of heat: when friction
draws them together, they set the woods ablaze.
But if, in fact, flame lay locked in the forest,
not for a minute could fire be kept constrained: 905
everywhere forests would burn, trees turn to ashes.
And now do you see what I said a bit before:
it often matters much how given atoms
combine: in what arrangement, with what others,
what impulse they receive, and what impart,   910
and the selfsame atoms, slightly interchanged,
may build both fire and wood. Just like the terms
themselves: we slightly interchange the letters
to spell the separate words *ignis* and *ligna*.[7]
Lastly if no phenomenon you observe   915
could occur, you think, unless your basic stuffs
had characteristics like your visible things,
here's how your basic stuffs would meet their end:
something would strike them odd; they'd shake with laughter
until they flooded their faces with bright tears.   920
    Come now and learn, and hear the rest more clearly.
Nor am I deceived how dark my subject; still
high hope of praise strikes hard upon my soul
and also drives into my heart sweet love
of the Muses; steeped in this, with mind alert,   925

7. The two Latin words aptly illustrate Lucretius' point; they both contain the combination of letters *ign* but otherwise are made up of different letters. *Ignis* means "fire"; *ligna*, "wood."

I travel the Muses' pathless places; none
before has walked where I walk. I love to find
new founts and drink, to gather fresh, new flowers
and seek the laureate's crown whence Muses never
till now have veiled the brow of any man.   930
For first I teach of weighty things, and work
man's heart free of religion's garrotte-knot;
and, next, I turn the bright light of my verse
on darkness, painting it all with poetry.
This, too, I think, is not without good reason.   935
For just as doctors, who must give vile wormwood
to children, begin by painting the cup-lip round
with sweet and golden honey; thus the child,
young and unknowing, is tricked and brought to set
the cup to his lip; meanwhile, he swallows the bitter   940
wormwood, and though deceived is not infected,
but by this trick grows well and strong again:
so now, since my philosophy often seems
a little grim to beginners, and most men
shrink back from it in fear, I wished to tell   945
my tale in sweet Pierian song for you,
to paint it with the honey of the Muses,
hoping that thus I might fix your attention
upon my verse until you clearly saw
how all of nature is arranged and shaped.   950
    But since I've shown that matter is atoms, solid,
always in motion, forever undestroyed,
now let us turn to whether the sum of them
has any limit, or not; likewise, the void
(or "place" or "space," in which events occur)—   955
let us observe if it has bounds and base
or stretches wide and deep, an endless waste.
    The All-that-Is, wherever its paths may lead,
is boundless, for then it would have to have an end.
But there can be no end to anything   960
without something beyond to mark that end
and show where nature and sense can go no further.
But we must admit there's nothing beyond the All;
it has no end, has then no bound nor limit.
Nor does it matter at which point one may stand: 965
whatever position a man takes up, he finds
the All still endless alike in all directions.
Further, if we should theorize that the whole
of space were limited, then if a man ran out
to the last limits and hurled a flying spear,   970
would you prefer that, whirled by might and muscle,

the spear flew on and on, as it was thrown,
or do you think something would stop and block it?
One or the other you must assume and grant.
But either cuts off escape and forces you   975
to grant that the All goes on and has no bounds.
For whether your spear is checked and stopped by something
from tracing its path and landing at its goal,
or flies free, where it started was not the end.
So it will go: no matter where you spot   980
the end, I'll ask, "What happens to my spear?"
Thus nowhere will a boundary stand firm:
a hidden escape route always will be found.
Lastly, we see that one thing limits another;
the air walls off the hills, and hills, the air.   985
Land limits the sea, the sea bounds all the lands;
outside the All, there's nothing to mark an end.

    Further, if all the space of all the Whole
on all sides were enclosed within fixed bounds,
and thus were finite, all matter long since   990
had settled, in leaden lumps, down to the bottom,
and nothing had happened under heaven's vault,
and there would have been no sky, no light, no sun;
for all matter would lie piled up, inert,
where it had sunk down, down through boundless time.   995
But now, you see, no rest is ever granted
to prime bodies, for there's no base nor bottom
where they might run together and settle down.
All things are brought to being through endless motion
in all directions; from the bottomless pit   1000
beneath come speeding fresh supplies of atoms.
This, then, is the nature of the deeps of space:
bright lightning could not cross them, though its path
flash on forever down time's endless track,
nor render less the traverse still remaining.   1005
So vast, all ways, extends the room for things,
and bounds are abolished toward all points alike.

    Furthermore, that the All may not itself
set limits, Nature has ruled, for she compels
void to be bounded by matter, matter by void,   1010
one by the other, and thus is the All made endless;
or else the one, if the other should not bound it,
would extend, in single substance, without end[8]

                        *   *   *

8. At least one line is missing here, something to the effect that both the void and the atoms
must be infinite; otherwise . . .

nor sea, nor land, nor heaven's light-filled zones,
nor humankind, nor sacred stuff of gods   1015
could last the scanty space of one lone hour.
For sundered from its junctures, the supply
of matter would travel aimless through the void;
or better, it never would have joined to make
one thing; so scattered, it could form no junctures.   1020
For surely not by planning did prime bodies
find rank and place, nor by intelligence,
nor did they regulate movement by sworn pact;
no, changing by myriads myriad ways, they sped
through the All forever, pounded, pushed, propelled,   1025
till, trying all kinds of movements and arrangements,
they came at last into such patterned shapes
as have created and formed this Sum of Things.
And it will last down through the long, long years,
once it has launched out into the needed movements;   1030
it makes the streams and rivers in full flood
refresh the sea; it warms the earth with sunshine
till it brings forth new life, and animals grow
and flourish, and heaven's fires glide on alive
This they could no wise do, if infinite   1035
supply of matter did not keep rising up
to help things in good time repair their losses.
For just as animate nature, wanting food,
will lose flesh and collapse, so must all things
be broken up once matter somehow strays   1040
from the path and fails to bring them fresh supply.
Nor could surrounding outside pressures keep
our Sum of Things intact once it was formed.
They might strike many spots and hold them firm
until fresh atoms came to fill up the Sum;   1045
still sometime they'd perforce leap back, bestowing
on primal bodies an opportunity
for flight, to travel away free of their bonds.
So, over and over, fresh atoms must come forth;
yes, even to maintain those very pressures,   1050
limitless matter must pour in from all sides.
    One theory, Memmius, you must not accept—
that in the Sum, all things press toward the center,[9]
and thus the world keeps stable without pressures
external to it, nor could it, bottom or top,   1055
be anywhere raveled, since all things push toward center

9. Refutation of the centripetal theory of atomic movement. Lucretius' difficulty here seems to be that he confuses our world, in which centripetal force—i.e., gravity—does operate, with the universe, which as he correctly sees, has no "center" toward which all movement might take place.

(if you think things can stand upon themselves),
and heavy things below the earth all press
upwards, and cling to earth there upside down
like the reflections of objects seen in water.   1060
In the same way, they claim the animals walk
back-down, yet cannot drop off from the earth
to the sky below, no more than can our bodies
of their own will fly up to heaven above.
When they are seeing the sun, we see the stars   1065
of night; by turns, they share with us the hours
of heaven, and pass nights equal to our days.
But a fool has proved these things to stupid people . . .[1]
because they have embraced false reasoning.
For there can be no middle, since the All   1070
is infinite. Nor if there were a middle
could anything rather find a foothold there
than in quite different fashion be repelled.
For all of "place" or "space" which we call "void"
through middle, through non-middle, must permit   1075
all objects alike to pass, as movement drives them.
Nor is there a place where bodies may arrive
and, losing weight, stand stock-still in the void;
nor can what is void support a single thing,
but as its nature demands, must let all pass.   1080
By no such system, then, can things be held
in congress, faint with lusting for the center.
   Besides, they do not tell us that *all* bodies
press to the center—just those of earth and liquid,
sea-wet and billowing waters from the hills,   1085
and matter that might be called the stuff of earth.
But they declare that breezes of thin air
and heat of fire alike flow *from* the center,
hence round us heaven is all alight with stars,
and sun-flame browses through the deep blue sky;   1090
heat, fleeing the center, has all foregathered there.
Nor at treetop could branches put out leaves
unless they slowly drew up food from earth[2]

*   *   *

lest, like flames, the walls of the world take wing
and suddenly scatter in fragments through the void
and all the rest trail after in like fashion;

1. Lines 1068–75 are either omitted or muti-
lated in the MSS. The translation given here is
based on restorations by H.A.J. Munro.

2. An unknown number of lines, the content
of which can only be conjectured, have been
lost here.

lest, too, the heavens, high home of thunder, tumble,   1105
and earth be ripped from under our feet, to fall
amid the crumbling wreckage of an earth
and heaven confounded, down through the empty deeps,
to leave, in a second, no remnant of themselves
except blind atoms and abandoned space.   1110
For wheresoever you first allow a shortage
of atoms, there you open a door to death,
and through it all matter will madly whirl away.

    Thus will my poor little poem lead you to learn:
one fact will light up the next; night will not blind you   1115
nor rob you of the way: you'll see straight through
to the ends of Being, as truths light lamps for truth.

Book II

It's sweet, when winds blow wild on open seas,
to watch from land your neighbor's vast travail,
not that men's miseries bring us dear delight
but that to see what ills we're spared is sweet;
sweet, too, to watch the cruel contest of war   5
ranging the field when you need share no danger.
But nothing is sweeter than to dwell in peace
high in the well-walled temples of the wise,
whence looking down we may see other men
wavering, wandering, seeking a way of life,   10
with wit against wit, line against noble line,
contending, striving, straining night and day,
to rise to the top of the heap, High Lord of Things.
O wretched minds of men, O poor blind hearts!
How great the perils, how dark the night of life   15
where our brief hour is spent! Oh, not to see
that nature demands no favor but that pain
be sundered from the flesh, that in the mind
be a sense of joy, unmixed with care and fear!
     Now for our physical life, we see that little—   20
so little!—is needed to remove our pain.
For Nature does not ask that vast delights
of a more tickling kind be spread before us,
even if through the house there are no statues
of golden boys with flaming lamps in hand   25
to furnish light for banquets all night long,
and there's no silver to glitter nor gold to gleam,
no lyre to echo from coffered, gilded ceiling.
Why! Men can lie on soft turf side by side
under a tall tree's branches near a stream,   30
and easily, pleasantly, care for creature needs—
especially when the sun shines, and the year
in season sprinkles the fresh green grass with flowers.[1]
     Nor do hot fevers leave our flesh the sooner
if we lie tossing on crocheted quilts and sheets   35
of purple, than if our bed is shabby stuff.
And so, since wealth's no profit to the flesh

---

1. This passage embodies a central Epicurean doctrine—that pleasure, which is the only true criterion of the Good, is an absolute, admitting of no degrees. It is, in fact, a negative, consisting of the absence of pain. In its crudest form, it is "the pain you don't have": cf. 2.1–13. See Introduction, p. xiv. Mark Twain phrased it less elegantly but just as forcibly: "We all like to see people in trouble, if it doesn't cost us anything." (*Following the Equator*, Chap. XLVIII).

whatever, nor noble blood, nor royal power,
it follows that they can't benefit the soul,
unless on seeing your legions in the field   40
at charge and countercharge of wild war games,
backed by cavalry staunchly massed. . . .[2]
full-armed alike with weapons and with courage . . .
you see your far-flung fleet come boiling in,   43ᵃ
then your religion terrified by these sights
flees fluttering from your soul, and fears of death   45
then leave your heart released and free of care.
But if we see that this is foolishness,
that in fact men's fears and cares are always with them,
and fear no rattling sabres or savage spears
but live quite boldly with the lords of earth   50
and kings, all unabashed by gleaming gold
and the splendor of a gorgeous purple robe,
why doubt that only reason can help us here,
above all, since man's life labors in darkness.
For as in the dead of night children are prey   55
to hosts of terrors, so we sometimes by day
are fearful of things that should no more concern us
than bogeys that frighten children in the dark.
This fright, this night of the mind must be dispelled,
not by the rays of the sun, nor day's bright spears,   60
but by the face of nature and her laws.
    Now, by what movements do creative bodies
produce things, and destroy them, once produced?
What force drives them to do this? Whence derived
their power of moving freely through the void?   65
I shall explain; attend, and hear my words.
Now surely matter is not all packed together
in permanent form, for we see things grow smaller,
and everything melt, so to speak, as years go by.
The old and worn slip from our sight away,   70
and yet the Sum, it seems, stays undiminished.
Why? Because atoms, departing, make one thing
smaller but render the thing they come to larger;
they make the one grow grey, the other bloom
and then move on. Thus is the world renewed   75
always, and mortal things trade life for life.
One nation grows, another wastes away;
the ranks of the living change in one brief hour;
like racers, they hand along the torch of life.
    If atoms, you think, can cease to move, and ceasing   80
can then set matter to moving in new ways,

---

2. The last part of this line, and perhaps three additional lines, have been lost here.

you've wandered away from truth, far from the road.
For atoms, since they wander the void, must all
be driven along either by their own weight
or perhaps by striking another. They often meet,   85
colliding at high speed and then at once
spring wide apart. No wonder! They're very hard,
heavy and solid, with nothing behind to block them.
All atoms of matter are constantly in motion.
To see this better, remember: in the All   90
and Sum, there is no bottom where prime bodies
may come to rest, since space is limitless,
stretching unmeasured toward all points alike;
this I've repeatedly shown and proved by logic.
Since this is true, nowhere in all the void   95
have our prime bodies a resting place assigned;
rather, they dash on, onward, this way, that way,
sometimes to dart in safety, far apart,
some at close quarters to meet, clash, and collide.[3]
All those that meet and mass in closer context   100
dart in and away on brief trajectories,
entrapped within their own complex formations;
these form tough-rooted rock and particles
of savage steel and other things like these.
The rest, some few that roam the boundless void,   105
leap far, far out, and from far out race back
in long trajectories; these build thin air,
all that we need, and sunlight, clear and bright.
And many besides that roam the boundless void
have been cast off from compounds but could find   110
no others to join in partnership of movement.
I'll show that this phenomenon always has
a pattern and image that stands before our eyes.
For watch whenever the bright rays of the sun
pour shafts of light into a darkened house: 115
you'll see a thousand motes a thousand ways
commingling in those very shafts of light,
engaged in battle and blow as if in strife
eternal, host against host, without a pause,
uniting, dividing, swiftly, again and again;   120
from this you may conjecture of what sort
is the endless movement of atoms in the void.
To such extent can small things show the likeness
of larger and the steps that lead to knowledge.

3. Atomic motion. According to Epicurean theory, the atoms are always in motion, never at rest, even when they are enclosed within compounds which to our senses appear to be solid and stationary. The sources of atomic motion are twofold: (1) their own weight, and (2) impulse from other atoms. See Introduction, p. xii.

So much the more should you observe these motes   125
that are seen swirling about in rays of sunlight
because their swirl reveals that, all unseen,
under the surface, atoms are on the move.
You'll see many motes propelled by unseen forces,
changing direction, turning, bounding back,   130
whirling now here, now there, now everywhere.
And this, you know, is how all atoms move:
To begin, prime bodies are of themselves in motion;
next, those that gather together in little groups
and are, so to speak, just above atoms in size,   135
are further propelled by blind atomic blows,
then they themselves strike those of larger size.
Thus movement ascends from atoms bit by bit
to the level of our senses, till the motes
we see in sunlight, too, are set in motion,   140
yet by what blows they do this is not clear.
   Now what velocity is assigned to atoms,
Memmius, you may learn in brief from this:
when dawn first sprinkles the earth with fresh, new light,
and bright-colored birds fly through the pathless woods   145
and morning air, filling the world with song,
we see how quickly the sun, just rising then,
colors and curtains the whole world with its light,
for this is clear and manifest to all men.
But the heat and clear, pure light the sun emits   150
pass through no empty void: they are slowed down,
as they must be, whipping their way through waves of air.
Besides, the atoms of heat do not move singly
but interwoven and closely intertwined,
at once impeding themselves and being blocked   155
from without; this makes them move more slowly still.
But atoms are of solid, single substance;
they pass through empty void, and are slowed down
by nothing external; singly, all parts together,
they travel to that one place toward which they started.   160
Therefore they must have greatest velocity
and travel at higher speed than does the sunlight,
racing through far more space in no more time
than sunlight takes to flash across the sky.[4]

*   *   *

4. The speed of atomic motion must be greater than that of light, for light being itself atomic in nature, must make its way through and past other atomic substances, whereas atoms move through void, empty space, and hence are not retarded in any way. After line 164, an unknown number of lines have been lost. The content of the lost lines cannot be satisfactorily conjectured.

nor do they follow the single atoms through 165
that they may see the cause of each event.
Some people, again, in ignorance of matter,
believe that nature, unhelped by godlike power,
could not, so consonant to the needs of man,
have ordered the seasons and created fruits 170
and other things toward which we men are urged
and escorted by holy pleasure, life's true guide
(and teased through sex to reproduce our kind,
lest man die out). When, on these grounds, men fancy
that gods began it all, in all respects 175
they've slipped far off, I think, from truth and reason.
For though I were ignorant of the basic stuff,
still, just from heaven's behavior, I would dare
affirm, and assert on many other grounds,
that gods most certainly never made the world 180
for you and me: it stands too full of flaws.
This, Memmius, I shall soon make clear to you.
Right now, I'll finish my theory of motion.
Now here is the place, I think, in my account,
to state this fact: by its own power, no form 185
of matter can travel upward, or move up;
and don't let bodies of fire deceive you here,
because they start and grow with upward movement,
and gleaming grain grows up, and so do trees,
yet weight itself will always travel downward. 190
We must not think, when fires leap toward the roof
with flame that hurries to taste of board and beam,
they do this by themselves, pushed by no force.
It's just like blood that from our body pours
pulsing and bubbling up and splashing red. 195
See too with what force water tosses back
our boards and beams. The deeper we press them down
and push on them in a body, and heave and strain,
the more it blithely throws them up and sends them
leaping in air, well over half their length. 200
Yet we don't doubt, I'm sure, that of themselves
these things all travel downward through the void.
So too must flames by force of pressure rise
up through the moving atmosphere, although
their weight, of itself, would struggle to draw them down. 205
Don't you observe how torches flying high
in heaven by night draw trains of flame behind them
toward any quarter where nature shows a path?
Haven't you noticed that meteors fall toward earth?
Yes, and the sun from heaven's height throws heat 210

in all directions, sowing the land with light;
the heat of the sun, then, also veers toward earth.
You'll note that lightning flashes athwart the rain:
bolts burst from clouds, now here, now there, and race
to meet in a flaming mass, then fall to earth.   215
    Here too is a point I'm eager to have you learn.
Though atoms fall straight downward through the void
by their own weight, yet at uncertain times
and at uncertain points, they swerve a bit—
enough that one may say they changed direction.[5]   220
And if they did not swerve, they all would fall
downward like raindrops through the boundless void;
no clashes would occur, no blows befall
the atoms; nature would never have made a thing.[6]
If someone thinks that heavier atoms fall   225
straight through the void, but faster, and can drop
from above on lighter ones, and so give rise
to blows that could produce creative movement,
he's drawn away from truth, far from the road.
For things that fall through water and thin air   230
must speed their fall according to their weight,
because the substance, water, and the essence,
soft air, could not impede each thing alike,
but give and yield to heavier bodies faster.
But on the other hand the empty void   235
could nowhere and never impede a single thing,
but, as its nature demands, must yield at once.
And so, through the blank of void, all things must fall
at equal speed, though not of equal weight.
The heavier, then, can never overtake   240
the lighter, causing by themselves those impacts
that start the myriad movements of creation.
And so again and again atoms must swerve
a little—the tiniest bit: we must not picture
crosswise movement, for facts would prove us wrong.   245
For this, we see, is obvious and clear:
weight of itself can never move transversely;
it drops from above straight down, as we observe.
But that no atom ever swerves at all
from the perpendicular, who could sense and see?   250
    To continue: if all movement is connected,
(new movement coming from old in strict descent)
and atoms never, by swerving, make a start

---

5. The "swerve" or "declension" of the atoms.
On this most important doctrine of the Epi-
curean system, see Introduction, p. xii.
6. The natural direction of atomic movement

is always downward, until it is deflected from
this path, either by the Swerve or by impulse
from other atoms. See Introduction, pp. xii.

on movement that would break the bonds of fate
and the endless chain of cause succeeding cause,   255
whence comes the freedom for us who live on earth?[7]
Whence rises, I say, that will torn free from fate,
through which we follow wherever pleasure leads,
and likewise swerve aside at times and places
not foreordained, but as our mind suggests?   260
Beyond all doubt, man's will begins all this
and sends a current of movement through his limbs.
Don't you see too, that though the barriers open
in seconds, the plunging horses can't burst forth
as much on the instant as their will demands?   265
All through their bodies the whole physical mass
must be alerted, so that, alert and tensed
in every limb, it follow the mind's desire.
See, then: the heart creates impulse to movement,
the soul wills it; from there it takes its start   270
and moves on into the body and every limb.
Nor is it the same as when some muscular man
strikes and propels us irresistibly on;
for then, clearly, our total physical being
is hustled involuntarily into movement   275
till over the limbs our will can gain control.
Do you see now: though outside force propel
people and push them willy-nilly on,
and hurry them headlong, still within our hearts
there's something that resists and can fight back,   280
and also of itself sometimes can force
our physical mass to bend in limb and joint,
to push to the fore, hold back, or fall to rest.
Thus to the atoms as well we must allow,
besides their weights and impacts, one more cause   285
of movement—the one whence comes this power we own,
since nothing, we see, could be produced from nothing.
Weight proves that all things are not caused by blows—
external force; that no internal power
controls the mind in every move it makes,   290
a helpless captive bound by what must be:
this comes from the tiny swerving of the atoms
at no fixed place and no fixed point of time.
    Nor was the supply of matter ever packed
more tightly nor, again, more widely spaced,   295
for it has neither increased nor suffered loss.
Therefore the basic bodies show the same
patterns of movement now as in time past

7. On this, the Epicurean doctrine of free will, see *Intro.*, p. xv.

and will always travel the same way in the future;
and what has been brought to be will be again   300
on the same terms, and exist and grow and flourish,
as much, each one, as nature's law allows.
Nor can any power alter the Sum of Things,
for there's no place where matter of any kind
could escape outside the All, nor any source   305
from which new force might break into the All
to change nature and rearrange her patterns.
    One problem here must not cause wonder: why,
though all the basic particles are in motion,
their total seems to stand at total rest,   310
except what moves by its own bodily impulse.
Atomic nature all lies far below
our powers of observation; hence since atoms
cannot be seen, their movements, too, escape us.
Why, yes! Things we could see may often fail   315
to reveal movement when placed some distance from us.
For often upon a hill the fleecy flock
cropping lush lands move slowly where the grass
bespangled with fresh dew calls invitation,
and lambs with a bellyful frisk and tease and nudge;   320
our distant view sees this all run together,
a patch of white pinned bright on deep green hills.
Further, when armies charge full tilt across
the plain, to fill the fields with games of war,
the flash reflects toward heaven, and all the earth   325
mirrors the shining bronze, while from the troops
comes the heavy tramp of feet. Men shout; the hills
re-echoing hurl their voices toward the stars;
the cavalry wheel, then suddenly post and pound
with earthquake power across the open fields.   330
Yet high in the hills there is a place from which
they seem a motionless bright spot on the plain.
    Now learn of the atoms, source of all that is:
what sort they are, in shape how widely varied,
how different in their multifarious forms;   335
not that only a few are of like shape,
but that in general all do not match all.
This is not strange: their number is so great
that, as I proved, it has no end nor sum;
hence all, you see, could not be just like all,   340
of matching size, made form and form alike.
Besides, the human race, and those mute swimmers,
the scale-clad clan, fat cattle, and wild beasts,
the varicolored birds that throng rich waters,

circling the river banks, the springs and swamps 345
and those that flock and fly through pathless woods:
choose any of these, select one single kind
still you will find them differing in appearance.
In no other way could young ones know their mothers
or mothers their young; yet this we see they can: 350
just as do men, they come to know each other.
For often at some handsome holy temple,
near altar and incense, a slaughtered calf has died
while blood flowed hot and bubbling from its throat;
but its mother, bereaved and roaming the fresh green fields, 355
searches the ground for prints of a cloven hoof;
eying each corner, she seeks a glimpse somewhere
of the little one she lost. She stops and fills
the leafy wood with moans, then turns again
back to the barn: grief for her calf strikes deep. 360
The tender willow, the grass crisp with the dew,
rivers in spate at banktop—none have force
to lighten her heart or avert the stroke of pain.
Other calves, spied across the rich, lush lands
cannot deflect her thoughts nor ease her sorrow: 365
so does she yearn for the thing she owns and knows.
Furthermore, tender kids with tremorous cries
know their own horned mothers, and butting lambs
their bleating kin: thus, as nature demands,
each (mostly) trots to his proper milk-filled udder. 370
Finally, take any grains of wheat: you'll see,
though one of kind, they are not all alike;
between the shapes a difference intervenes.
In the same way we see the seashell tribe
painting the lap of earth, where ocean waves, 375
soft on a crescent shore, slake thirsty sands.
Thus, once and again, in just this way, since atoms
are what they are by nature, and not cut
by hand to a single predetermined pattern,
some of them must have shapes unlike some others. 380
    By reasoning we may readily comprehend
why lightning-fire is much more penetrating
than ours that comes from torches here on earth.
For one may say that lightning-fire is finer
(being of heaven) and made in smaller shapes, 385
and thus can pass through openings that our fire
cannot, sprung as it is of wood and torch.
Furthermore, light can pass through horn, but rain
is halted. Why, if not that atoms of light
are smaller than those of water, liquor of life. 390

And wine, we see, will flow on the instant through
a sieve, but oil is hesitant and slow,
either because its particles are larger,
or else more hooked and tightly intertwined;
and this is why they can't be pulled apart   395
so quickly into separate single atoms
that seep through single openings, one by one.
Add this: that liquids such as milk and honey
are pleasurably sensed by tongue and mouth;
but nauseous wormwood and that savage herb   400
centaury rack the mouth with fetid tastes.
Thus you may readily see; the round and smooth
make things that touch the senses pleasurably;
but things that are perceived as harsh or bitter
are built of the hooked and tightly intertwined,   405
and hence they commonly lacerate the paths
of sense and, when they enter, scratch our flesh.

   Lastly, the pleasant to touch, and the unpleasant,
always have different shapes and always fight:
you must not think the harsh, hair-raising screech   410
of a saw consists of particles as smooth
as tunes the instrumenalist awakes
and shapes with nimble fingers on his strings;
you must not think that atoms of like form
enter the nose when corpses stink and scald   415
as when the stage is drenched with Asian crocus
and altars breathe Panchaean frankincense;
you must not judge that pleasant colors—food
fór the eye—consist of atoms just like those
that sting the sight and make the tears well up,   420
or show us the ugly, frightening, or obscene.
For every shape that makes sensation pleasant
has been created from atomic smoothness;
but those that trouble us, that we know as harsh,
are found to be composed of scabrous matter.   425
Then there are some not rightly counted smooth
and yet not hooked at all, nor sharp, nor jagged,
but rather with small projections such as might
tickle the senses more than cause them pain—
the flavors of lees and rue[8] are of this kind.   430
Lastly, the heat of fire and cold of frost
are toothed to puncture the flesh, but differently;
in each case, touch is proof of this to us.
For touch, yes, touch, by all the powers of heaven,

---

8. Strictly speaking, elecampane, an herb not commonly known in America. A bitter herb is meant.

is what we sense, either when things outside   435
penetrate the flesh, or something within offends us
or, leaving us in the act of love, gives joy.
Sometimes a blow upsets our body atoms,
sending them crazily spinning and darting away:
this you yourself may discover if you strike   440
any part you wish of the body with your hand.
In shape, the atoms then must differ widely
since they produce sensations so diverse.
　　To continue: things we see are hard and dense
must be composed of particles hooked and barbed   445
and branch-like, intertwined and tightly gripped.
Now foremost in this class is granite-rock:
its very surface, we know, makes mock of blows;
then too there's flint, and iron, strong and hard,
and bars of bronze that chatter in the lock.   450
Others, again, must be made of more smooth
and spherical stuff: the liquid things that flow.
For poppy-seed is fluid, just like water:
when piled in a heap, it will not keep its shape,
and a flick of the finger sends it rolling down.   455
Finally, everything that we see dispersed ·
quickly, like smoke and clouds and flames, must be,
if not all made of particles round and smooth,
at least not of the tangled and intertwined;
thus they may puncture flesh and pass through stone   460
yet do not cling together: all such we see
* * *　one can easily observe[9]
they are of pointed but not tangled atoms.
Now things you see are bitter but also fluid,
like salt sea-water: think them not strange at all.   465
Whereas they flow, they're made of round and smooth
atoms, but numbers of rough ones interspersed
cause pain. These can't be hooked or interlocked:
though they are rough, you see, they must be round;
thus they may roll but also cause us pain.   470
And that you may better see how rough and smooth
are mixed to make the bitter stuff of Neptune,
there is a way to separate them. Observe
how water, when it has seeped through many strata
of earth, flows as through filters and grows sweet: 475
it leaves behind the atoms of foul brine,
for they, being rough, cling faster to the earth.
　　Since I have proved this point, I next move on
to its dependent theorem: that the atoms

9. The first part of this line is garbled and unintelligible.

exist in a finite number of different shapes.   480
If this weren't so, some atoms, by turnabout,
would have to be of infinite magnitude.
You see, within the limits of small size
the shapes of matter cannot vary much
one from another. Suppose our basic bodies   485
possess three minimal parts, or slightly more.
When you arrange those parts within one body,
spotting them top and bottom, right and left,
you will have found the shapes that each arrangement
of that one body can give—all that there are.   490
If beyond that you seek to make more shapes
you'll have to add more parts; it follows then
that likewise the series will demand still more
if you shall seek to make still further shapes.
In sequence, then, new shapes imply increase   495
in mass. Therefore you have no right to think
atoms may vary infinitely in shape;
else you may force some to assume portentous
vastness—but this I've shown cannot be true.
Why! Your outlandish robes, your Melban[1] reds   500
dipped till they glow in conch of Thessaly,[2]
your peacock-kind, colored all golden-gay,
would be surpassed by things of novel hue;
we'd scorn the odor of myrrh, the taste of honey.
The song of the swan, the magic strings and tunes   505
of Phoebus, would lie, they, too, suppressed and mute;
each one would be surpassed by some new brilliance.
Again things could regress, move toward the worse,
all of them, just as we said they could grow better.
Each backward step would be the fouler then   510
to nose, to ears, to eyes, and to the palate.
But since this is not so, since on both sides
things show a clear-cut limit, you must grant
that matter differs in shapes of finite number.
Lastly, from fire to winter and chill and frost,   515
limits are set, and in reverse, like fashion.
For all degrees of heat and cold and warmth
lie in an orderly scale and make a total
with finite space between the two extremes.
For at either end there is a clear-cut mark: 520
here, made by flame; there, by the freezing cold.
    Since I have proved this point, I next move on

---

1. Strictly, *Meliboean*. Meliboea was a town in Thessaly, but the point of the reference is unknown.
2. The "conch" or sea-snail (*murex*) from which purple dye was made is commonly said to come from Tyre, not from Thessaly. The point of Lucretius' reference is unknown.

to its dependent theroem: that the atoms
made in one shape alike, identical,
are infinite, for though the differences   525
in shape are finite, those alike must be
infinite; otherwise the Sum of Being
is finite; but I've proved this cannot be.
My verses show that particles of matter
out of infinity constitute the Sum,   530
impinging here, there, everywhere, forever.
Whereas you see some animals are rare,
and observe they are less fecund in their nature,
yet in some other spot, some far-off land,
there may be many such, to fill their number.   535
Take quadrupeds: prime instance of this kind
we see in "snake-hand" elephants[3]; by thousands
they build for India an ivory wall
that cannot be penetrated, so vast the horde
of beasts, yet rare the specimens we see.   540
But still, to grant a point: let anything
be quite unique, sole creature of its kind,
which has no like in all the circling world;
yet if there were not endless lots of atoms
from which to beget and bear it, it could not   545
be made, nor, further, feed itself and grow.
Let me assume that atoms for one lone thing
were tossed in finite number through the All:
how could they meet or by what force combine
in that vast sea and alien swirl of matter?   550
They'd have, as I think, no way of joining ranks;
but as when many great ships have met disaster,
the great sea scatters abroad their hulls, their ribs,
rigging and stem and spar and floating oar,
and flotsam litters the seashores of the world,   555
that men may see and learn the proffered lesson:
"The sea is faithless, strong, a trap, a snare:
avoid her, trust her at no hour, and never
when peaceful, laughing waters lure you on,"
so if you once declare one class of atoms   560
finite, they will be scattered for all time
by shifting tides of matter (this must be)
so that no force could make them meet nor hold them
once met, nor add new matter to make them grow.
Yet both these things occur, as plain facts show: 565

3. As far as is known, this picturesque epithet *not appear again until post-classical times, and (anguimanus)* of the elephant was peculiar to *then in obvious reminiscence of Lucretius.* Lucretius, who may have invented it. It does

things come into being and, having come, can grow.
Thus, clearly, the number of atoms of any type
is infinite; and hence all needs are met.
  Further, destructive movements cannot always
prevail, nor sink sound structure in the tomb,   570
nor can creative and augmentive movements
preserve forever intact what they have made.
And thus with forces evenly matched, the atoms
wage war that started when boundless time began.
Now here, now there, the vital force prevails   575
or is defeated; death mingles with the wails
that babies raise on viewing the coasts of light;
no night has followed a day, nor dawn a night
that has not heard, mixed with those bitter cries,
the sobs that march with Death on his dark day.   580
  One point in all of this must be held fixed
firmly and placed in mind to be remembered:
there is no thing, whose nature is clear to see,
that is built of just one single kind of atom,
nor anything not of mixed and varied seed.   585
And the more a thing possesses many traits
and powers, the more it shows itself possessed
of many kinds of atoms and different shapes.
To begin: the earth has in it those prime bodies
by which cool fountains day by day renew   590
the endless sea; has, too, the stuff of fire.
For in many spots the soil is burning hot
and fires deep down feed Aetna's[4] force and fury.
Besides, earth has the stuff from which to raise
rich orchards and sleek grain for humankind,   595
stuff too for fountains, foliage and lush grass
to feed wild animals wandering in the hills.
Hence earth is called at once "great mother of gods,"
"mother of beasts," "life-giver of mankind."
  The ancient poets of Greece have sung of her[5]   600

                        *   *   *

enthroned in her chariot, driving her yoke of lions.
The poets teach that earth hangs in midair
for all its weight: earth cannot rest on earth.[6]
They added the lions since, however savage,

---

4. The reference here, and elsewhere in Lu-
cretius, is to the volcano in Sicily. See note 1,
p. 18.
5. After this line, at least two lines have been
lost. The reference is to Cybele, the Great

Mother of the Gods. See note 9 below.
6. Although editors in general make no note of
the fact, I am convinced that these two lines are
out of place here.

the child must bow before the parent's love.   605
Her head they circled with the mural crown
because with hill and wall she guards their cities:
Wearing this emblem, through the world she rides,
their Mother Divine; men quake before her idol.
Polyglot peoples keep her ancient rite,   610
call her "Mother of Ida," and surround her
with hordes of Phrygians, since that land, they say,
first planted grain and gave it to the world.
Her eunuch priests are sign that those who break
"Our Mother's" law, and prove themselves "ungrateful   615
to father and mother," must be declared unfit
to bring live offspring to the coasts of light.
Palms pound the parchment drumhead, rounded brasses
ring, and the horn makes hoarse, hair-raising howls,
while rhythmic Phrygian flutes drive men insane.   620
The priests bear knives, mark of their mad derangement,
to drive the "hard of heart" and "rude of mind"
to panic in terror of the goddess' power.
So when she makes her way through mighty cities,
without one word mutely making men whole,   625
wherever she goes they strew the ways with money
to make her treasury burst, and with the rose
weave canopies for their "Mother" and her priests.
Here men at arms perform a weapon-dance,
shouting with joy at the blood, and in a frenzy   630
convulsively shaking their fearsome, feathered caps.
Greeks call these dancers "Phrygian Curetes,"[7]
recalling perhaps that at the birth of Zeus
on Dicte in Crete, "Curetes" hid his wails:
boys danced and leaped about the baby then[8]   635
and beat their brazen shields with brazen blades,
that Saturn might not find him and devour him
and deal his mother's heart a cureless wound.
Hence men-at-arms accompany the "Great Mother"—   640
or else they symbolize her holy law
that men must bravely fight for fatherland
and be to their kind a bulwark and an honor.[9]
Though men may style this noble and inspired,
yet it is far removed from truth and reason.   645
For of itself all godhead must possess

7. Hesiod speaks of these as semidivine crea-
tures, who protected Zeus at his birth from the
fury of his father, Kronos. The origin of the
name is unknown. Strictly speaking, the Cu-
retes were devotees of Rhea, rather than of
Cybele, but the two were commonly identified:
see note 9 below.

8. Line 636 is generally regarded as an interpo-
lation and has been omitted.
9. The reference is to Cybele, the Great
Mother of the Gods, whose cult centered on
Mt. Ida in Phrygia, and to her orgiastic worship.
She was identified with Rhea, the earth god-
dess, whose cult centered on Mt. Ida in Crete.

immortal life and perfect peace and joy,
cut off from human affairs and sundered far.
Gods know no suffering, they know no dangers,
their self-engendered power needs naught of us;   650
we cannot win their love or rouse their anger.
And earth? It is insensate, now and always;
it holds within it the atoms of countless things,
and hence brings vast variety to the light.
If a man insists on calling the ocean "Neptune"   655
and grain "Ceres," and rather than use the word
proper to liquor, perversely names it "Bacchus,"
let us allow him to call this orb of earth
"the Mother of Gods," provided that in the fact
he never infects his mind with foul religion.   660
    Yes, often from one lone field beneath one sky
the woolly sheep, the warlike equine breed,
and cows (those hornèd heads) will crop the grass,
and from a single stream will slake their thirst,
yet keep identity, kind by kind preserving   665
their parents' nature and holding to their ways:
so vast and various is the tale of matter
in a single kind of grass and in one river.
And any one of the lot is also built
of bones, blood, veins, heat, water, guts, and sinew   670
from the same source, yet all dissimilar far,
made up of atoms arranged in different patterns.
Then, too, all things that are consumed by fire,
if nothing else, yet store within their mass
the source of power to put forth flame and light,   675
to shoot the spark and send the ashes flying.
Take all things else; survey them with like logic:
you'll find they hide within their mass the seeds
of many things, arranged in varied patterns.
You see many things as well that give off taste,   680
color, and smell together. First are the gifts[1]

*   *   *

These then must be composed of varied shapes;
smells enter the body in ways that color can't;
color and taste have each their special paths
to the senses: hence, in basic shape, they differ.   685
Dissimilar shapes, then, gather into one
conglomerate, and things are of mixed seed.
Why, yes! In the very verse I write, you see

1. After this line, at least one line has been lost.

dozens of letters shared by dozens of words,
and yet you must admit that words and verses 690
consist, now of these letters, now of those;
not that few letters rarely run through all,
or that no two have letters all alike,
but that in general all do not match all.
So too with other things: although they share 695
many an atom with many a thing, yet still
in total constitution they may be
unlike; thus, rightly, man and corn and tree
are said to be composed of other things.
Yet still we must not think all things can join 700
all ways, for we'd see monsters everywhere:
creatures would grow half-man, half-beast, and tall
branches would sometimes sprout from living flesh;
land-limb and sea-limb often would be conjoined,
and ugly dragons breathing stench and flame 705
would range and browse an omniparient earth.
Clearly, this never happens, since each thing
sprung of its own specific seed and parent,
grows always true to type, as we observe.
The process, of course, must follow clear-cut laws. 710
Foods are absorbed; from these the proper atoms
spread to the body's parts, combine and cause
suitable movements. Alien stuff is cast
by nature back upon earth; much substance flees
the body unseen, impelled by unseen blows— 715
atoms all unabsorbed that could not catch
or imitate the inward pulse of life.
And do not think that only animate creatures
follow these rules: the same law governs all.
For just as all created things are different 720
one from another in every way, so each
must have its own distinct atomic pattern;
not that only a few are of like shape
but that in general all do not match all.
Since atoms differ, they must be different too 725
in spacing, direction, texture, weight, and impact,
in speed and force; these make the different types
of animate creatures, keep all earth and sea
distinct, and hold the heavens clear of earth.
    Come now and hear the words I chose with joy 730
and care. Before your eyes you see white objects:
you must not think the white comes from white atoms,
or that black atoms make black objects black;
and anything else of any other color:

do not believe its substance wears this hue 735
because its atoms are tinted with like color.[2]
For atoms of matter have no color at all,
not like the color of things, and not unlike.
And if you think the mind can't come to grips
with atoms like these, you've wandered far astray. 740
For since the blind-from-birth, who've never seen
the sunlight, can distinguish things by touch
from childhood on, without the aid of color,
you can be sure our minds can also grasp
the concept of atoms wholly devoid of hues. 745
Further, things we ourselves in blinding night
touch, we perceive, although they show no color.
Since I've established this, I now will prove[3]

* * *

In general, all things suffer change of color,
but this our basic particles must not do. 750
For something must survive unchangeable,
lest everything in the world be turned to nothing.
For whatever changes and leaves its natural bounds
is instant death of that which was before.
Hence never stain the seeds of things with color, 755
lest everything in the world revert to nothing.
    Further, if to the atoms is assigned
no color, and they're endowed with different shapes,
creating hence all types and shapes of colors,
then—since it matters much how given atoms 760
combine: in what arrangements, with what others,
what impulse they receive, and what impart—
you can explain outright with greatest ease
why things which moments ago were black in color
can all at once turn gleaming marble-white: 765
    Witness the sea: when storm winds ruffle its planes
it turns to white-capped waves, with marbled gleam.
Take, then, a thing we normally see as black;
stir up its substance, alter its arrangement
of atoms, add or take away a few: 770
we'll see it turn at once a shining white.
But if the level sea were made of blue
atoms, by no device could it turn white.
For, tumble how you will things that are blue,

---

2. Atoms possess only size, shape, and weight. They do not possess any secondary qualities: color, temperature, sound, taste, smell, life, and sentience are all produced by combinations of atoms and void.

3. After this line, at least one line has been lost.

they'd never move across to marble-white.   775
But if atoms now of this hue, now of that,
make up the ocean's one consistent color,
as commonly out of different shapes and forms
we make an object single and four-square,
then, as in four-square objects we perceive   780
those varied shapes, so should we, in the sea
or anything else of one consistent color,
see many different, widely varied hues.
Further, the different shapes do not prevent
our object's being perfectly square outside,   785
but varied colors do impede and stop
a thing from being wholly of one hue.

Still more: the cause that draws and lures us on
sometimes to endow our primal stuff with color,
falls down, for white things do not spring from white   790
nor black from black, but from all sorts of colors.
Why, yes! White things more readily will arise
from something colorless than from something black,
or from any other that fights or blocks the way.
Further, since colors, now, cannot exist   795
when there's no light, and atoms don't come to light,
you'll understand that colors don't paint the atom.
For in blind night, what colors could there be?
Why! In broad daylight colors change because
they reflect the light directly or obliquely.   800
Take pigeons: watch their plumage in the sun;
the feathers that make a ring all round the neck—
sometimes you'll see them turn bright ruby-red,
and then again you'll sense a change, and see
pink coral intermixed with emerald-green.   805
And peacocks' tails, when sunlight shines full on them,
will likewise, as they catch the light, change color;
now since these colors come when light has struck,[4]
without it, we must conclude, they could not be.
And since the eye receives one kind of impulse   810
when it is said to sense the color "white,"
and different kinds for "black" and all the rest,
but it doesn't matter, when you touch a thing,
what color it is, but rather what its shape,
you may be sure the atoms need no color,   815
but vary impact by their variant forms.[5]
Further, since no fixed color is assigned

4. Lucretius here makes the astute observation that color is produced by the reflection of light, and cannot be observed in the absence of light.
5. The point here is that sight is only a second-ary sense; like all the senses, it is dependent on touch. Only touch—i.e., impact of material bodies—is primary and fundamental. See 1.302–4.

to a given shape, and any configuration
of atoms may be present in any hue,
why do not things composed of atoms show,   820
alike in all their types, all kinds of colors?
Why! Then, at any time, a flying crow
might get white feathers and show the color white,
and swans, from atoms of black, turn black themselves,
or green, blue, orange, brown—what shade you like.   825
    And further, the more a given thing is shredded
finer and finer the more you can observe
its color fade and gradually disappear,
as happens when purple cloth is torn to bits:
the red, the scarlet color so bright and clear,   830
as we pick it to single threads, is all destroyed.
Hence you can see that fragments lose all color
before they are broken down to single atoms.
    Lastly, since you concede that not all things
emit a sound or an odor, you would never   835
attribute noises and odors to everything.
Likewise, since we don't sense all things by sight,
we know some things exist as much devoid
of colors as others of odor and of sound,
and that the mind as shrewdly tells their names   840
as it marks out things deprived of other signs.
    But lest you think that atoms are deprived
only of color, they are devoid as well
of warmth; they have no cold nor scalding heat.
They're sterile of sound; we say they "thirst for taste;"   845
their substance gives out no distinctive odor.
As when you would concoct seductive perfumes—
marjoram, say, or myrrh, or *fleur de nard*
("breath of the nectar")—you must first search out,
as far as it may be found, an oil by nature   850
odorless, wafting nothing to the nose,
so that when scents are stirred and steeped in it,
its sluggish flow may touch but not destroy them;
for just this reason, atoms must not bring
scent or sound of their own to things they make   855
since they can throw off nothing from themselves,
and in like fashion bring no flavor, either,
nor cold nor heat, of high degree or low.[6]

* * *

the rest are such as to be clearly mortal—

6. I follow Giussani in assuming the loss of several lines here.

unstable, weak, soft, pliant, porous, light—   860
and from the atoms must all be kept distinct,
if under Being we mean to set a base
immortal, a resting place for permanence,
lest everything in the world revert to nothing.

Now all we know as sentient is composed   865
of insensate atoms; this you must admit
in every case. Plain facts do not refute it;
it's not opposed by things we clearly see:
rather, they guide and force us to believe
that, as I say, life springs from the insensate.   870
Why, of course! You may see living worms emerge
from rotting manure, when earth has found itself
all wet and stinking from untimely rains.
All other things as well transform themselves.
The flowing stream and foliage and lush grass   875
turn into cattle; cattle turn their substance
into our flesh, and often from our flesh
wild beasts and feathered kinds build flesh and strength.
So nature turns all food to living flesh,
and in the living creates the powers of sense,   850
almost exactly as she breaks dry wood
down into flame, and turns it all to fire.
Now do you see, then, that it matters much
how atoms are arranged, and how combined,
how they are moved, and how set others moving?   885

Further, what is it that hits you in the heart,
troubles you, drives you to feel in many ways
that the insensate can't produce the sentient?
Just this: if sticks and stones and earth are mixed
together, they still produce no life nor feeling.   890
In this respect one point must be recalled:
I did not claim that all things which create
the sentient always do so out of hand,
but that it matters much how small may be
the creators of sense, and with what form endowed,   895
and what may be their movements and arrangements.
Those requisites we don't see in wood and soil,
yet when they're rotted, so to speak, by rain
they bring forth worms, because their atoms, moved
by new conditions from their ancient patterns,   900
now join in ways that must make living things.
Next: Those who claim that sentient things do spring
from sentient, and these from others that can sense[7]

*   *   *

7. Editors indicate the loss of several lines here.

they make them soft. For sense is always joined
to viscera, sinews, veins; all these we see   905
created soft and made of mortal substance.
But grant that these things could go on forever:
then they must either own sense in some part
or else be sentient like whole living creatures.
But parts cannot be sentient by themselves;   910
the sentience of our parts depends on us:
neither a hand nor any other part
cut off from us stays sentient by itself.
It follows they must be like whole living creatures,
to share throughout their substance life and sentience.   915
How could they be called primal matter, then,
and not face death, since they'd be living beings,
and living beings are also mortal beings?
Suppose they could; still when they joined and met,
they'd make just this: a lot of living beings.   920
For men and beasts both wild and tame, create
by mutual meeting not one different thing.
So primal matter would feel just what we feel.
But if, perhaps, they lose their native sense
and acquire another, what need to grant the sense   925
we take away? Besides, as we have seen,
since we observe that birds' eggs turn to living
nestlings, and that earth seethes with worms when rains
out of due season cause it to decay,
we rightly conclude that sense comes from non-sense.   930
  But if someone should say that sense can rise
from non-sense only through the power of change,
or through extrusion by some kind of birth,
it will suffice to show and prove to him
that birth must be preceded by coition,   935
and that no change takes place without joint action.
In the first place, no senses can exist
in matter before we have a living creature,
because, of course, its substance is dispersed
in air, stream, earth, and things born of the earth,   940
and hasn't foregathered nor made those balanced movements
proper to life, that start sensation, guard
all-watchful, guardian of each living thing.
  Further, take any form of life: a blow
too heavy for it will damage it forthwith,   945
distorting sentience all through mind and body;
their atoms lose their relative positions,
and movements proper to life are checked or stopped,
till substance, shaken in all its members, breaks

the bonds of life twixt soul and flesh, ejecting 950
the shattered soul piecemeal through every pore.
For what else do we think a proffered blow
would do except to shatter and destroy?
Often, besides, when blows less hard have struck,
some vital movements are left to win the day, 955
yes, win, and heal the wound's huge dislocations,
call substance back into its proper paths,
and, though death now is dominant, knock its routes
awry, and kindle senses almost lost.
How else should man have power to marshal mind 960
and rather, at death's door, turn back to life,
than run to the end a course so nearly finished?

　　Further, since pain occurs when in our parts
and organs, atoms of matter are disturbed
and shaken from location by some force, 965
but pleasure results when they drop back in place,
you'll see that atoms cannot be attacked
by any pain, nor, of themselves, gain pleasure,
since, out of all the atoms, there are none
whose movements could, by change, be rendered painful, 970
or garner the fruits of sweet life-giving joy.
Atoms must not, then, be endowed with sense.

　　To continue: if, for animals to be sentient,
we must attribute sentience to their atoms,
what of the atoms that go to build mankind? 975
Of course! When something strikes them odd, they laugh
until they sprinkle their faces with bright tears;
they lecture sagely and long on mixing matter,
and seek to discover what the atoms are.
Since they are likened to mortal things throughout, 980
they must be made of other elements, too,
and those, of others; you'd find no stopping place:
whatever you say can speak and laugh and think,
I'll claim is made of others that do the same.
But if we observe that this is foolish nonsense; 985
if man, made of nonlaughing stuff, can laugh,
and think, and couch this thought in artful speech,
though made of atoms that neither think nor speak,
why cannot all the sentient things we see
be put together of atoms void of sense?

　　To continue: we're all sprung of heavenly seed; 990
one is father of all.[8] From him the earth,

8. By "heavenly" (*caeleste*) Lucretius of course does not mean "divine," but simply "coming from the sky." The rain, coming from the sky (the "father") joins with the substance of the earth (the "mother") to create all the forces of life; cf. 1.250–61. Conversely, death is not destruction but rather the dissipation of the compounds formed by the joining of "sky" and "earth."

life-giving mother, receives bright liquid drops,
then, pregnant, bears lush fruits and shining corn,
the race of man, and every kind of beast;   995
she gives them food by which they all are fed,
lead happy lives, and propagate their kind;
quite rightly, then, she gains the name of "mother."
Then, too, what came from earth before returns
to earth, and what has dripped from heaven's bounds   1000
is taken once again back to the skies.
Yet death, in killing things, does not destroy
their atoms, but only dissipates their compounds.
By joining one to one, one to another,
she makes them change their colors and their forms,   1005
gain sense, and lose it in a minute's time.
Know then, it matters much how given atoms
combine: in what arrangements, with what others,
what impulse they receive, and what impart.
Don't think the superficial characteristics   1010
we sometimes see, that come and go in things,
can be firm-fixed to the eternal atoms.
You see, in the very verse I write, it matters
how letters are arranged and how combined:
the same ones token earth, sky, sea, and stream,   1015
the same the sun, the animals, grain, and trees;
they match—not all the way, but in large part:
by their positions, they tell us different things.
Likewise in things themselves, if change is made
in joinings, motion, position, patterns, shape[9]   1021
of substance, then the things, too, must be changed.
    Now grant me your attention: hear the truth.
A new idea is pressing to be heard,
a new aspect of nature to be revealed.   1025
But there's no thought so simple that at first
it won't be difficult to accept, and none
so vast, so wonderful, that bit by bit
it won't seem less astounding to us all.
To begin, the clear, clean color of the sky,   1030
and all it contains, the ever-wandering stars.
the moon, yes, and the sun's bright gleaming light:
if all these things were, without warning, now
tossed all at once before man's mortal eye,
what could be called more marvelous than this,   1035
what would man less have dared expect to see?
Nothing, I think: so strange had been that sight.
Yet no one now, for weariness of looking,

9. Line 1020 is omitted by editors.

lifts up a jaded eye to heaven's bright sphere.
Then don't, in terror at sheer novelty, 1040
hound reason from your heart, but weigh my words
with finer judgment, and, if you find them true,
surrender, or if false, take arms against them.
Intelligence asks for answers: since this whole,
outside the walls of the world, is infinite, 1045
what is there to act as guideline for the mind?
Where will objective thought speed to its goal?

   To begin: in all directions everywhere—
this side and that, above, below, throughout—
there is no end; I proved it, and plain fact 1050
proclaims it; the nature of outer space is clear.
In no way, now, will logic let us think,
since empty space runs endless everywhere,
and atoms in countless count speed through the depths
of the All a thousand ways, and never rest, 1055
that only our earth and sky have been created,
and all those atoms of matter out there do nothing;
after all, our world was made by nature, when
atoms, meeting by chance, spontaneously,
and joined in myriad useless, fruitless ways, 1060
at last found patterns, which when thrown together
became at once the origin of great things—
earth, sea, and sky, and life in all its forms.
And so again and again you must admit
that other meetings of matter exist elsewhere 1065
like this of ours which ether holds close-gripped.

   Furthermore, when much matter is on hand,
when space is there, and neither law nor substance
hinders, events must happen and things be made.
Now if the atoms exist in such great numbers 1070
that all our lifetimes could not count them through,
if nature and the power that could cast
atoms into relations such as those
they're cast in here persist, you must admit
that other circled earths exist elsewhere 1075
and other nations of men and kinds of beasts.

   Now add that in the Sum there's not one thing
that could be born and grow unique and single,
but must be of some class, with countless others
of that same kind. Consider animals first. 1080
You'll find a "genus" of mountain-faring beasts,
and men in "races," and similarly the mute
scaly creatures and all the flesh that flies.
Therefore in similar wise you must admit

that sky, earth, sun, moon, sea, and all the rest   1085
are not unique but numberless in number;
for their life's limits are as deeply set
and their identities are as much created
as all our myriad things here, kind by kind.
    If you have grasped this well, you see that nature,   1090
free in a world no lords and masters rule,
does everyting by herself, without the gods.
For, by the gods, those holy, tranquil hearts
that pass their days in peace, and live serene,
who now could rule the Infinite? Who could hold   1095
in hand and govern the guidelines of the deeps,
move all those heavens in harmony, and beneath
the fires of space plant all those fruitful earths,
be present in every place at every hour,
make night with clouds, shatter the clear, bright sky   1100
with thunder, hurl the lightning, throw down temples—
often their own!—then flying to lonely spots
savagely practice with shafts that often spare
the guilty and murder misused innocence?.
    Now since the world was born, and since the birthday   1105
of land and sea, the day the sun first rose,
new matter has come from space, as countless atoms
were added that the universe hurled this way;
hence land and sea could grow, hence the broad sky
come into view and raise her vaulted halls   1110
high above earth, and hence could air rise up.
For all these atoms, from whatever place impelled,
move toward their own, each seeeking out its kind:
water joins water, while atoms of earth cause earth
to grow; fire forges fire, and ether, ether,   1115
until creative nature ends her work
and brings them all to growth's last boundary;
this happens when no more than what escapes
is added to the vital flux within.
In all things here, the span of life must end;   1120
here nature curbs increase by her own power.
For all things that you see so gaily growing
and step by step climbing to full-formed life,
take to themselves more atoms than they lose
as long as food moves freely to every channel,   1125
and they're not stretched so thin that they lose much,
and pay out more than the process of life takes in.
For you must allow that many atoms flow
away from things; but more must come to them
until they reach the highest peak of growth.   1130
Then little by little time breaks their full-blown strength

and powers, as life grows weaker and melts away.
Yes, and the bigger a thing is at full growth,
and the broader it is, the more it sprinkles atoms
in all directions, a loss from its own substance;   1135
nor does its food move freely to every channel,
nor, in view of its vast and surging losses,
can it find supply and source to meet its needs.
Such things are bound to die when they've been weakened
by losses and overcome by outside blows,   1140
since finally in old age they lack for food,
and atoms outside them, pounding endlessly,
strike them, weaken them, damage and master them.
So, too, the walls round this great world of ours,
once taken, will crumble to ruin and decay.   1145
For food must make things whole, renew them all,
food must sustain and food support all things;
yet in the end their channels can't supply
the needed resilience, or nature the needed food.
And now earth is so weakened and worn out   1150
she scarce creates small creatures, she who once
made every kind and bore enormous beasts.
For, as I think, it was no golden chain[1]
dropped mortal kinds to earth from heaven above,
nor sea nor moaning floods created rocks,   1155
but earth who feeds them now begot them then.
Further, for mortal men she first created,
of her own will, lush vineyards and sleek grain,
herself produced lush pastures and sweet produce.
Yet now these scarcely grow for all our toil;   1160
we weary our oxen, sap the farmer's strength,
wear plows away in fields that scarce support us,
so niggard the crops, our labors so increased.
The aged plowman sighs and shakes his head
again and again—all that work gone for naught!—   1165
compares the present times with times gone by,
and often remarks how lucky his father was.
Discouraged, the vintner tends his tattered vines,
curses the weather, and prays till heaven is tired;
he growls of an age long gone, when men were good,   1170
and found life easy though their world was small,
and the land that each man held was then far less.
He does not see that all things slowly weaken
and fall to ruin,[2] worn out by ages past.

---

1. The idea is derived from Homer, *Iliad* 8.19.
It was widely propagated in antiquity, notably
by the Stoics, as an allegory of the divine nature
of life.

2. This is my guess at the meaning of what-
ever text the MSS *ire ad scopulum* may conceal.

Book III

Out of deep darkness you were first to lift
that light whose beam illumines the good in life;
you, glory of Greece,[1] I follow, and in the marks
your feet have pressed, I set and mold my step;
I strive to do as you did, not so much   5
in rivalry as in love: how could the swallow
vie with the swan or, in a race, the kid
match spindly legs against a great strong horse?
You are our father, founder, patron, teacher;
yours are the precepts; from your sacred page,   10
as bees in meadows taste of every flower,
we likewise feed on all your Golden words,
golden, most worthy of eternal life.
For when your Reason, sprung from godlike mind,
begins to formulate Nature's Law, at once   15
the heart's terrors disperse, the walls of the world
draw back; I see things happening all through space.
There shine the gods in glory, and their blest home,
which neither wind can shake nor storm bestrew
with clouds; nor snow crystaled by cutting frost   20
fleck with a fall of white; its roof is a heaven
cloudless forever, a gay expanse of light.
Nature supplies their every need, and nothing
takes from their peace of mind at any hour.
But nowhere do we glimpse the halls of hell,   25
though Earth's not there to block our view of all
that happens under our feet down through the void.
At this, a feeling of godlike awe and pleasure
grips me, because through you the world of Being
stands wide, distinct, revealed on every side.[2]   30
      And since I've taught what bodies begin all things,
what sort they are, how varied in their forms,
how, self-impelled, they speed and never rest,
and how from them each thing may be created;
after these topics, my task must be to show   35
in this my poem the nature of soul and mind,[3]

1. Epicurus.
2. Epicurean Theology: the gods exist; they live
a life of eternal peace and tranquillity. But they
are without either the will or the power to affect
our world in any way. A more detailed account
of the gods is given 5.146–234 and 6.70–75.
3. Latin *animus* and *anima*. In general, the
ancients did not distinguish between soul and
mind, but regarded both as appropriate names
for the incorporeal aspects of human life. To
the Epicureans, of course, soul and mind were
corporeal, made up of atoms, like all other
forms of Being. Later on in his argument
(3.136–51) Lucretius will use the terms *animus*
and *anima* in a specialized sense, to denote the
parts of the soul. Still later (3.417 ff.) he will
reverse the process and use the terms inter-
changeably.

and drive outside, headlong, that fear of hell
which, top to bottom, muddies the life of man,
roiling it all with death's dark murk, and leaving
no single pleasure pure and unalloyed.   40
For though men often claim to fear a life
of illness or disgrace more than death's darkness,
and say they know the substance of the soul
is blood or even wind—just take your choice!—
and have no need at all of my fine "reason,"   45
you'll see that this springs more from vanity
and thirst for praise than from sincere conviction.
Put these same men in exile, drive them far
from the sight of man, disgrace them, call them felons,
put them to every torment, still they live,   50
wherever they find themselves, poor fools, and pray,
and kill black cows, and send death offerings down
to the ghouls and ghosts: misfortune stirs their hearts
to even keener zeal for their religion.
Yes, it is better to watch a man in doubt   55
and danger, see what he is when all's gone wrong;
for only then will truth come from the heart,
the mask be torn away, the man remain.
Greed, too, and blind passion for public office,
that make poor fools transgress the bounds of law,   60
and sometimes join to serve a criminal cause,
contending, striving, straining night and day
to rise to the top of the heap: these ulcered lives
are nourished in no small part by fear of death.
The man forgotten is shamed, the poor man bleeds;   65
such lives seem far from sweet stability,
like early dalliers at the gates of death.
When men, driven by unreal terror, seek
to flee from here and move far, far away,
with blood of friends and neighbors they buy wealth,   70
then greedily double it, piling murder on murder.
A brother dies: they weep with heartless joy;
they loathe a kinsman's board, and fear to share it.
In similar wise often through that same fear
they're racked with envy to see some man gain power,   75
to see men watch him march to fame and glory,
"while we must grovel," they whine, "in muck and darkness!"
Some give their lives for statues and a name.
And often through fear of death men come to hate
life and the sight of the sun so bitterly   80
that in a burst of grief they kill themselves,
forgetting it was this fear that caused their cares,

troubled their conscience, broke their bonds of friendship,
and overturned all sense of decency.
Often men have betrayed both fatherland   85
and family, seeking escape from hell's grim halls.
For as in the dead of night children are prey
to hosts of terrors, so we sometimes by day
are fearful of things that should no more concern us
than bogeys that frighten children in the dark.   90
This fright, this night of the mind must be dispelled
not by the rays of the sun, nor day's bright spears,
but by the face of nature and her laws.
    First I speak of the soul (sometimes called "mind"),
in which life's thoughts and government are placed;   95
it's no less part of a man than hand and foot
and eyes are parts of the total living creature.[4]

                        *   *   *

that the sentient soul is not placed in some part
but is a condition of the living flesh
(Greeks call it a "harmony") that gives us life   100
and sentience, though we've nowhere any "mind";
as when we commonly say we "have" good health,
though health is no *part* of a healthy man.
Thus they assign the soul to no fixed place—
in which, I think, they err in several ways.   105
Often our visible surface-parts are ill
while deep in the inner man we feel content;
and then in turn the opposite often happens:
the soul may suffer, when with the flesh all's well;
precisely as, when a sick man's foot feels pain,   110
there is in his head perhaps no pain at all.
Besides, when we've surrendered to sweet sleep,
and wearied flesh lies limp without sensation,
there's something within us still that at such times
keeps constantly moving, to each pulse of joy   115
susceptible, and to all the heart's vain cares.
Now learn how soul is one among our members,
and that no harmony makes the body sentient.
To begin: though large part of our flesh be lost,
yet often life still lingers in our limbs;   120
but again when some few particles of heat
have fled, and through the mouth air[5] has escaped,

4. After this line, an unknown number of lines are lost. The sense of the missing lines would have been "others disagree, and insist . . ."
5. Heat and air are two of the basic constituents of the soul. Lucretius sometimes seems to work too hard at finding synonyms for these words: at 126, he calls them "warmth" and "wind." For a complete account of the atomic constituents of the soul, see 3.231–57, and note 7 below.

life leaves at once, deserting vein and bone.
Learn hence: all atoms do not play all parts
alike, nor all alike support well-being;   125
rather, atoms that make up wind and warmth
take care that life may linger in our limbs.
Therefore, within our bodies there is heat
and vital wind that leave us when we die.
And so, since mind and soul are found to be   130
part, so to speak, of man, hand back that word,
harmony, from high Helicon sent to tunesmiths
(or maybe they got it elsewhere and transferred it
to a thing that then possessed no proper name;
in any case, let them keep it!) Hear the rest.   135
    I now declare that mind and soul[6] are joined
together, and form one single entity,
but the head, so to speak, that rules in all the body,
is counsel, mind, and intellect, as we say,
and this is placed midway within the breast.   140
For here leap terror and panic, this spot feels
sweet joy; here, then, are intellect and mind.
The rest of the soul, dispersed through all the body,
obeys the mind and moves to its command.
For mind thinks its own thoughts, knows its own pleasures, 145
when nothing has stimulated soul or body.
And as when injury attacks our head
or eye, they hurt, but we're not agonized
all over, thus the mind sometimes feels pain
or joy and strength, when other parts of soul   150
in limb and joint have felt no novel impulse.
But when the mind is deeply stirred by terror,
all through the body we see the soul affected;
we pale, and over all the body sweat
pours out, the tongue stumbles, voice goes awry,   155
eyes are befogged, ears ring, the knees give way,
yes, from sheer terror of mind we often see
men fall in a faint; thus readily we perceive
the union of soul and mind, for soul, when struck
by mind, in turn strikes body and makes it move.   160
    This argument also proves that soul and mind
are physical things. Clearly, they move our limbs,
arouse the body from sleep, change our expression,
and guide and govern the man in all his being.
Yet without touch, we see, such things can't happen,   165

6. As here stated, the "mind" is the central, governing entity, located (naively) by Lucretius in the breast. The "soul" is the diffused entity, scattered throughout the body. In function, Lucretius' "mind" is similar to the brain, his "soul" to the nervous system, but neither he nor Epicurus ever made this association.

nor touch without matter; must we not then admit
the soul and mind in fact are physical things?
Besides, we see that in our bodies, soul
and body act and react in sympathy.
If a bristling spear has driven deep, exposing   170
sinew and bone, and yet not taking life,
still faintness follows and sweet swooning down
to earth, and there a sense of rocking motion,
sometimes with vaguely felt desire to rise.
And so the soul must be a physical thing,   175
since physical weapon and wound can make it suffer.
     I'll now proceed to argument and proof
of what makes up the soul, and what its substance.
To begin, I say the soul is subtly built
of infinitesimal atoms. You may see   180
and learn that this is so from what's to come.
Nothing whatever, we see, can move as fast
as the mind when it conceives and starts an action;
thus nothing whose nature clearly lies within
our range of vision moves faster than the mind.   185
But whatever is so mobile must be made
of very round and very tiny atoms,
so that the slightest impulse starts them moving.
Yes, just a touch makes water move and flow:
it's made, you see, of small-sized shapes that roll.   190
But the nature of honey tends to be more stable;
its fluid is thicker and less disposed to move.
For all the atoms of its substance cling
more closely, being of particles less smooth,
you see, and not so delicate or so round.   195
Take poppyseed: a gentle puff of air
at the top will blow a tall heap helter-skelter,
but not, on the other hand, a heap of stones
or grain. According, then, as particles
are smallest and smoothest, they will move with ease.   200
But on the other hand, as some are found
rougher and heavier, so are they more stable.
Now since the soul has been revealed to be
uncommonly mobile, we must grant it made
of atoms very tiny, smooth, and round.   205
Take this to heart, good friend; in many ways
you'll find it a useful, helpful thing to know.
This fact, too, tells the nature of the soul,
how fine its fabric, and in how small a space
it could be held, if it were all rolled up: 210
when once the carefree peace of death has seized

a man, and the substance of soul and mind has left him,
from his whole body you'd see nothing lost
in appearance or in weight; death leaves him all
but the humid heat and sentience that mean life.   215
The entire soul, then, must consist of tiny
atoms, strung out through sinews, vitals, veins,
since, when it all has gone from all the body,
the outer dimensions of body-parts remain
unaltered, and not an ounce of weight is lost.   220
It's such as when bouquet of wine floats off,
or breath of perfume is wafted to the winds,
or when from a substance flavor dies away;
to the eye, the physical thing appears no smaller
for all of that, and suffers no loss of weight.   225
Why? Because many minuscule atoms make
flavors and scents throughout the range of things.
Thus you may know the substance of the mind
and soul, I insist, is formed of most minute
atoms, for, slipping away, it steals no weight.   230
    But don't conclude that soul's a single substance.[7]
When we are dying a delicate "wind" deserts us;
it's mixed with "warmth" and "warmth" draws with it "air."
No form of heat exists not mixed with air.
Since heat has porous structure, many atoms   235
of air are bound to circulate within it.
We find that soul, then, has a threefold nature.
And yet all three cannot create sensation,
for none of these conceivably could cause
sense-bearing movements[8]   240

*   *   *

There must be another substance, then, a fourth,
added to these, and this one has no name.
There's nothing more mobile or tenuous than this,
or made of smaller or smoother particles;
this starts sense-bearing movements through our bodies,   245
for this, built of small shapes, is first to move.
It then sets heat, and wind (the unseen power)
in motion, and then air, then all things move:

7. The four elements that make up the soul are (1) "wind," Latin *aura*, i.e., moving air, a cooling element; (2) "air," Latin *aer*, static air, a stabilizing element; (3) "warmth," Latin *vapor*, heat, a stimulating element (in its extreme form, it is the source of strong emotions); and (4) the "fourth nature," Latin *quarta natura*, to which Lucretius can give no name and which he can only describe as "more mobile or tenu-ous" (243) than any of the others. It is tempting to see it as the atomic substance of life itself—as made up of "atoms of life"—although neither Lucretius nor Epicurus ever expressed the idea. Variations in proportion and prominence of these four elements account for variations in personality: see 3.294–322.
8. The latter part of this line is hopelessly garbled.

the blood surges, and all our inward parts
feel it; last to be stirred are bone and marrow,   250
whether by pleasure or its opposing blast.
Pain cannot pierce that deep nor acrid evil
seep there, without such total dislocation
that no room's left for life; the shattered soul
runs out through the body's every pore and passage.   255
But sometimes, just at the surface, movement stops
and thus allows us to retain our lives.
    Next, how these elements of the soul are mixed
and arranged to give them power, I'd like to tell,
but the poverty of my native tongue forbids it;   260
still, best as I can, I'll touch the salient points.
The atoms of the elements race down paths
so interlocked that none could be exsected,
nor could their separate powers be marked off;
they're like one thing with many characteristics.   265
As in the parts of animals, commonly
there's odor, heat, and taste, yet from all these
together, a single complex is composed.
Thus heat and air and wind (the unseen power)
might join to make one substance, plus that mobile   270
force[9] that initiates movement for the others,
whence through the body sense-bearing movement starts.
This force, you see, is hidden deep, deep down;
it is the inmost element in the body,
and is, beyond that, the soul of all the soul.   275
As in our parts and the body as a whole
the force commingled of mind and soul lies hidden
because its atoms are small and widely spaced,
just so this nameless substance made of tiny
atoms, lies hidden and is, as it were, the soul   280
of the total soul and rules our total being.
In similar fashion, wind and air and heat
must show a corporate power in our bodies;
one may lie under the others or rise above
so that they all three seem to become just one,   285
yet heat and wind alone, or air alone,
single and separate, would destroy sensation.
Heat, now, the soul does have, and puts to use
when wrath boils up and eyes flash hot with fire;
wind it has, too, cold comrade of our fears,   290
that makes us shiver and unstrings the knees.
And then there's air, pacific, static thing,
that comes with tranquil mind and smiling face.

9. I. e., the "fourth nature." See note 7, above.

But they have more of heat whose hearts burn high
and with slight cause flare up and seethe with fury.   295
High among these we rank the savage lion,
who often roars to burst his lungs, and snarls,
and can't contain the wrath that floods his breast.
But in the deer's chill heart there's more of wind;
it sends swift icy currents through his flesh,   300
and causes a trembling motion in his limbs.
But cattle are governed more by placid air;
the torch of wrath is never thrust too close,
spreading its clouds of black and blinding smoke,
nor are they numbed by terror's icy shafts: 305
they stand midway twixt deer and savage lions.
Just so with man, though education give
whole groups a like high gloss, still there remain
in each man's heart marks of his basic nature.
Never imagine all vice can be uprooted.   310
One man too readily flies to wrath and rage,
one is too quickly troubled by fear, a third
takes things a bit more calmly than is right.
In other ways, too, the natures of men must vary,
each having its consequent traits of character.   315
I cannot now expound their hidden cause
nor find a name for each configuration
of atoms, from which these varying traits arise.
This one thing, though, I see I can affirm:
in human nature, the problems that remain   320
insoluble by reason are so petty
that nothing prevents our living as gods should live.

　　This nature, now, is gripped by all our flesh,
is source of the body's welfare, and its guard;
for roots common to both hold them enlaced,   325
nor can they be pulled apart and not be damaged.
As myrrh cannot be readily stripped of scent
without destruction of its substance, too,
so mind and soul cannot be readily drawn
out of the body but that all three must die.   330
From the very first their atoms are so entwined
together that life becomes a partnership;
and neither body alone nor soul alone
without the other's help can cause sensation,
for movements common to both merge into one,   335
to hasten sentience through our inward parts.
Besides, in isolation, body can never
be born or grow or, after death, persist.
It's not like water, that often loses heat

it has received, and is not harmed thereby   340
but stays intact—not so, I say, can flesh
suffer departure and divorce of soul.
No, it will be disrupted, die, decay.
From the first moment, body and soul conjoined
one with the other, learn how life must move,   345
still deep in the mother's body and her womb;
sunder them, and they sicken and waste away.
You see, then, since their welfare lies in union,
their substance must be unified as well.

    Further, if anyone says that flesh can't feel   350
and thinks that soul, mixed with the flesh throughout,
picks up the movement that we call sensation,
he battles against the manifest facts and truth.
"Flesh feels": what ever will tell us what that means
except what the facts have plainly shown and taught us?   355
"But send off soul, and body is all insensate!"
Yes! It has lost what it never owned in life,
(and much else, too, when it is expelled from life.)[1]

    Further, to say eyes have no power to see,
but soul looks through them as through open doors,   360
is wrong, for the sentient act refutes this view.
That act remands us to the eye, the organ,
especially since we often can't see bright things
because their gleam curtains the gleaming eye.
With doors, this doesn't occur; when doors are opened   365
to let us see, they suffer no distress.
Furthermore, if our eyes are just like doors,
then, with the eyes removed, the soul should see
still more, since the very door-posts would be gone.
Here, too, is a theory you must not accept   370
(Democritus, saintly man, thought it correct):
that atoms of soul and body alternate
singly, one with the other, to shape our limbs.
In the first place, atoms of soul are much, much smaller
than those which build the body and inward parts.   375
They're fewer in number, too; just here and there
an atom scattered through flesh. Rest then assured:
the size of bodies that, impinging on us,
can start sense-bearing movements in our body,
shows us how far apart soul-atoms lie.   380
For often we fail to feel the dust that clings
to the body, or powder that strikes and settles there;

1. The point is that sensation is a function of body and soul *in combination*; neither one, if divorced from the other, has sensory powers. The last two lines of this passage seem a gratui- tous addition to the thought. The idea seems to be that the body does not "own" the soul, or any other part of its make-up; its properties are the result of fortuitous combinations of atoms.

to notice the mist at night, or feel the fine
web of the spider, netting us as we pass,
or his dried-up coat that drops upon our heads,   385
or feathers of birds, or floating thistledown,
that for vast lightness grudgingly descends.
Nor do we feel the passage of crawling creatures
(just any kind) nor the separate single footsteps
that gnats and the like set down upon our skin.   390
To such degree must many atoms be stirred
within us before, commingled with our flesh,
the particles of soul are roused to sentience,
before, too, chains of impulse race across
the spaces, and meet, and then bounce back again.   395
   Now, too, the mind, for maintenance of life
and its control, is stronger than the soul:
without intelligence and mind, no part
of soul can live one moment in the body,
but follows them out and scatters to the wind   400
and leaves the body cold in icy death.
But he remains alive whose mind remains.
Lop off his limbs all round, leave him a bloody
torso, take out the soul from all those parts;
he lives, and breathes the vital breeze of heaven.   405
Deprived, if not of all, yet of large part
of the soul, he stays alive and clings to life.
Just like the eye: cut round it; if the pupil
remains unharmed, the power of sight lives on.
Only, you must not damage the eye's whole sphere—   410
cut *round* the eyeball, leave it alone untouched
(and even this is dangerous for the organ).
But if that tiny central part is punctured,
light dies at once, and darkness then ensues,
though the eye is otherwise unhurt and bright.   415
Such everlasting bond links mind and soul.
   Come now and learn that mind and soul (slight things)
are born in living creatures and must die.
For this, I spent sweet hours of toil to find
verses worth your perusal: here they are!   420
Be sure that under one name you join the two,
and when, proving them mortal, I say "the soul,"
believe that the word will mean "the mind" as well,
since both make up a unit, a thing conjoint.[2]
To begin,[3] since I have proved it delicate   425

2. On the distinction between "mind" and "soul", which Lucretius here eliminates, see note 3 p. 57.
3. Lucretius here launches into a long series of proofs of the mortality of the soul. With great ingenuity, he bases a number of these proofs on the very characteristics of the soul that, to the "orthodox" Roman, proved its *immortality*. For a convenient summary of the latter, see Cicero *On Old Age* IV. xxi. 78.

and made of tiny atoms—particles
much smaller than those of clear and fluid water,
or fog or smoke, for it is far more mobile
and moved by impulse far more delicate.
Why! it is moved by the *image* of smoke and fog!   430
Just as when asleep and deep in dreams, we see
altars breathing out vapors and making smoke,
these come to us, no doubt, as images.
Now since, from jars all badly cracked, you see
water leak out and liquids flow away,   435
since fog and smoke, too, scatter to the winds,
be sure that soul disperses even faster
and dies more quickly, dissolving into atoms
once it has gone and left our human frame.
Now since the body—the soul's jar, so to speak—   440
when somehow badly damaged and left porous
by drainage of blood, cannot contain the soul,
how do you think a thing like air could hold it,
a substance much more porous than our flesh?
    Further, we sense that body and mind are born   445
together, develop together, and age alike.
Children's bodies are weak, unsteady, soft:
just as their minds and thoughts are unsubstantial.
Then as they grow in bodily strength and years,
their minds increase in wisdom, wealth, and power.   450
Later, when heavy blows of time have damaged
the body, blunted its powers, and made it droop,
intelligence limps, tongue stumbles, reason slips,
then all together the whole complex collapses.
It follows that all the substance of the soul   455
dissolves like smoke into the tall fleet air;
for body and soul, we see, are linked in birth,
in growth, and in the weary waste of years.
    Add now that we may see how, just as body
suffers portentous illness and harsh pain,   460
so soul knows acrid care and grief and fear;
therefore, by logic, it shares in death as well.
Further, when body is ill, soul goes awry
often; it raves and utters foolishness,
and sometimes lethargy weighs it down to deep   465
and endless sleep, when eye and will are lost;
from there it hears no word, and cannot tell
the faces of those who, calling it back to life,
stand round while tears bedew their eyes and cheeks.
And so we must admit: soul, too, dissolves,   470
because contagion and disease can reach it.
For pain and disease are builders, both, of doom,

as we have long since learned from countless deaths.[4]   473
Why, too, when the bite and burn of wine have reached   476
into a man and spread out through his veins,
do limbs grow heavy and legs impede each other
and wobble, the tongue turn dull, the mind go sodden,
the eyes flow over, shouts, sobs, and curses rise   480
and other consequences of this kind—
why do they happen, except that wild rude wine
must always muddle the mind inside the body?
But things that can be muddled and tangled up
show us that if a somewhat harsher cause   485
slipped in, they'd perish, deprived of further life.
Yes, often a man seized suddenly by disease
falls as we watch, as if a thunderbolt
had struck him; he foams, he groans, his body trembles,
he babbles, turns rigid, and writhes; his breathing comes   490
in gasps, and muscular spasms tire his limbs.
The disease, you see, has spread out through his body,
attacking the soul * * * on the salty sea
when winds blow wild, the hissing waves run high.[5]
He utters a groan because his flesh is racked   495
by pain—in sum, because his atoms of voice
are unseated, massed, and forced out through the mouth,
the path they take, so to speak, by use and training.
Madness comes on because the soul and mind,
confused and, as I've shown, riven apart,   500
are wrenched and tattered by that same toxic force.
Now when the disease relents, and the acrid humors
that attacked the man return to their hiding-holes,
the victim gets up, unsteadily at first,
then slowly recovering sense regains his mind.   505
And so, when the soul is racked within the body
by such disease, and wretchedly wrenched and vexed,
how can it, outside the body, in open air,
maintain its life, do you think, where wild winds blow?
And since disease of soul, like bodily illness,   510
can be, we observe, by medicine checked and cured,
this fact as well suggests that soul is mortal.
For whoever starts and attempts to change the soul
or seeks to alter any existing thing,
is bound to add some parts or change their order[6]   515
or else subtract some fragment from the whole.   516
But deathless things will not permit their parts

4. Line 474 (=510) and 475 have been omitted by editors.
5. The text is corrupt, and the ineptness of the reference to the sea suggests to me that at least one line has been lost here.
6. For the sake of clarity, I have transposed lines 513–14 to follow 515–6.

to be moved about, augmented or diminished,
for whatever changes and leaves its natural bounds
is instant death of that which was before.   520
Thus, whether soul falls ill or is restored
by medicine, it has proved its mortal nature.
To such extent, we see, truth obviates
false reason and blocks its access to escape:
a dilemma refutes it and proclaims it false.   525
    Further, we often observe that men will die
slowly, and limb by limb lose vital sense.
First, in the feet the toes and nails turn blue,
then feet and legs: they die; next through the parts
remaining, the trace of icy death moves on.   530
Since, here, the soul is broken, and comes out
not whole nor all at once, it must be mortal.
Now if you think the soul might, through the limbs,
draw inward and contract its parts to one,
thus taking sentience from our total being,   535
but then that spot, where all that mass of soul
was pressed, should have, it seems, much heightened sentience.
But that "spot" doesn't exist, for, as I showed,
the soul, torn up and scattered abroad, has died.
Why no! If it please us now to grant the false   540
and say soul can be massed inside the bodies
of those who, leaving the light, die bit by bit,
you must concede, still, that the soul is mortal:
what matter whether it's lost, dispersed in air,
or drawn in, crushed, contracted into nothing?   545
In the whole man, the senses more and more
are failing, and less and less is left of life.
    And since mind is one part of man, and stays
fixed in its proper place, like ears and eyes
and all sense organs else that guide our lives;   550
and just as the hand and eye or nose, when severed,
cannot still sense and live apart from us,
but in brief time must soften and rot away,
so the soul can't live by itself, without the body,
without that man who is, so to speak, its "jar"—   555
or think, if you wish, of things more intimate,
since soul and body cling and are closely joined.
    Further, the living power of body and soul
have strength and life by virtue of their union;
for without the body, the soul cannot alone   560
of itself produce life-movements, nor the body,
stripped of the soul, survive or have sensation.
Of course! Just as an eye, torn from its roots,

cut off from the body, could of itself see nothing,
so mind and soul by themselves are powerless.   565
After all, commingled with the flesh and veins,
sinew and bones, they're locked throughout to body;
their atoms cannot leap free, far, and away.
When thus confined, they execute sense-bearing
movements, which after death, in open air,   570
outside the body, they cannot execute,
because they are not in similar wise restrained.
Air would be body, and animate, if the soul
could hold together and make those locked-in movements
which it had made before in flesh and sinew.   575
Say it again: when all our fleshy husk
is loosened, and the breath of life cast out,
you must admit that sensate soul and mind
break up; a single life links soul and body.

    Further, since body cannot stand divorce   580
from soul, but that it stink and rot away,
why doubt but that the soul, from deep within,
began to diffuse and trickle out like smoke;
and hence the body, so changed by rot and ruin,
collapsed, because its basic stuff and structure   585
were wrenched awry as soul seeped from the parts
through all the body's labyrinthine paths
and pores? Thus you may learn that many ways
soul was divided as it passed through flesh
and, still in the body, was torn apart before   590
it slipped and floated out to open air.
Further, while soul yet lies within the bounds
of life, we often see that, by some cause
weakened, it seeks release from all the body:
the face turns ashen as in life's last hour,   595
and every limb falls flabby and bloodless down.
This happens, as people say, when "soul is smitten"
or "heart has failed"; then everyone, in panic,
tries to restore that final link with life.
For then the mind and soul, in all their power,   600
are shaken and shattered, and with them the body, too,
and a slightly heavier blow could break their bonds.
Why do you doubt, then, that the poor, weak soul,
pushed from the body, uncovered, in open air,
not only could not survive throughout all time,   605
but couldn't maintain itself for one brief moment?
For no man dying ever feels his soul
step out of all his body in one piece,
or move up to his throat, then to his mouth;

rather he feels it fail fixed in its place,   610
as, each in its proper spot, he notes the senses
destroyed. But if we had immortal souls,
at death they wouldn't complain of their destruction,
but step out and slough their clothing, like a snake.

Further, why don't the intellect and mind   615
grow in the head or feet or hands, but always,
in everyone, cling to a single, special region,
if everything hasn't its special spot assigned
for growth, where, once created, it persists,
and things have parts so manifold, so discrete,   620
that nothing is ever outlandishly arranged?
Things come in logical sequence: flames don't rise
from rivers, nor ice commonly form in fire.

Besides, if the soul in substance is immortal
and, set apart from the body, is sentient still,   625
we must, I think, endow it with five senses.
In no other way can we here theorize
that, down below, souls wander in Acheron.
Thus painters and poets of an earlier day
have laid before us the souls endowed with senses.   630
But souls cannot have separate eyes or hands
or noses—no, nor separate tongues or ears;
and so, by themselves, they neither can sense nor be.

And since we note that vital sense inheres
in all the body, and all the body has soul,   635
if on a sudden some force, with lightning blow,
should cut it at midpoint, leaving it in two halves,
doubtless the soul, too, would be sliced and severed
into two parts, dismembered with the body.

But anything cut to sections of any size   640
disclaims eternal nature for itself.
Men tell how scythe-armed chariots, spattered hot
with blood, will often lop off a limb so fast
that, cut from the body, it falls to earth and lies there
twitching, while yet the man, alive and strong,   645
fails through speed of the wound to feel its pain—
besides, his mind's absorbed in zeal for battle.
With all that's left, he heads for the fight and kill,
unaware that a passing team, with wheel and scythe,
have carried away his left arm, shield and all.   650
Another climbs on, unaware of a lost right hand,
another tries to rise on a missing leg
(dying, it lies on the ground, the toes still dancing);
and the head cut off from a body still warm with life
keeps on the ground wide eyes and lifelike look   655

until it has shed the last remains of soul.
See, too, the flickering tongue and thrashing tail
of the snake, and as he lifts his body high
cut him to many pieces with your blade:
you'll see each separate section, freshly wounded,   660
wriggle and writhe and spatter the ground with gore, ·
and the head-part, turning about, attack the tail,
slashing at it in fiery fury of pain.
Are we to say that a soul resides complete
in each of the pieces? But this compels conclusion   665
that a single animate body has many souls.
A single soul, then, living inside the body,
was cut up, and hence we deem both must be mortal
since both alike are separable into parts.

   Further, if we declare the soul immortal   670
and slip it into our bodies at their birth,
why can't we remember a life led previously?
Why have we no trace of what we did before?
For if the mind's potential is so changed
that all recall of previous acts is lost,   675
this seems, I think, to stray not far from death.[7]
And so you must admit what was before
has perished, and what is now was now created.

   Further, if into a body fully formed
a soul possessed of life and power enters   680
at the moment when we are born and come to life,
it wouldn't be logical that, along with body
and flesh, the soul should grow right in the blood,
no, logic would place it in some cavity
by itself—yet body must all abound with sense.   685
Once more, then: soul must not be held exempt
from being born, or privileged not to die.
We must not think that souls so closely knit
to the body could ever have slipped in from outside;
plain facts declare against this whole idea.   690
For soul is so bound to viscera, sinew, vein,
and bone, that even the teeth share in sensation:
witness decay, the shock of ice-cold water,
and the harsh crunch of a bite on grit in bread.
The soul is part of the fabric; it can't leave   695
undamaged, you see, or free itself intact
from all our sinews, all our bones and joints.

   But if you theorize that the soul slips in

---

7. Lucretius here attacks the theory, held by the Pythagoreans and by Plato (*Phaedo* 72c–77a; *Meno* 81 ff.) that learning is at least in part simply memory of things known in a previous existence.

from outside, filtering down and through our bodies,
so much more must it perish, fused with the flesh.   700
For all that filters, breaks up, therefore dies.
As food, distributed down the body's paths,
and thus apportioned to every limb and joint,
disappears, but out of itself creates new substance,
so mind and soul, however whole and new   705
they enter the body, in filtering must break up
as they are apportioned in particles to our parts
down paths, and thus create this living soul
which governs within the body now, the product
of soul-stuff lost when apportioned to our parts.   710
And so the entity, soul, is not deprived
of a day of birth, we see, nor free from death.

   Now further: do atoms of soul remain, or not,
in a dead body? But if they remain, still present,
we may not properly deem the soul immortal,   715
since it has gone but left some parts behind.
But if it has fled with all its parts intact,
leaving no single particle in the body,
how can a corpse all rotting come alive
with worms? Whence comes this mass of living things,   720
boneless and bloodless, squirming in bloated flesh?
But if you believe that souls outside slipped in
to the worms and came thus singly to their bodies,
and give no thought to why those myriad souls
flocked to a place whence one had fled, it seems   725
we still must ask and ultimately decide
whether those souls went hunting for atom on atom
of worm, and built for themselves places to live,
or slipped into creatures virtually full-formed.

   Why they should do this or go to all that effort,   730
no one can say. For while they're free of body
they flit, untroubled by illness, hunger, cold.[8]
These, now, are faults of the body, its native ills;
the touch of body brings many a pang to soul.
But grant to the soul much profit from building bodies   735
to enter: I see no way this could be done.
No, souls do not build bodies for themselves.
They could not form the delicate connections
and contacts that make feelings truly shared.   740

   To go on: what makes the lion-breed bloodthirsty
and cruel? The fox, crafty? Speed is the deer's
birthright; ancestral panic spurs his flank.

---

8. A dig at the Platonic doctrine that the soul is free only when it has been released from the body by death. Cf. Plato *Republic* 611–12.

All other such things, the heritage of the flesh
and intellect: why do they start when life begins   745
if not because the soul, a thing unique,
self-seeded of its own atoms, grows with the body?
If, now, it were immortal and could exchange
bodies, the animate world would show mixed traits:
hounds by Hyrcanian breed would often run   750
attacked by the antlered deer; high in the air
a fluttering hawk would flee the dove's approach;
men would be fools; wild beasts, philosophers.
For a faulty logic claims the soul immortal,
yet has it adapt itself to change of body;   755
for all that is changed, breaks up and therefore dies.
For the parts are shuffled and their order altered;
hence they can be dispersed throughout the body
and all, with the body, in the end must die.
But if they say that human souls pass always   760
into human bodies, I'll yet ask why the wise
may become the fool, why no child is sagacious,[9]
why new-born colts lack a great stallion's cunning.   764
Their refuge, of course, will be: "A tender mind   765
in a tender body." But then they must admit
that the soul is mortal, since it changed so much
in the body and lost its earlier life and sense.
And how, in pace with the body, will the soul
gain strength and reach that longed-for bloom of life,   770
unless they are partners from the very start?
And why would the soul leave bodies now grown old?
Does it fear to stay locked up in rotten flesh?
Fear lest its "house," grown weary and waste with years,
collapse? But the deathless are exempt from danger!   775
    To continue: that at the sexual act or birth
of animals, souls stand by, is utter nonsense—
immortal souls waiting for mortal bodies
in numberless numbers, or running races to see
which should be first, which favored to slip in!   780
Or do the souls have contracts, signed and sealed:
"The soul that swoops in first shall have first chance
to enter: no pushing or shoving, no argument!"
    To go on: trees can't exist in air, nor clouds
in the ocean deeps, nor fish live in the fields;   785
there can't be blood in wood or sap in stones.
It's fixed and ordered where things may grow and be.
Thus without body the soul alone can't start
to live, nor exist apart from flesh and blood.

9. Line 763 = 764, and is omitted by editors.

For if it could, far sooner that very soul   790
might live and flourish in head, shoulders, or feet,
and grow as a matter of course in any organ,
still staying in that same person, that same "vessel."
Since, clearly, within our bodies it's fixed and ordered
where soul and mind, each in its place, may live   795
and grow, far more we deny that as one unit
they may be born and endure outside the body.
And so when the body dies, we must admit
the soul dies too, dispersed throughout the body.

    Of course, to think that mortal and immortal   800
could live, sense, act, in mutual partnership
is nonsense. What could be more inconsistent,
more paradoxical, more at odds with self,
than mortal and eternal, deathless things
united in sufferance of life's raging winds?   805
Further, things lasting and eternal must
either, because they're solid, repel all
and allow nothing to enter them that, once in,
could ravel their tight-knit structure, like the atoms
of matter, whose nature we've already shown;   810
or have the power to last throughout all time
because immune to impact, like the void,
which stays untouched, and suffers never a blow;
or else because there is no space around them,
where things might escape, so to speak, or break away   815
like the Sum of Sums Eternal: outside this,
there is no room for escape, nor are there bodies
that could collide and strike and crack its fabric.
But if we should rather think the soul immortal
because it is walled around by living substance   820
or because it meets nothing to hurt its health,
or because what it meets goes somehow on its way,
repelled before we note how it might harm us[1]

*   *   *

Besides that it sickens with the body's ills,
things often occur that put it on the rack   825
with apprehension, fear, care, and fatigue,
and the sins of yesteryear return to plague it.
Add madness of mind and loss of memory;
add that it sinks beneath black waves of gloom
    Death, then, is nothing, concerns us not one bit,[2]   830

---

1. After this line, several lines are missing.
2. Having proved to his satisfaction that the soul is mortal, Lucretius now ends Bk. III with a series of exhortations to men to abandon their foolish fears of death.

since the soul has proved to be a mortal thing.
Just as in time gone by we felt no pain
when Punic hordes came crashing from every quarter
and everything quaked and shook with the shock of war—
a world of ruin and terror beneath high heaven—   835
and none were certain under whose domination
on land and sea the human race must fall,
so, when we shall not be, when the body and soul
which, joined, made us unique have been divorced,
then nothing whatever to us, who shall not be,   840
can happen, you see, or rouse us to sensation,
not if earth clashed with sea and sea with sky.
And even if those entities, soul and mind,
when torn from the body, still had sentient powers,
this would be nothing to us, who are unique,   845
formed of *that* soul, *that* body, in *that* conjunction.
Even if after our death time should assemble
our atoms, and set them again as they now stand,
and the light of life were given once more to us,
this wouldn't affect us—no, not even this,   850
once our link with the self had been destroyed.
Right now we have no bond with the "we" that was
before, nor fear for the "they" that then shall be.
For when you think of the whole measureless span
of time gone by, and of matter—how it moves   855
in myriad ways, then you may well believe
that these same atoms of which we're now composed
were often arranged just as they are today.
And yet we cannot remember and recall this,
for a break in life has occurred, and every movement   860
of sentience has gone, hither and yon, astray.
For if a man is to suffer and feel pain
he must at the time exist, that trouble then
strike him. Since death prevents this, and forbids
existence to him who might incur discomfort,   865
know that there's nothing for us to fear in death,
that a man who doesn't exist can't be unhappy,
that for him it's just as if he'd never been born,
once deathless death has taken his life away.

Hence when you see a man distressed because   870
once he is dead and his body interred, he'll rot,
or perish in flames, or between the jaws of beasts,
know that he won't ring true, that in his heart
deep down, something is rankling, though he swear
he doesn't believe in sentience after death.   875
He's not convinced of his theory or its grounds;

he doesn't truly cut himself off from life,
but unwitting lets some part of himself live on.
For when a living man imagines the future—
how birds and beasts, in death, will slash his flesh,   880
he pities himself: he doesn't remove or cut
the self from the cast-off body, but imagines
it's he, and stands there thinking it feels as he does.
Hence he is angry at being born to die,
nor sees that in real death there'll be no other   885
himself to live and mourn that he is gone,
to stand and grieve that he lies bloody or burning.
For if in death it's painful to be mauled
and bitten by beasts, why would it be less cruel
to be laid on a pyre and roast in searing flames,   890
or be put to smother in honey, or grow stiff
with cold atop a slab of icy stone,
or be squeezed and crushed beneath a load of earth?
   "No more will happy home or loyal wife
greet you, nor will sweet children run to catch   895
first kisses, and touch your heart with wordless joy.
Works, wealth, and family—you'll not be their strength
and bulwark. Tragic soul! One tragic day
of doom," they say, "stole all life's blessings from you!"
But here they fail to add, "Nor do you have   900
still in you the slightest longing for these things."
If they could clearly see and speak this thought
they'd free themselves of much heartache and fear.
   "Asleep in death"; so shall you be for all
that's left of time, exempt from grief and pain.   905
But we—in the cold, cold tomb we laid your ashes,
and wept, but could not weep enough: no day
will take this endless sorrow from our hearts.
And so let us ask this man what is so harsh
and cruel (if everything ends in sleep and peace)   910
as to make man waste his life away in tears?
   Here's something else men do: at feast they drink
toast after toast, and shade their heads with flowers,
and say with a sigh, "How short man's life is here;
it's gone tomorrow, forever beyond recall."   915
As if in death they would be chiefly troubled
by thirst that scorched and parched them, poor, dry souls,
or still feel yearnings for sundry other things.
Yet never a man misses his life and self
when soul and body alike lie lulled in sleep.   920
But we shall sleep like this throughout all time,
and we'll not miss ourselves—not in the least.

And even so, the atoms in our parts
cannot be straying far from paths of sentience,
since we collect ourselves when suddenly wakened.   925
Far less, then, must we think death means to us—
if what we see is nothing can be less.
For death is followed by greater dislocation
and loss of atoms; no man can rise again
once he has crossed that ice-cold blank in life.   930
    Then, too, if Nature suddenly should raise
her voice, and take someone to task like this:
"What troubles you, man, that you should thus indulge
in bitter tears? Why weep and wail at death?
For if your earlier years of life were happy   935
and all your blessings haven't proved thankless—lost,
drained off, as if poured into a punctured jar—
why not, like one filled at life's table, leave
in peace, you fool, and take your carefree rest?
But if the joys you knew have all run out   940
and life's a burden, why will you add still more,
to see it again turn sour and all be lost?
Shouldn't you rather set end to life and labor?
For there is nothing further I might find
or invent to please: all things are ever the same.   945
If years don't wither your body, and your limbs
aren't weary and worn, yet all things stay the same
if you should live a life beyond all lives,
and even more, if you were never to die."
What shall we answer but that Nature's charge   950
is just and that she pleads the cause of truth?
And if one truly full of years should fret
and wail at death, poor soul, more than is right,
what has he earned but sterner reprobation:
"Away with your tears, you fool, and stop your wailing.   955
You've had all life could offer; now you're tired.
You've wanted what isn't; scorned what is; hence life
has slipped through your fingers, shapeless and unlovely,
and now you're amazed that death stands near, before
well-filled and sated, you might depart this world.   960
Now banish all thoughts unsuited to your years
and in good spirit yeild * * *[3] you must."
Just, her complaint, I think, just, blame and censure.
For in this world the new drives out the old
always; one thing must die to build another.[4]   965

---

3. The word *magnis*, which appears in the   emended.
MSS at this point, is generally regarded as   4. See note on 1.263–64, above.
spurious, and has never been satisfactorily

Nothing goes down to darkness and the Pit;
there must be matter that worlds to come may grow;
they too will run their course and follow you.
Before your day, men died, and men will die;
there's never an end; one thing grows from another.   970
Life is no grant in freehold: life's a loan.
Think back to ancient times, the endless past:
how little that means to us, before our birth.
Here nature holds her mirror to the future:
so will it be for us when we are dead.   975
Where here is the grim and ugly face of terror?
Is this not a state more peaceful than all sleep?

    And all those things men tell of down in hell,
far under the earth, are right here in our lives.
No Tantalus[5] fears a boulder beetling high   980
(so goes the tale) or huddles in hollow terror;
but rather, in life, vain awe of gods oppresses
man, and he fears what blows of fate may fall.
No Tityos[6] lies there, target of hellish buzzards:
even in that huge torso they'd not find   985
throughout all ages something to pick and tear.
However monstrous vast his body lay,
not spanning a mere nine acres with his limbs
spread-eagled, but the whole round world and wide,
he'd not have strength to bear such pain forever,   990
or to offer his flesh for food eternally.
No, here's our Tityos—one laid low by love,
slashed at by birds, devoured by pain and fear,
or cut to the quick by care and vague desire.
Sisyphus[7] too lives right before our eyes;   995
he pants his plea for the people's heartless rods
and axes, but always ends the downcast loser.
Yes, to seek power that's vain and never granted
and for it to suffer hardship and endless pain:
this is to heave and strain to push uphill   1000
a boulder, that still from the very top rolls back
and bounds and bounces down to the bare, broad field.
And then, to feed forever a thankless heart
and with good things to fill yet never fill it

---

5. According to the version of his story here referred to, Tantalus was punished for stealing the ambrosia and nectar of the gods by being suspended under a boulder that seemed always about to fall and crush him. The more familiar version has him endlessly trying to catch the water and fruits that forever eluded his grasp.
6. Because he attempted to assault Leto, Tityos was condemned to be shackled to the ground for all eternity while buzzards fed on his liver—liver, because to the ancients this organ was the seat of sexual passion.
7. The famed "Trickster" of ancient legend. Because he tricked others—including, apparently, Zeus himself—he is condemned to be endlessly tricked by the boulder he tries to roll up the hill.

(as do the yearly seasons, circling round 1005
to bring us fresh life and color and loveliness
yet never to fill us with the fruits of life)
this, I think, is the myth of maidens, young
as flowers, who carry water to punctured jars
that never in any fashion can be filled.[8] 1010
Cerberus,[9] too, the Furies, the Dearth of Light,
Tartarus[1] retching and vomiting tides of terror

* * *

which nowhere exist, which simply cannot be.
But in life, the fear of penalty for our sins
is great in the greatest: crime and crime's atonement, 1015
prison, the terrible hurling from the Rock,[2]
the lash, the hangman, stake, pitch, iron and brand.
And take these away: the heart knows what we've done
and plies the goad and lash to make us cowards,
yet never sees where stands the stone that marks 1020
the end of pain, the bounds of punishment,
but fears these may grow heavier still in death.
Hell is right here, the work of foolish men!
And sometimes, too, remind yourself of this:
"Even the eye of Ancus the Good[3] grew dark, 1025
and he was your better—for shame!—a thousand ways.
And other thousand kings and potentates
have died, the governors of mighty nations.
He, too, who once paved highways over the sea
and built his legions a road across the deep 1030
(taught them to walk atop the pools of brine,
sent prancing horse to spurn the ocean's roar)
fell ill, saw daylight fade, and breathed his last.[4]
Scipio,[5] thunderbolt-warrior, scourge of Carthage,
gave bones to earth just like the meanest slave. 1035
Add the discoverers of truth and beauty;
add Helicon's Host,[6] of whom great Homer sole
earned knigship: like them all, he rests in peace.

8. The daughters of Danaus (Danaids), who at their father's orders murdered their husbands on the wedding night. Their futile activity in Hades is symbolic of the emptiness and futility of their lives on earth.
9. The three-headed dog who guarded the entrance to the underworld. Furies: the goddesses of vengeance, who punish men for their acts of violence. Dearth of Light: the Underworld itself, which is perennially dark and shadowy.
1. The Underworld, Hades. After this line, some lines have been lost. They must have embodied a connective clause of some kind.
2. The reference is to the Tarpeian Rock, a cliff at one corner of the Capitoline Hill in Rome, from which convicted traitors were hurled to their death.
3. The fourth king of Rome, called "the Good" because of his generosity toward the plebeians. He founded the port city of Ostia.
4. The reference is to Xerxes, king of the Persians, who built a bridge across the Hellespont in order to move his armies into Greece (480 B.C.). He was ultimately defeated by the Greeks in the Battle of Salamis.
5. Publius Cornelius Scipio Africanus the Elder (236–184 B.C.). In the Second Punic War, he inflicted final defeat on the Carthaginians under Hannibal, at Zama, 202 B.C.
6. The poets.

Then, too, Democritus,[7] when ripe old age
warned him that mind and memory were fading,   1040
went freely to place his person in death's path.
Epicurus himself died when life's light ran out,
he who in mind surpassed all men—eclipsed them
all, as the sun hung high in heaven, the stars.
Will you hang back, indignant that you must die: 1045
Alive and awake, you live next-door to death;
you waste the greater part of life in sleep,
and, even waking, you snore, and dream, dream on;
you wear a heart confounded by empty fears
yet rarely can tell what caused them, when oppressed   1050
and drunk and wretched with unremitting cares
you wander, waver, and wonder where to turn.
    If men, who clearly sense the weight that rests
upon their souls and drags them weary down,
could also know what causes this, and whence   1055
this pain that lies like lead upon their hearts,
they would not live as commonly now we see them,
not knowing what they want, in endless quest
of change, as if by this to slough their burden.
Day after day, the great man leaves his palace,   1060
bored sick with home, yet comes right back again
because he finds no better world outside.
He drives his nags top-speed out to his villa,
as if it were burning, and he to put out the fire;
he's yawning before his foot has passed the door;   1065
in weary search for oblivion, he sleeps,
or turns and gallops away to town again.
Thus each man runs from himself—the self, of course,
he can't escape but must hold close; he hates it
because, being sick, he can't know why he's sick.   1070
If he could see this clear, he'd drop all else
and plunge into learning the nature of the world,
for through eternity, not one hour, extends
the state we're questioning in which all men,
once they have died, must be, time without end.   1075
    Then, too, mid all these dangers, doubts, and fears,
what vile, perverted lust for life subdues us?
The end of life stands fixed for every man;
death cannot be avoided: we must meet it.
Besides, we spin on the same spot, round and round;   1080
we live, live on, but forge no new delights.
The thing we want but don't possess seems far
the best; we get it, and beg for something else;

7. See Introduction, p. xi, *et passim.*

we're held slack-mouthed with endless thirst for life.
Yet we don't know what fortune years may bring,   1085
what may befall us or what end await.
Nor do we by dragging out our lives take off
one second from death's term; we have no power
to shorten somehow our prisonment in death.
Live on, then! Bury what spawn of men you will!   1090
The death that awaits will be no less eternal;
nor will that man, who made an end of life
today, not-be a shorter time than he
who died a thousand years and months before.

Book IV

No paths in the Muses' places! None before
has walked where I walk. I love to find new founts
and drink; I love to gather fresh new flowers
and seek the laureate's crown whence Muses never
ere now have veiled the brow of any man;   5
for, first, I teach of weighty things, and work
man's heart free of religion's garrotte-knot,
and next I turn the bright light of my verse
on darkness, painting it all with poetry.
This, too, I think, is not without good reason.   10
For just as doctors, who must give vile wormwood
to children, start by painting the cup-lip round
with sweet and golden honey: thus the child,
young and unknowing, is tricked and brought to set
the cup to his lip; meanwhile, he swallows the bitter   15
wormwood, and though deceived is not infected,
but by this trick grows well and strong again.
so now, since my philosophy often seems
a little grim to beginners, and most men
shrink back from it in fear, I wished to tell   20
my tale in sweet Pierian song for you,
to paint it with the honey of the Muses,
hoping that thus I might fix your attention
upon my verse until you clearly saw
the nature of things and understood its value.   25
    And since I've taught what bodies begin all things,[1]
what sort they are, how varied in their forms,
how, self-impelled, they speed and never rest
and how from them each thing may be created,
and since I've taught what nature the soul possesses,   30
what atoms it owns, how bound to the body, what powers,
and how, torn free, it reverts to primal stuff,
I'll now discuss a matter of vast import:

1. In Bk. III, Lucretius had discussed the soul
(*animus, anima*: see note 3, p. 57) primarily as
the life principle; in Bk. IV he will discuss it as
the intellect and the organ of sense perception.
He uses the same Latin terms (*animus, anima*)
in both books; in Bk. III, the more appropriate
translation seemed to be "the soul," in Bk. IV
"the mind," since in the latter Lucretius dis-
courses on the Epicurean theory of psychologi-
cal phenomena. He views these as a species of
perception: we perceive ideas exactly as we do
things, that is, by physical contact. Imagina-
tion, thought, dreams, and all related phe-
nomena are caused exactly as is sense percep-
tion. The mind experiences physical contact
with corporeal agents, exactly as the eye does in
seeing. The only difference is that the mind is a
very fine and delicate construct, and is capable
of receiving impulses from atomic entities far
more tenuous and delicate than those that affect
the senses. These entities are envisaged as films
of atoms cast off from things, floating every-
where, bypassing the senses and impinging di-
rectly upon the mind itself.

there are what we call the "images" of things,
and these, like membranes torn off from the surface   35
of things, flit this way, that way, through the air;
they strike our minds and frighten us when we lie
wakeful, and often we see them in our dreams—
strange shapes, the "images" of lightless creatures,
which often rouse us in terror from the sleep   40
of fever: we're not to think that souls have fled
from Hell, or that ghosts flit among the living,
or that, *post mortem*, something is left of us,
when soul and body-substance both have died,
dispersed alike into their primal stuff.   45
   I say, then: shapes of things, and delicate casts
are freed by things from the surfaces of things;
we might denote these "membranes," "husks," or "rinds,"[1a] 50
because they're "likenesses," with the shape and form
of the bodies from which, sloughed off, they wander free.
And here is proof for even the dull of mind.
Take first the obvious cases: many things
cast particles off, sometimes in loose diffusion,   55
as firewood casts off smoke, or fires, heat,
sometimes close-knit and dense, as when cicadas,
some summer's day, put off their tube-like coats,
and calves at the moment of birth cast membranes off
from their body-surfaces, and the slippery snake   60
leaves his cloak on a bramble: many a time
we've seen the thorn hung with his fluttering spoils.
Since all these happen, a delicate "likeness" too
must be released from the outer planes of things;
for why the former should fall and leave things, more   65
than those so delicate, there's no power to tell;
especially since, on the surface of things, are countless
small bodies that could be freed in that same order
they had, and keep the same prefigured shape—
so much more readily as, being few and placed   70
right on the top, they would be less entangled.
For we see many things scattered and cast abroad
not only from deep within, as said before,
but from the surface, even color itself.
A common example are red, yellow, and brown   75
awnings when, stretched across great theatres,
flung wide over poles and beams, they ripple and flap.
For they dye the whole thing under them: people, pit,
stage, and scenery * * *[2]

1a. Lines 48–49=33–34 and are omitted by   2. The rest of this line is unintelligible.
editors.

and make it flow with bands of their own colors.   80
And the more the walls of the theatre are enclosed
around, the more all that's inside is gay
and flooded with beauty when it has caught the light.
And so, since canvas from its surface casts
color, all things must cast off effigies   85
as well, since they are loosed from every surface.
Things, then, free clear-cut tracings of their shapes
that flit fine-textured speedily everywhere
yet separately and singly can't be seen.
Furthermore, odors, smoke, steam, and all else   90
like them billow diffuse from things, because
starting from deep inside and coming out,
they're torn by twisting paths: no straight road leads
to the exits where, once started, they seek to leave.
But when the delicate surface-film of color   95
is cast, there's nothing that could damage it,
placed as it is at the surface, right on top.
Lastly, the likenesses that we see in mirrors,
in water, in anything shiny: it must be,
since they possess the shape and sheen of things,   100
that they consist of images cast from things.[3]
There are then delicate shapes and effigies   104
resembling things, which singly none can see,   105
yet when they have been bounced back, time and again,
from polished mirrors, they create preception,
nor could they otherwise be preserved, I think,
to take on shapes so like each single thing.
    Come now and learn how delicate is the nature   110
of images. And to begin: atoms are far
below our sentient powers and much smaller
than things the eye first starts to fail to see.
But to confirm this once again, learn briefly
how fine are the atoms of all forms of matter.   115
First there are animals—insects—some so small
that their three parts can no way be distinguished.
What size do you think the guts of these must be?
The globe of heart, the organs, eyes, and joints?
How tiny are they? Further, what kind must be   120
the atoms of which their souls and minds consist?
You see how infinitely small they'd be.
Further, all things that from their substance breathe
harsh odors: panacea, stinking wormwood,
foul artemisia, bitter centaur-weed,   125

---

3. Lines 102–103 = 65–66, and are omitted by editors.

any one of which if you should barely sniff[4]

* * *

you'd sooner deem many images of things
float all around, devoid of force and feeling.
   But don't think, now, that floating images
of things are only those that come from things: 130
there are also those spontaneously formed,
self-constituted in this sphere, the air.
In many shapes and forms they ride the sky,
fluid, free-moving, with ever-changing face,
taking the outlines of all kinds of shapes.   135
Thus we see clouds sometimes grow effortlessly
in heaven, and mar the firmament's clear face
with air-caressing movement. Often faces
of giants seem to float and cast wide shadows;
sometimes great mountain-shapes and rugged crags   140
block out the mountains and rise past the sun,
then other clouds parade like tethered beasts.
   How quickly, now, how easily these are formed
and ever flow from things, and float away[5]

* * *

for always, atop all things, there's something extra   145
for casting off. When this meets other things,
it passes through them—glass is our best example.
But if it meets rough rock or timber, then
it's torn and no longer represents an image.
But if it's stopped by things compact and bright   150
(our best example: a mirror) no such thing happens:
it can't pass through it like glass; it can't be torn,
either: high sheen knows how to keep it safe:
and thus sends images to us, wave on wave.
And however quickly, at any time, you set   155
something to face a mirror; its image appears.
Know then: from surfaces forever flow
these films of things, fine-textured, finely shaped.
Thus in a flash are many images formed,
and we may rightly style them instant-born.   160
   As in brief time the sun must send up light
in abundance, that the world be ever full,

4. After this line, a number of lines have been
lost. They probably brought to a conclusion
Lucretius' proofs that very small, even invisible,
substances demonstrably affect the senses, and
led to the analogical argument that even smaller
and more delicate substances (e.g., the "im-
ages") must affect the mind-soul.

5. After this line, a number of lines have been
lost, probably to the effect that films of atoms
delicate enough to affect the mind could be cast
off from things without perceptible effect on the
appearance, weight, or other characteristics of
those things.

just so from things at any point of time
in similar fashion images must flow
countless in countless ways and all directions;   165
yes, toward whatever shapes we turn a mirror,
it will reflect things of like form and color.
Further, just when the climate of the sky
is clearest, it turns most suddenly dark and foul.
You'd think Hell's barren shadows all escaped   170
and filled the caverned vastness of the sky,
for in that filthy night of clouds there hang,
hosted above us, faces of black fear.
How tiny a part of these the image is
there's none could say, or render account in words.   175
    Come, now: how swift the images may ride,
what speed is granted them as they traverse
the air, so that long distance takes brief time,
wherever, however, singly impelled, they go,
I'll tell in lines more sweet than numerous: 180
better the swan's brief note than that loud call
of the crane, wind-driven through the clouds of heaven!
To begin: we often observe that things light-weight
and built of small-sized particles, are swift.
In this class is the sun's light, and its heat,   185
because they're made of microscopic atoms
which are, so to speak, hammered; through empty air,
they speed across unchecked, struck from behind.
For light by new light speedily is supplanted
and lightning, so to speak, goads lightning on.   190
Thus images in similar wise must have
the power to race through space beyond all telling
in no time at all, first, because some impulse
small and far back starts them and drives them on;
for the rest, because they fly with speed of wing;   195
then, too, because they're thrown off with a fabric
so fine that they can penetrate every kind
of matter, and seep, as it were, through empty air.
Further, if atoms launched deep down in things
and hurled outside, as are the light and heat   200
of the sun, are seen to speed in one bright moment
and spread themselves across the sky's whole void,
and fly over land and sea, suffusing heaven,
what of those atoms placed right at the top,
when they are loosed with nothing to block their launching?   205
They must go faster and farther (don't you see?)
and cross far greater distance in the time
it takes the light of the sun to fill the sky.

And here seems further and prime valid proof
how fast the images of things must move: 210
the instant that shining waters lie beneath
clear skies, the sparkling constellations find
bright answer in the waters of the world.
Can you see, now, in what brief time the image
falls down from heavenly coasts to coasts of earth?   215
And so you must—yes, must—admit that atoms
are freed to strike the eyes and goad our sight.
From certain things, too, odors ever flow,
as cold from rivers, heat from the sun, and tides
from the sea, that eat away the longshore dikes;   220
and the air is ever filled with winging words.
Besides, to the lips comes often a damp, salt taste
when we walk beside the sea; and when we watch
wormwood stirred and dissolved, bitterness hits us.
To such degree from every source things stream   225
away, and are released in all directions
with never a halt or rest allowed their flowing!
for sentience in us is constant: we can see
all things always, and smell, and sense their sounds.

    Take, further, a given object; handle it   230
in darkness; we'll know it identical with the one
we saw by the light of day. Hence it must be
that similar causes stimulate touch and vision.
If, then, square objects tell us they are square
when handled in darkness, what will identify   235
a thing as square in daylight but its image?
Clearly the image, then, is stimulus
to vision; without it, nothing can be seen.

    Now what I call the images of things
ride everywhere and are scattered in all directions.   240
But since we see things only with the eyes,
this means that only where we turn our gaze
do all things move in color and form to meet it.
The image, too, provides that we may see[6]
and determine how far away from us things are.   245
For, once released, it pushes ahead of itself
the air that lies between it and our eyes,
and all this air glides through our visual organs,
one might say "washes" the pupils, and moves on.
Thus we are made to see how far away   250
a given thing is: the more air driven ahead,

---

6. Here Lucretius introduces his "air-theory" of depth perception. Its mechanics should be obvious if we remember that the films that cause vision (or any other type of perception, including the purely psychological) are actual, physical things, made up of atoms, and hence entirely capable of pushing other atomic constructs, *e.g.*, air, ahead of them as they move.

the longer the column of air that "washes" our eyes,
the farther away we see each thing removed.
All this, now, happens with consummate speed:
at once we identify things and judge their distance.   235
In this connection it must not cause wonder
that single images, as they strike the eye,
aren't visible, yet we see the things themselves.
For wind, too, beats us bit by bit, and cold
flows over us keen, yet we don't commonly sense   260
each separate particle of wind or cold
but rather one whole, and see blows then inflicted
upon our flesh, as if some single thing
were striking and telling us of its presence there.
When, further, we stub our toe on stone, we touch   265
the outmost surface of rock, and its top texture,
yet rather than feeling this by touch, we sense
the inner hardness of rock, deep, deep inside.
    Come now and learn why the image is seen behind
the mirror; for surely we see it deep inside.   270
It's just like things we really see outside
when through a door we're given an open view
and a chance to see various things outside a house.
For here, too, sight is effected by twofold air.
For first we observe the air this side the doorposts,   275
then come the doors themselves, to left and right;
next outdoor light and a second air wash over
the eyes, and the things we really see outside.
So when a mirror first casts off its image
it moves toward the organs of sight, pushing before it ·   280
the air that lies between it and the eyes,
and causes us to sense the entire column
before the mirror. But when we sense the mirror
straightway the image that travels from us to it
arrives, is reflected, and visits our eyes once more;   285
it drives and rolls ahead of it one more air
and makes us see this before itself; that's why
it appears an equal distance behind the mirror.
And so it is not, *not* right for us to wonder[7]

*   *   *

which from polished mirrors create perception,   290
for this is effected by two airs, both times.
Now those parts of our bodies on the *right*
appear as *left* in a mirror for this reason:
When an image comes and strikes the mirror-surface

7. After this line, at least one line has been lost, to the effect that the *apparent* depth of the image behind the mirror is effected in the same way as the *actual* depth of an object seen through a door.

it isn't reversed intact; instead, it's punched   295
straight back, as though, before a plaster mask
were dry, someone should press it on post or beam,
and it should still keep right configuration,
and show itself punched backward, but the same.
Thus what before was *right* eye, now will be   300
left, and that on the *left* is changed to *right*.
An image, too, may pass from mirror to mirror,
so that five likenesses, or six, are made.
For all that lie concealed, far back inside,
from there, though deep removed down angled paths,   305
will be brought out by routes complex and shifting
and make the house seem filled with things and mirrors.
From mirror to mirror the image will be reflected;
what was produced as *right* will turn to *left*,
and then revert to first frontality.   310
In addition to this, there are these "sided" mirrors,
curved in an arc like that of our own flank;
these send our likeness back with right side right,
either because this mirror mirrors the image,
which flies back twice-reflected, or because   315
when the image gets there, it turns around because
the mirror's curved face tells it to turn toward us.[8]
Further, conclude that images set the foot
just as we do, and imitate our gait,
because if you move from the mirror anywhere,   320
at once from there no image can be reflected;
for nature demands that the angle of approach
and of repulsion be for all things the same.
    Further, our eyes shun looking at bright lights.
The sun, too, blinds us if we look straight at it,   325
because, with its huge power, its images
fall heavily from great height through empty air
and, striking the eye, damage its parts and functions.
Further, things bright and shiny often hurt
the eye because they're peppered with seeds of fire   330
which slip inside the eye and cause it pain.
Further, the jaundiced, looking at things, will see them
tinged with yellow because their flesh throws off
thousands of bits of yellow that block the path
of images; yellow, too, mixed in their eyes,   335

8. It is hard to see just what Lucretius means here. Apparently he thinks of the image as first striking one side of a concave mirror, with the usual *reversed* frontality, and then being reflected from that side to the other side, thus producing an image with *correct* frontality, which is then reflected to the eye. Or does Lucretius mean not a simple, concave mirror, but one with three panels, like those employed today in clothing stores? If this is his meaning, his explanation is entirely acceptable.

contaminates all the images with its color.
   From darkness, now, we see things in the light
because the closer air, all black and cloudy,
comes first to the open eye and fills it full;
next quickly follows a bright and shining air   340
that purges the eye, dispelling the lightless shadows
of that first air, for the second is many ways
more mobile and finer, and has much greater power.
Soon as it fills the ways of the eye with light,
and opens the paths clogged hitherto by black air,   345
at once the likenesses of things that lie
in the light come after, and spur us on to see.
But out of light into dark we can't do this,
because the air that enters second is cloudy
and coarser, too; it fills up every pore   350
and clogs the ways of the eye, so that no image
of any kind can strike and stimulate it.
   When from afar we see a town's square towers
it often happens that they seem round, because
all angles, viewed far off, look blunted down.   355
Or, better, the angles aren't observed; their force
is lost, and their impress doesn't reach our eyes,
because the images, traveling through much air,
lose clarity as the air rains blows upon them.
Thus, since the angles all elude our sight,   360
the towers of stone are ground as on a lathe,
still, not like things seen close and truly round,
but similar—like their shadows, so to speak.[9]
   Our shadows in sunlight likewise seem to move   365
and follow our steps and imitate our gestures,
if you believe that air deprived of light
can walk and follow men's movements and their gestures.
For it can be nothing else but air devoid
of light, this thing we commonly call a shadow.
The earth, you see, in clear, successive steps,   370
is cut off from the sunlight as we move
and block it, then filled again where we have passed;
that's why we see that what has been the body's
shadow follows us, changing place for place.
For endlessly fresh rays of light pour in,   375
and the first are lost, like wicks drawn into fire..
And so the earth is readily stripped of light,
then filled again, and sloughs black shadows off.

9. The important point here is that the eye is
never deceived; sense perception is always true.
What appeared to be errors in perception are
caused either by imperfections in the effective
agent (as in 356–59, here) or by faulty interpre-
tation of the received image (as in 354–55, here,
and, more explicitly, in 462–521.).

Nor will I grant at all that eyes may err.
"Where is it light? Where dark?" This is for eyes   380
to tell; but whether the light's the same or not,
if the darkness that was *here* has now moved *there*,
or rather if what I've just described has happened—
this, after all, our reason must decide:
the eye can't comprehend the laws of nature.   385
Don't fasten the mind's mistake upon the eye.
The ship we ride on moves, but seems unmoving;
the one fast-moored we think is passing by.
Toward ship, it seems, come racing hill and plain
as we row by, or glide past under sail.   390
The stars seem sluggish, fixed in heaven's vault,
yet all and singly are in constant motion,
for they must rise, and travel far, and set,
when their bright bodies have traversed the sky.
Likewise the sun and moon appear to stay   395
fast-moored, yet simple fact shows that they travel.
Far off, from mid-sea waters, mountains rise;
navies ride free the wide sea-lanes between them,
yet they appear conjoint, a single island.
Rooms spin, and columns run the racetrack round   400
so fast, it seems to boys, when they have stopped
spinning themselves, that they can scarce believe
the whole house won't come tumbling down upon them.
When nature lifts her first red flush toward heaven
and raises shifting fires above the mountains,   405
you watch, and the sun seems then to touch their tops
and, rising, to brush them with its own bright flame:
they're scarce two thousand arrow-shots away,
or better, scarce five hundred javelin-casts.
Yet twixt them and the sun lie monstrous seas,   410
spread level under the huge confines of heaven;
between them too are miles and miles of land,
where dwell ten thousand tribes of men and beasts.
And yet a puddle no more than a finger's depth,
held in the street between the paving-stones,   415
lets us look down into earth and see as far
as yawning heaven spreads high and wide from earth;
one seems to look *down* on clouds and sky and bodies
lurking in mystic heavens under the earth.
Then too, when in midstream our horse has reared   420
and balked, and we look down on rushing waters,
some force appears to carry the stock-still horse
sideways, and send him rushing against the current,

and no matter where we turn the eye, all things
seem floating and streaming along just like ourselves.   425
Although a portico is of equal width,
and rests on columns of equal height throughout,
still when we look from the end down its whole length,
top, sides, and bottom shrink to a tapering cone;
top joins with bottom and right side all with left,   430
till they contract to a conical vanishing-point.
To sailors at sea the sun appears to rise
from water and set in water and bury its light,
since they see nothing, of course, but sea and sky:
don't lightly conclude their senses gone awry!   435
And landlubbers think that ships in port are crippled;
their oars, where they meet the water, are broken and bent!
For whatever part of the oar stands out above
the brine, is straight, the rudders above, straight too.
But where they enter the water, they seem to break   440
and all of them bend, turn upward, and lie flat,
bent back and floating just beneath the surface.
When winds blow scattered clouds across the sky
in time of night, the shining stars appear
to glide against the clouds and pass above them   445
in ways far different from their actual movement.
And if we place a hand beneath one eye
and press, somehow sensation makes all things
that we observe seem doubled to our sight:
double, the lamps blooming with fire-flowers,   450
all through the house, the furniture double twinned,
and everyone has two faces and twin bodies.
Then too, when sleep has sweetly wrapped our limbs
in rest, and the body lies in deep repose,
even then we think that we're awake, with limbs   455
in motion; and in the viewless murk of night
we think we see broad daylight and the sun;
within four walls, sea, sky, and hill and stream—
new scenes; we think we're tramping overland,
and hearing sounds, when night hangs round us, grim   460
and still, and answering, though we speak no word.
We see many other like things that make us wonder,
all trying to shake our faith in sense perception;
wrongly, since most of the errors they have caused
spring from our minds, that add their own conclusions,   465
and make what sense has not perceived seem true.
For nothing is harder than separating truth
from the hasty, hazy additives of the mind.

If, too, men claim to know nothing, they don't know
they know this, either, admitting that they know nothing.[1]   470
With them, then, I'll forbear to plead my case:
they stand themselves on their heads, right in their tracks.
　But let me grant they know this, still I'll ask
one question: since thus far they've seen no truth,
how can they know what "know" and "not-know" mean,   475
what thing creates the concepts "false" and "true,"
what proves the dubious different from the sure?
You'll find the concept "truth" was first created
by the senses, nor can we prove the senses wrong.
We'd have to find that thing worth greater trust,   480
which by its single truth could conquer falsehood.
Now what, than the senses, may we hold more worthy
of trust? Could reason sprung from false sensation
refute the senses from which it wholly sprang?
Unless sensation is true, all reason is false.[2]   485
Can ears reprove the eyes? Can touch reprove
the ears? Can taste-in-the-mouth charge touch with error,
or nose refute it, or eyes proclaim it wrong?
Not so, I think, for each has powers discrete
and apart, its separate force; it must then be   490
that to sense the soft, the cold, the hot, is one thing,
and quite another to sense the different colors,
and to see the properties that belong to color.
Yes, taste has force discrete; odors exist
discrete; sounds are discrete. It must be, then,   495
that one sense cannot prove another wrong.
Nor can a single sense refute itself;
for we must trust them equally all the time:
whenever they judge a thing is true, it's true.
And if our logic can't explain the reason   500
why what is square close-by, when viewed afar
looks round, we'd better say that faulty logic
has rendered a false account of form, both times,
than ever let manifest truth fall from our grasp,
destroy primary faith, and make a shambles   505
of the base whereon man's life and reason rest.
All sanity would collapse, and life itself
would drop in its tracks if we can't trust the senses,
avoid pitfalls, and all else of the sort

1. This is Lucretius' most explicit declaration
of the absolute necessity of accepting sense per-
ception as true. We must accept it, he says,
even if sometimes we cannot thereby give a
completely satisfactory explanation for every
phenomenon, for if we do not accept it, all
rational explanation collapses.

2. In this connection, it is essential to re-
member that according to Epicurus, reason,
like all other thought processes, is based on
physical impulse and on the mind's reaction to
it.

that we must shun, and take the opposite path.   510
For you, then, all that mass of words is vain
which men have devised and ranged against the senses.
In a building, too, just draw the baseline wrong,
and lay the ruler askew and out of place;
and let the plans be somewhere not quite right: 515
the whole thing's bound to be a jumbled error,
crooked and shaky, a hindside-foremost mess,
looking about to fall—and fall it will,
betrayed from the very start by faulty judgments.
Thus any account of things you'll find distorted   520
and wrong that springs from senses wrongly read.
    Now takes the other senses: how they do
their work demands no thorny train of thought.
    First: we hear sounds and speech when, having entered
the ear, by physical impact they cause hearing.   525
For speech and sound are matter: this we must
accept as fact, since they can strike the senses.
Sometimes, too, speaking rasps the throat, and shouts
proceeding outward roughen its passageways;
for atoms of voice then, gathered in greater mass,   530
are forcing their way out through a narrow place:
they fill it from end to end and rasp its outlet.
There's no doubt, then, that words and speech consist
of atoms—the basic stuff—and hence cause pain.
Nor are you unaware what men may lose   535
in weight, in muscular vigor, in sheer strength,
through speech that lasts till night's black shadows fall
from the hour when dawn rose up and shed first light,
especially speech delivered at full lung-power.
Speech, then, is matter; this we must admit,   540
since he who speaks at length loses some weight.
Now harshness of the voice results from harshness
of atoms; and just so smoothness comes from smoothness.
Nor are the atoms that enter the ear alike
in shape, when trumpets blow a deep bass blast   545
(and raucous barbarous bawls reverberate)
and when, from Helicon, interlacing tones
raise a sad strain with clear and poignant note.[3]
    Now, then, when we produce these sounds inside
the body, and send them out straight through the mouth,   550
the nimble, magical tongue molds them to words,
and in their turn the lips take form to shape them.
Now when the space from source to destination

---

3. The text of lines 546–48 is badly damaged. My version is an attempt to approximate the meaning
of the passage.

of a given word is short, we're bound to hear
each word, each syllable, clearly and distinctly,   555
for they retain their pattern and their shape.
But if too long a space is interposed,
the words will be confused by all that air,
and the sound garbled, gliding athwart the breeze.
Thus you can hear the sound but can't discern   560
the separate words or apprehend their meaning:
so much is the speech confused and tangled up.
Besides, sometimes, in crowds, one single word
from the lips of an auctioneer will strike all ears.
For that one utterance, scattered into hundreds,   565
has parceled itself into each single ear,
marking the words distinct in form and sound.
But all of the sounds that fall upon no ear
pass on to be lost and scattered to the winds.
Some, striking solid places, are thrown back   570
as echoes: at times, these "mirror-words" deceive us.
When this you've understood, you can explain
to yourself and others how in lonely spots
cliffs may repeat our words in form and order,
when in dark mountain-vales we search for friends   575
scattered and lost, and call them with loud cries.
I've seen spots echo six, yes, seven times
at a single cry, as hill to hill repeated
the words, taught them to echo, and tossed them back.
People nearby fancy that goat-foot satyrs   580
and nymphs live in these hills. They talk of fauns
that wander by night, and swear it is their shouts
and dancing and singing that shatter peace and quiet:
they sound the string and make the sweet, sad strains
that pour from a flute stopped by a player's fingers.   585
The farmers everywhere know, they say, when Pan,
shaking the pine that wreathes his half-wild head,
sends curved lip racing across the hollow reeds
to flood the world with piping of woodland song.
They talk of other such marvels and miracles, too,   590
lest they be thought to live in lonely spots
that even the gods forsook. That's why they tell
wild tales—or something else persuades them, since
all humankind much love a willing ear.
    Further, we need not wonder by what means   595
voices can pass and rouse the ear through places
through which eyes can't discern the clearest thing.
Often we "see" a colloquy through closed doors,
because, of course, through winding pores of matter

the word may pass unharmed, the image won't.   600
For the image is torn unless it swim straight channels,
like those of glass, through which all figures float.
Now words divide themselves in all directions,
since one begets another; a lone word starts,
then bursts apart into many, as a spark   605
of fire often sows fires just like itself.
Thus places hidden behind are filled with words,
seething with sound, and echoing to its impact.
But images always keep straight down the path
down which they started; hence men cannot see   610
over a wall, but can hear words outside it.
And yet words, too, when passing through enclosures
in houses, are blunted and reach the ear confused:
we seem to hear a noise instead of words.

    Nor is it the least bit harder to explain   615
how with the tongue and palate we sense taste.
We first sense taste in the mouth when we press food
in the act of chewing, as if with the hand one pressed
a sponge full of water and tried to squeeze it dry.
Then what we press all passes through the pores   620
of the palate and through the labyrinthine tongue.
When the atoms of the trickling juice are smooth,
then they touch gently, gently deal with all
the moist, saliva'd temples of the tongue.
But again, the atoms sting and rasp the sense   625
to the degree that roughness fills them full.
Now pleasure from taste is limited to the palate;
when juices tumble beyond, down through the throat,
and pass on into our parts, there is no pleasure.
Nor does it matter what food may feed our flesh   630
if we can digest what's eaten, and absorb it,
and keep concoctive movement smooth and fluid.

    Now I'll explain why one man's food is poison
to another, and why what some find harsh and bitter
may seem to others most agreeable.   635
So far apart these things, so different,
that one man's meat is another man's cold poison.
Just like the snake: touched by the spittle of man
it dies: it bites until it kills itself.
Further, to us, hellebore is cold poison   640
but it fattens the goat and makes the quail grow plump.
That you may understand what makes this so,
remember, first, what I have said before,
that things have atoms in countless combinations.
Further, all animate creatures that take food,   645

just as they differ outwardly, and by kinds
keep within fixed extremes of physical form,
so are they built of atoms in varied patterns.
Now since the atoms are different, they must differ
in spacing and passages—what we call the "pores"—   650
in all our parts, in mouth and palate, too.
Some must be smaller, then, some must be larger,
and others square, some must be triangular,
many are round, some many ways angular.
For, as their patterns of motion and shape demand,   655
so must the different shapes have different "pores,"
and passages vary according to their structure.
Hence what is sweet to some is bitter to others.
For him who finds it sweet, the smoothest atoms
must enter the palate's paths caressingly,   660
but those who, taking the same thing, find it sour
are stung in the mouth by atoms rough and barbed.
With this for a start, the rest is easily learned.
Take one with a fever, victim of the bile,
or felled by illness from some other cause: 665
his body is all confusion then, and all
his patterned system of atoms is changed around;
substances once agreeable to his tastes
no longer agree, and others are now preferred
which penetrate and produce a harsh effect.   670
In the taste of honey, both qualities are combined;
this I have often shown you, just above.
Come now, I'll tell you how a jetted odor
touches the nose. First, many things must exist
from which flow undulant streams of different odors;   675
we know they're everywhere, wafted, thrown off, scattered,
but to breathing creatures some seem better than others
because of their different shapes. Thus, through the air
bees are drawn for miles by the scent of honey,
and buzzards by carrion. Then, where wild beasts set   680
their split-hoof footprints, unleashed dogs are drawn,
and from far off the scent of man is caught
by a goose, white savior of our Roman walls.
Thus by the scents they catch are creatures led
each to his food, and from foul poison forced   685
to shrink; this way, wild animals save their lives.
    Now these very odors, that stimulate the nose,
may be released, some farther away than others,
but scarcely a single one can travel as far
as noise, as speech, to say naught of those things
that strike the eye and stimulate our sight.   690

For scent, being slow and errant, fades away
as, little by little, soft breezes dissipate it.
Starting inside its source, it struggles out;
for proof that odors flow from deep in things   695
is seen in the fact that broken things smell stronger
always, as do things crushed, or cracked by fire.
Besides, you see that odors are made of atoms
larger than those of speech, for they can't pierce
stone walls, where speech and sound pass commonly.   700
Hence you'll see too that smells can't be tracked down
so easily to the place from which they come.
For, passing slow through air, their force grows cold;
it won't race hot to the nose to tell of things.
Thus dogs sometimes go wrong and search for tracks.   705
   Yet still this is not true of tastes and odors
alone; some kinds of things and colors, too,
don't all so mesh with every creature's senses
that some are not more harsh to view than others.
Take even the cock, whose wings drum out the night,   710
who with loud crowing daily summons dawn:
the savage lion can't stand up to him
or look at him;[4] no, he thinks at once of flight,
because in the cock's body there are these atoms,
you see, which, once they enter the lion's eyes,   715
dig deep down into the pupils, and cause pain
so sharp, that even the savage beast can't stand it.
And yet these atoms never hurt our eyes,
either because they don't pierce through, or, piercing,
they find free exit; not remaining there,   720
they cannot hurt the eyes at any point.
   Now hear what things can stir the soul, and learn
briefly whence come those things that come to mind.
I say first: images of things float free,
countless in countless ways and all directions,   725
fine fabrics combining readily in the air
whenever they meet, like cobwebs or gold-foil.
You see, they're far more delicate in their texture
than those that capture the eye and stir the sight,
for they penetrate the porous flesh and rouse   730
the fine soul-stuff within, and stir the senses.
Hence we see Centaurs and a Scylla's body,
dog-snouts of Cerberus, likenesses of men
whose bones the earth holds locked in death's embrace.
Yes, images of all kinds float everywhere,   735

4. This curious bit of nonsense seems to have been widespread in antiquity. For the references, see
Bailey's note on this passage.

some formed spontaneously in the very air,
some pulling away from different kinds of things,
some built by the joining of their several shapes.
For Centaur-images can't be formed from life
since such a beast has never lived or breathed,   740
but when, by chance, horse-shape and man-shape meet,
at once they simply merge, as I've explained,
because of their delicate substance and fine texture.
All other things like this are formed this way.
Since they are nearly weightless and move with ease,   745
as I showed before, each delicate shape among them
by one light impact stimulates our soul,
for the mind itself is fine and strangely mobile.
    Now hear sure proof that my account is true:
so far as mind and eye see things alike,   750
the means by which they see must be alike.
And since I've proved that I identify
the lion by images that rouse the eye,
you'll know that in like manner the mind is moved:
by image it tells the lion and all else   755
no less than the eye, but sees more delicate kinds.
And not otherwise, when sleep has loosed our limbs,
is the mind awake; no, these same images
we see when awake, now stimulate our souls
so much we truly think to see that man   760
who, gone from life, is owned by death and earth.
This, nature compels to happen, because the senses,
throughout our sleep-drugged limbs, are all at rest
and can't make truth prevail against the false.
The memory, too, lies dull and drugged by sleep   765
and fails to mark as long since dead and gone
that man the mind believes it sees alive.
It's not strange, either, that these images move,
and gesture with arm and leg in rhythmic manner.
The image appears to do this in our dreams,   770
for when one vanishes and a second follows
differently posed, the first seems to have moved.
You know, of course, this takes place very fast,
so mobile are these things and so abundant,
and at any moment of sensing, such a mass   775
of atoms is present that every need is filled.
    Much questioning here occurs, and we must make
much clear, if we're to give plain explanations.
We're asked first, why, whatever thing a man
may wish, his mind thinks of that thing at once.   780
Well, do the images wait upon our will,

and, soon as we wish it, come to us post-haste,
whether we want the sea, the earth, the heavens?
Crowds of people, fights, revelry, parades—
does nature make and provide them all on order?   785
Especially when, in a single place, the minds
of different people all think of different things?
What, too, when in our dreams we see a dance
of images, see them move their lovely limbs,
by twos nimbly enlacing their lovely arms,   790
watching the movements, matching them step by step?
The images must be artistis, schooled and trained
to stage performances for us by night!
Or is it rather true that in the moment
of sentience (that is, when one word is uttered)   795
lurk many moments, found there by our reason;[5]
and hence it happens that at any moment
images are on hand in every place:
so mobile are these things and so abundant.
For when one vanishes and a second follows   800
differently posed, the first seems to have moved.
And since they're delicate, if the mind's not tensed
to discern them, it will miss them; all the rest
are lost but those for which the mind is ready.
It will make ready and expect to see   805
what follows a given idea—and see it will.
And watch the eyes, too: when they try to see[6]
delicate things, they tense and ready themselves: 809
without this, you observe, we can't see clearly.   810
And even in obvious things, we know quite well,
if we don't pay attention, it's as if
the thing were years away and far removed.
Why is it strange, then, if the mind will miss
all but the things on which it concentrates?   815
By petty signs, too, we adjudge great things,
letting ourselves slip into fraud and error.
    Sometimes it occurs, too, that an image comes
not of the same kind: what was female once
seems in the ghost-world to come up as male   820
or trades with another in features or in years.
We're never surprised: sleep sees that we forget.
    One error here you must with might and main
avoid—in fear and trembling flee this fault:
do not imagine the eyes' bright gleam created   825

5. This is the Epicurean's not too lucid way of
saying that words have many meanings and
many associations; no word is an isolated utter-
ance.
6. Line 808=804, and is omitted by editors.

in order that we might see, or that we might
step the long stride: for this, thigh ends in calf,
and calf in foot, firm-based yet flexible;
or that our arms were strung with brawn and muscle
and hands bestowed, our servants, left and right,   830
that we might do what life required of us.
These and all other like interpretations
are falsely reasoned and preposterous;
no part of us grew there that we might use it,
but what grew there created its own use.   835
There was no seeing before the eye took form,
no words, no pleas, until the tongue was made;
tongues, rather, came into being far ahead
of speech, and ears took form long, long before
a sound was heard. In short, each of our parts   840
existed, I think, before its use arose;
they can't have grown, then, to fulfill a function.
Per contra, battle and fight with hand and fist,
slashing the body, staining the flesh with blood,
took place long, long before bright weapons flew;   845
instinct had made men shrink from wounds before
the left hand learned to hold the shield and parry.
And of course to lay one's weary flesh to rest
is older far than beds all softly spread,
and slaking of thirst was born before the cup.   850
Credibly, then, we learned these things to turn them
to use—things taught us by the world and life.
All others are different; they were first created,
then later gave us a concept of their use.
First in this class we see our parts and senses;   855
hence we must keep ourselves far from belief
that they could have taken form to serve a purpose.
    Nor must we wonder why, by very nature,[7]
the body of every living thing seeks food.
I proved, you recall, that atoms come and go   860
in a thousand ways from things, but most of all
from living things: because they keep in motion,
they sweat and lose many atoms, squeezed from within,
and tired and panting, breathe many out by mouth.
These ways the body grows porous; its whole substance   865
is undermined; the consequence is pain.
That's why food is taken: it permeates,
to rebuild flesh and strength, and dull that love

7. Lines 858–76 may be misplaced. Some editors bracket them; others try to relocate them elsewhere, e.g., after 906. Bailey suggests that they would go better after 2.1118, but also—and sensibly—advocates leaving them as they stand.

of eating spread through every limb and vein.
Water as well diffuses to every part   870
that asks for water: when many atoms of heat
roll up in a mass to make our stomach burn,
water will scatter and put them out like fire,
that heat no further may parch and scorch our organs.
You see, thus panting thirst is washed away   875
from our bodies, thus our hunger-lust is filled.
     How it happens now that we can take a step
when we wish, whence comes our power of random movement,
and what force learns to push our heavy mass
of body forward, I'll tell: you hear my words.   880
I say that first an image of walking comes
to our mind and strikes it, as I said before.
The wish comes second, for no one starts an action
before the mind first sees what it desires.
The thing it sees is image of that action.   885
Thus when the mind, self-moving, wills to walk,
at once it strikes the soul, that power dispersed
throughout the body, through every part and limb—
easily done, since they are held conjoint
Thereafter, soul strikes body, and bit by bit   890
the entire mass is pushed and set in motion.
Besides, the body rarefies then, and air
(as must, you know, a thing so mobile ever)
comes flooding in, down through the opened pores,
and scatters thus to every tiny part   895
of the body. Both these forces, then, are cause
that body is moved, like ship by wind and sail.
Nor, in this matter, should we be surprised
that particles so small can wrench a body
so large, and make our whole mass twist and turn.   900
Why not? The gentle breeze, so soft of substance,
sets a great ship, great burden and all, to moving;
whatever her speed, one hand controls her helm
and one lone rudder alters her course at will;
the sheave, the tackle, the windlass make light work,   905
again and again, of shifting heavy weights.
     Next, sleep: in what ways it can flood our flesh
with peace, and free the heart and soul from care,
I'll tell in lines more sweet than numerous:
better the swan's brief note than that loud call   910
of the crane, wind-driven through the clouds of heaven!
Just grant me a humble ear and thoughtful mind;
don't flatly reject what I say can be; don't turn
away with heart dead-set against my truth,

when you are the one at fault, and just can't see.   915
To begin: sleep comes[8] when through our flesh the links
of soul are weakened: part is forced outside
and part is driven deeper in tighter union.
Our body structure then turns loose and fluid.
For doubtless it is by virtue of the soul   920
that we have senses, and when sleep impedes them
we must conclude our soul has been disturbed
and forced outside—not all of it, for the body
would then lie under death's cold, eternal stream.
For if no part of soul were left concealed   925
in the body, like fire deep buried under ash,
whence could sentience so quickly be rekindled
in us, as flame leaps up from hidden fire?
    But by what means this strange state is produced,
and how the body and soul grow weak and troubled,   930
I'll explain: don't let my words drift with the wind.
First, on the body's outward parts, since they
are in close contact with the air, there must
be a constant pulse and pounding from that source.
That is why nearly all things are protected   935
by skin or shell or horny hide or bark.
Yes, and for those who breathe, this same air beats
on the inward parts, when drawn in and blown out.
Thus two things happen: blows rain on the body
and also, through narrow channels, penetrate   940
to the basic parts and elements of our bodies;
then, little by little, our physical frame collapses,
for atoms of body and soul are knocked about
and disarranged. Part of the soul is then
ejected, and part draws inward into hiding;   945
part, too, wide-scattered through the limbs, can't be
interconnected or answer move with move,
for nature bars it from the paths to union.
Sensation turns about then, and submerges,
and since, as it were, the limbs thus lose their props,   950
the body falls weak, and all our flesh turns tired;
arms slacken, eyelids droop, and we lie down,
as tendons, calf and thigh, relax and soften.
Now sleep follows on food because our food
does just what air does, as it finds its way   955
into our veins; and much the deepest sleep
comes when we're full or tired, because most atoms
are then displaced, disturbed, and knocked about.

8. To Lucretius, as to the ancients in general, sleep and death are different only in degree, not in kind.

In the same way part of the soul contracts and sinks
deeper, and more of it still is cast outside,   960
and it is more cut and torn apart within us.
    And, mostly, the interests that we hold the closest,
or those on which we have long dwelt before,
in which our minds have felt most satisfaction,
are those we normally seem to meet in dreams.   965
Lawyers plead cases and put briefs together;
generals plan compaigns and march to war;
sailors wage ancient battle with the winds;
I work at this, my endless quest of nature,
and tell my findings in my native tongue.   970
In this way, arts and interests often seem
to grip and bedevil the mind of man in dreams.
And those who day after day have sat and watched
the games of the circus, often, we observe,
after they've stopped this use of sense perception,   975
there still remain broad pathways in their minds
down which those same old images still may travel.
And so day after day these same things pass
before our eyes: we seem, when wide awake,
to see the dancers form their graceful figures,   980
to catch in ear the singing, ringing song
of lyre and lute, to see that vast assembly
and the beauty of color on color across the stage.
So much do our interests matter, and our pleasures
and all those things to which not only men   985
but every animate creature turns attention.
You'll see fine horses, when they lie at rest,
sweat in their dreams and snort, day after day,
and as if racing, marshall all their strength,

*   *   *

or, as if the stalls had opened[9]
And huntsmen's hounds often, when sound asleep,
suddenly move their legs and make quick sounds
of baying, and sniff at the air, and sniff again
as if they'd found and caught an animal-trail;
then, waking up, they often chase an image,   995
their dream of a deer, as if they saw it running,
till they recover themselves and shake off error.
But the gentler breed of dogs, used to the house,
will start, leap from the floor, and shake themselves[1]   999
as if they were seeing some stranger's face and form.

9. The latter part of this line is unintelligible.   1. Lines 1000-1003 = 992-995, and are omit-
                                                      ted by editors.

And the coarser each one of these bloodlines is,   1005
the more they show their fierceness in their dreams.
But bright birds take to flight, and with quick wings
affright the groves of the gods long after dark,
if in sweet sleep they had a dream of hawks
swooping, pursuing, attacking in flocks or singly.   1010
The minds of men, great thinkers of great thoughts,
are likewise busy in dreams with plot and act;
they drive out kings, are captured, join in battle,
they scream, as if their throats were being cut.
They fight to the death, sometimes, and moan in pain;   1015
and as if gripped by the jaws of savage lion
or panther, they fill the whole house with their screams.
Many mean speak in dreams of weighty matters,
and all too often betray their own misdeeds.
Many meet death; many, like those who plummet   1020
from mountain-top to earth, in all their flesh
know panic; they wake, but still entrapped in mind,
they scarce regain their wits for physical terror.
Men sit thirsting beside a lovely spring
or brook and nearly gulp the whole stream down.   1025
And innocents, sometimes, in the grip of sleep
thinking they lift their shirts by some latrine,
pour out the body's whole embladdered liquid,
and soak their gorgeous silken coverlets.
Then those whose semen for the first time flows   1030
into their youthful parts, now timely ripe,
encounter images, sloughed off from some person,
that tell of a lovely face and soft, smooth skin;
these rouse and tickle that place with seed full-swollen,
and often, as if the act were done, it spreads   1035
a stream, a surge, a flood, and stains the bed.
    That semen, as I've just said, is stimulated
in us when manhood makes our bodies strong.
Many things stir and stimulate other things;
man's power alone draws human seed from man.   1040
Soon as it's forced out from its starting points
all over the body, it moves through limb and organ
and, gathering at one special spot, at once
rouses the body's genital parts themselves.
The organ tickles and swells with seed; we will   1045
to eject it whither desire directs itself,[2]
straight toward the body that wounded us with love.   1048
For normally men fall *toward* a wound, and blood
wells outward *toward* the blow that wounded us;   1050

2. Line 1047 = 1034, and is omitted by editors.

yes, if the enemy's close, he's drenched with blood.
Thus he who's wounded by the bolt of love
(whether a boy with girlish limbs has struck him,
or a woman, darting passion from every pore)
turns toward the source of hurt, and aches for union,   1055
to jet his humors, body into body;
desire, though wordless, tells of joys to be.
    This we call "Venus," hence we speak of "love"[3]
and of that drop of passion, first and sweet,
that trickles into our heart and brings cold care.   1060
For if your love is absent, still her image
is with you and her name sings in your ear.
But we must shun these images and scare off
what feeds our love, and turn our thoughts elsewhere,
and jet our humors into someone's body,   1065
not keep them, and, once trapped by one lone love
save up sure woe and worry for ourselves.
For if the cancer's fed, it lives and grows;
in time, folly's a fever and pangs are millstones,
if fresh hurts aren't distracted by new bruises,   1070
and we don't take to the streets to cure young love
or else divert our thoughts and minds elsewhere.
    Nor, lacking passion, must one lose love's joys;
rather, one gains pure happiness, at no cost.
For certainly to the healthy, pleasure's purer   1075
than to the sick. In the moment of possession
impassioned lovers waver, blunder, stumble:
they can't decide where first to look and touch.
Whatever they seize, they crush, inflicting pain
of body; sometimes they press tooth into lip   1080
and kiss like a flail, for theirs is no pure pleasure:
in it are lash and goad, perforce to hurt
that object, whence this burgeoning madness rose.
But in the act, love gaily blunts these pangs,
lets pleasure in, and gently curbs distress.   1085
For there is hope that in that very body
that set us afire, the flame may be put out.
But nature battles against this whole idea;

3. This passage is often referred to as a "tirade against love" or (Bailey) an "attack on the passion of love." It is rather an attempt to analyze and explain, in Epicurean terms, the phenomenon of sex in all its aspects, beginning with the sexual dream (1030–36) and discussing the impulses toward and mechanics of sexual union, the causes of fertility and sterility, the problems of genetics, the transmission and inheritance of physical and psychological characteristics, and above all, the dangers that sex poses for the Epicurean ideal of pleasure. More than any other human activity, sex, pleasant in itself and therefore good, tempts us to overindulgence and thoughtless complaisance, thus exposing us to the danger of turning what was essentially pleasant and good into something painful and evil. The passage is one of the most brilliant parts of the entire poem, requiring hardly more than a number of changes in terminology to bring it into harmony with modern discussions of sex. It might properly be entitled "The Physiology, Psychology, and Philosophy of Sex."

love's the one thing, of which the more we have
the more the heart burns with insane desire.   1090
Now food and drink are taken into the body,
but since they settle in predetermined spots
our need for bread and wine is readily filled.
But from a human face and soft, smooth skin
the body gets nothing to use but images—   1095
slight things, poor hopes the wind oft whips away.
As one in dreams who, thirsting, looks for water
but finds none that might cool his fevered flesh;
(he struggles to reach the fluid—vain mirage;
midway a roaring river he drinks and thirsts)   1100
so Venus deludes fond lovers with simulacra.
They view bare bodies but get no fill of viewing;
hands chafe but win no substance from young flesh,
though they roam wildly over all the body.
Besides, when two lie tasting, limb by limb,   1105
life's bloom, when flesh gives foretaste of delight,
and Venus is ready to sow the female field,
they hungrily size each other, mouth to mouth
the spittle flows, they pant, press tooth to lip—
vainly, for they can chafe no substance off   1110
nor pierce and be gone, one body in the other.[4]
For often this seems to be their wish, their goal,
so greedily do they cling in passion's bond,
till pleasure loosens their limp and fainting limbs.
Yet, when impounded lust has burst from sinew,   1115
hot passion, just for a moment, makes a pause.
Then men go mad again, wild lust returns,
while even the passionate wonder what they want,
and find no artifice to assuage the pain,
so helpless, weak, and blind the wound has left them.   1120
 Add that they waste their strength, they strain, they die;
add that the will of a woman rules their life.
Fortunes go first, for Oriental robes,
then honor and reputation totter and fall.
Perfumes, fine slippers for her pretty feet,   1125
of course, and flashing emeralds, huge and green,
set in pure gold; blue gowns for everyday,
to be rumpled and sweat-soaked in the act of love.
A grandsire's hard-earned wealth turns into jewels,
a holiday dress, imported silks and satins.   1130
We buy fine food, fine clothes and entertainment,
garlands and perfumes, wines for everyone;

---

4. Milton's description of angelic love bears a curious, and probably not entirely coincidental, resemblance to this passage; *Paradise Lost* 8.618–629.

no use, since in the midst of bubbling joys,
bitterness rises and turns bright bloom to pain,
sometimes when conscience sets the tooth of guilt   1135
to self for useless living and wasted years,
or a girl has tossed some doubtful word, and left it
fixed in our foolish heart like living fire,
or cast too free an eye upon some rival,
or shown a trace of mockery on her face.   1140
    And these are thrills that plague acknowledged love,
when all goes well; but when love's poor and luckless,
you'll pick up troubles by thousands with the eye
blindfolded; better to be on watch before
and avoid the pitfall, in the way I've shown;   1145
to keep from falling into the snare of love
is not so hard as to escape the net
once caught, and burst the knotted bonds of Venus.
Yet, even snared and tangled, you can still
get free, unless you block your own way out,   1150
and start by ignoring every fault of mind
or body in her whom you desire and want.
For this men often do when blind with lust,
bestowing virtues where they don't exist.
Hence we see ugly, shapeless women loved   1155
like precious darlings, loaded with wealth and honors.
And some men mock their fellows, and bid them beg
Venus for mercy, so sick, so foul their love,
and never observe, poor fools, their own worse ills.
Sallow is "honeyed," unkempt, unwashed, "informal";   1160
she stares: "a goddess!" all bone and muscle: "a fawn!"
Dumpy? "She's exquisite! Tiny—but what a mind!"
Huge and clumsy? "Portentous! Pure dignity!"
Hare-lip? Tongue-tied? "No, lisping," "self-effacing!"
Shameless? A hideous bore? No, "Wisdom's lamp!"   1165
Stringy and thin? Not long to live? "She's dainty,
a darling!" Bad cough? One foot in the grave? No, "frail!"
Bulging? Huge-uddered? "A Ceres, suckling Bacchus!"
Pug-nosed? "A saucy nymph!" Thick-lipped? "For kissing!"
And so on and so on: the rest is long to tell.   1170
But grant her now the world's most lovely face,
let every inch of her flesh breathe forth love's power:
still there are others, still, we lived years without her;
still (and we know it) she does what the homely do:
drenches herself, like an idiot, with vile smells   1175
(her slaves slip out and titter behind her back).
But a shut-out lover tearfully loads her door
each night with flowers, and oils the heartless hinges

with perfume, and—fool!—plants kisses on her steps;
yet let him enter, and if one single whiff   1180
should meet him, he'd look for good excuse to leave,
forgetting the ballad he'd learned, wrung from the heart,
scolding himself for a fool, because he'd see
he'd granted her more than man may be allowed.
Nor does this escape our ladies: more than ever   1185
they struggle to hide these backstage bits of life
from the men they wish to hold fast-bound in love.
Vainly, for you by taking thought may draw
all this to the light, and analyze every smile.
If hers is a pretty wit, and herself not gross,   1190
let her go—her too; she's human: accept that fact.
     Now woman will sigh for love, not always falsely.
Embracing her man, she joins him, flesh to flesh;
kissing wet-lipped she covers his mouth with hers.
Often she acts sincerely; seeking joy   1195
for them both, she sends him racing down love's track.
Not otherwise, birds and beasts of field and forest,
cow, ewe, and mare, can move beneath their males;
their very female lust wells up and burns
and joys to feel and fondle their mounting lovers.   1200
Don't you see, too, how those whom shared delight
has linked and interlaced are racked with pain?
How often dogs in the street strive might and main,
pulling and panting, to go their separate ways,
yet still are helpless, locked in sex together.   1205
They'd never do this but for shared delights;
these trick them, throw them together, and hold them fast.
I say it again: the sexes share this pleasure.
     Now when at mingling of seed the female force
seizes, subdues, and dominates the male,   1210
the children, from mother's seed, are like their mothers;
vice versa, like their fathers. But those you see
like both, with features mingled of both parents,
grew from the father's flesh and mother's blood
when love-seed, roused and coursing through their bodies,   1215
met with equal ardor, united, lived,
and neither was dominant, neither one subdued.
Sometimes it happens that children may resemble
grandparents, or show a great-grandfather's face.
This is because our parents often carry   1220
a host of atoms combined in countless ways,
passed down the family line, father to son;
hence Venus at random draws resemblances,
the face of an ancestor, or his voice, his hair,

since these arise as much from special atoms   1225
as do complexion, body-type, and size.[5]
The female, too, comes from the father's seed
and males find origin in the mother's flesh,
for every child is born of twofold seed,
and every child resembles more that parent   1230
of whom it has more than half; this we observe
whether the child's of male or female sex.[6]

   Now godhead (that bugaboo) will never stop
conception, so that no sweet child ever calls us
"father," and love is sterile all our lives.   1235
Yet many believe so; saddened, they drench the altars
with blood, and with burnt offering fog the shrines,
for floods of seed to get their wives with child.
A waste of time, to weary the gods and fate!
The sterile, in part, have seed too coarse and heavy,   1240
or again, more thin and watery than should be.
This seed can't firmly fasten itself in place,
but slips right off, withdraws, and is expelled.
Coarse seed, again, comes in unwieldy masses:
it either can't be propelled with proper speed,   1245
or can't pierce through to the place, or having pierced,
can't mingle readily with the woman's seed.
Suitable union in sex takes many forms.
Some serve one woman better, some, another;
women grow pregnant better by different men.   1250
Many a woman, sterile though often wed,
finds later a man by whom she can conceive
children—treasures to fill their lives with joy.
And men to whom a train of fertile wives
have borne no child, find mates, they too, well matched,   1255
who'll bear them sons to comfort their old age.
So much it matters that seed be capable
of mixing with seed in modes of generation,
mesh coarse with watery, watery mesh with coarse.
It matters, too, what foods sustain our lives,   1260
for some will strengthen the seed within our bodies,
while others will make it weak and watery.
The modes of the act by which we gain sweet pleasure
are all-important too; in wild-beast fashion
and four-foot style, men commonly believe,   1265
our wives conceive more readily, for their parts

---

5. Here, without realizing it, Lucretius has described genes, and their role in the determination of physical characteristics.
6. Lucretius here shows an understanding, nearly unique in the ancient world, of the fact that both male and female contribute physical entities to procreation. He does not, to be sure, distinguish between ovum and sperm (both are called "seed"), but he is far in advance of ancient physiology in general, which taught that the "seed" came only from the male, who "planted" it in the female's body.

(breasts down, hips high) best take the seed this way.
And wives must make no lustful movements, either,
for women prevent conception, beat it back,
when for delight, their parts caress the man's,   1270
and liquid flows from lithe and twisting flesh;
for they throw the furrow awry and skew the path
of the plow, and make the seed-cast miss the place.[7]
For their own purposes, whores will make these motions,
to avoid conception and idle, pregnant days—   1275
and also to make love pleasanter for their men.
Of this, our wives clearly can have no need.

    Nor is it by hand of god and shafts of Venus
that a girl ill favored of form may yet find love.
For sometimes by her works and ways,   1280
by kindness, patience, neatness, and good taste,
woman may win you to share a life with her.
And anyway, habit's the builder of affection;
for things though lightly struck, yet constantly,
in the end are overcome and must give way.   1285
You see how even drops of water, falling
on stone, in course of time bore through the stone.

---

7. Lucretius here seems to be describing female orgasm, which he views as an attempt to prevent conception.

Book V

Who has the might of mind to write a poem
worthy of all the majesty here discovered?
Who has the power to marshall words of praise
meet for the merit of him whose mind sought out,
garnered, gained, and bequeathed such wealth to us?   5
No man, I think, born of mere mortal flesh.
Here stands a world revealed in all its grandeur.
Say it, Lord Memmius: "He was god—yes, god!"
who first unveiled that way of life and thought
we call "philosophy" now, and who, by science,   10
took life from storms so vast and such vast darkness
into a calm so great and light so clear.
Compare the old god-stories of other men.
Ceres,[1] so goes the fable, just gave grain,
and Bacchus[2] the vine-juice, wine, to mortal men;   15
yet even so, men could have lived without them,
as to this day, we're told, some people live.
But good life never could be without pure heart.
More properly, then, he seems to us a god,
for even today, spread through the great, wide world,   20
his sweet words comfort lives and soothe men's souls.
A Hercules[3], you think, might match his deeds?
Then you will travel far from truth and reason.
Lion of Nemea (those great gaping jaws)
Arcady's Bristle-pig: how could they harm us now?   25
The Bull of Crete, and Lerna's Pest, the Hydra
stockaded with poison snakes: what force have they?
What force three-chested Geryon, triple-twinned?[4]

*   *   *

so harm us, denizens of Stymphalus,
and Diomede's horses, with their fiery breath   30
in Thrace, near Ismara and Bistonea's plains?
The Guard of the Golden Apples of the West,
that scaly, hypnotic-eyed, gigantic snake,
coiled round his tree trunk—how could he do us harm
beside the Atlantic, shore of the Frowning Sea,   35

---

1. Goddess of grain, especially of wheat. She
was identified with the Greek goddess Deme-
ter.
2. The god of the vine, also called Dionysus.
His cult featured wild dancing and singing,
performed in mountain retreats by women (the
Bacchantes).
3. The Greek Heracles, famed for his "Twelve
Labors," some of which Lucretius mentions in
this passage.
4. After this line, at least one line has been lost.

where none of us goes, nor even the savage dares?
The rest of such monsters, dead now, after all,
if they had won and survived, how could they hurt us?
Not at all, I think. The world is crammed with beasts,
alive with them, even today, filled with stark terror   40
in grove and mountain and in the forest deeps,
all places that we commonly can avoid.
But if the heart's not whole, what struggles then,
what dangers must engulf us against our will?
How then will the stinging saber slash of lust   45
and guilt trouble a man, what fears besides?
And pride, bad temper, baseness, what disasters
can they inflict? What, sloth and self-indulgence?
He who drove all these evils from our hearts—
purged them with words, not weapons—should not he   50
be deemed one man meet to be counted god?
Especially since, about those deathless gods,
he never wearied of telling the godlike truth,
and with his words unveiled the world of Being.

His are the steps I tread[5] as I pursue   55
reason, and show how all things must remain
bound by the convenant that ruled their birth,
and none can repeal the changeless laws of time.
Here we at once discover that the soul
consists of substance created and compounded   60
and cannot remain undamaged down long years.
But images commonly trick the mind in dreams,
when we believe we see one lost from life.
For the rest, the order of argument now demands
that I explain our cosmos: how it's made   65
of mortal stuff, and had its day of birth,
and in what ways this matter came in congress
to form earth, sky, and sea, the stars, the sun,
the lunar globe; then, on our earth, what creatures
did come to be, and what were never born;   70
and how the human race, with varied speech,
began to treat together by naming things;
and in what ways this fear of gods engulfed
our hearts, with holy awe throughout the world
for shrines, lakes, altars, groves, and sacred idols.   75
And I'll explain how nature by her law

5. Lucretius here (55–63) briefly summarizes the contents of Bks. I–IV, and then goes on (64–90) to outline the subject matter of Bk. V. The fact that he presents such a summary here, and not elsewhere, suggests that Bk. V was intended to be the climactic and most immediately important section of his poem. At least two cardinal principles are enunciated: (1) that our world was brought into being by natural forces and natural law, and not in any degree or manner by divine intervention, and (2) that our world, since it is a *thing*—i.e., a conglomerate of atoms and void—is impermanent and must someday inevitably be destroyed.

governs the shifting course of sun and moon,
lest we imagine them free twixt heaven and earth,
by will of their own tracing their yearly course
with kind concern for growth of crops and creatures,   80
or think they revolve because some god so planned it.
   If people have learned that gods lead carefree lives,
and still, for all that, wonder by what means
phenomena may occur, especially those
they see in heavenly zones above their heads,   85
then they will slip back into their old beliefs
and take on heartless masters, whom they deem
almighty—poor fools, they don't know what can be
and what cannot; yes, and what law defines
the power of things, what firm-set boundary stone.   90
   To continue (no more promises and delays!)
begin by observing sea and earth and sky.
Their threefold substance, Memmius, those three bodies,
three aspects so dissimilar, three such fabrics
will die in a day; that great, geared world, held massed   95
and ordered for ages, will come crashing down.
Nor do I forget how strange, how weird, the thought
strikes us, that heaven and earth will be destroyed,
or how I must labor to win you to my view.
So is it with things ear has not heard before,   100
that can't be laid out either, for eye to see
or hand to touch—that road of faith paved straight
to the heart of man and the temples of his mind.
Yet I'll speak out. Events may prove my view;
perhaps some crash, some earthquake may occur,   105
and show you, in one short hour, a shattered world—
which Fortune, hand on helm, divert from us!
Let reason rather than actual fact be proof
that everything may collapse in screaming ruin!
   On this, I shall declare the dooms in words   110
more sacred and more certain far than all
the Pythoness prates from Phoebus' tree and tripod.
But first I'll write you skillful lines of comfort,
so that religion not hold you bound to think
that earth and sun and sky, sea, stars, and moon,   115
must be of godlike stuff, eternal, fixed.
You must not deem it just, that like the Giants,
all those be punished, as for a monstrous crime,
who, reasoning, knock the walls of the world awry;
who try to put out the shining sun in heaven   120
by giving immortal things mere mortal names,
things so widely removed from godlike power,

things clearly deemed not meet for heaven's roster,
we'd rather think they'd give us an idea
of something cut off from movement, life, and sense.   125
It can't be that just anything you like
be thought possessed of wisdom and soul-substance.
In air there are no trees; in the salt sea
clouds can't exist, nor fish live on dry land;
there can't be blood in wood, or sap in stone.   130
It's fixed and ordained where things may grow and live.
Soul, then, can't come to being without the body,
all by itself, far, far from flesh and blood.
For if it could, the soul could sooner function
in head or shoulders or the soles of feet,   135
and commonly come to being in any part,
staying, of course, within one man, one vessel.
Now since it's clear that even within our bodies
it's fixed and firm where soul and mind apart
can exist and grow, far more must we deny   140
that totally outside body and animate forms,
in moldering clods of earth or in sun-fires,
in water or heaven's high zones, the soul could last.
These things, then, aren't endowed with sense, like gods,
since they can't even have souls or be alive.   145
   Here's something else[6] you can't believe: that gods
have holy domiciles anywhere in our world.
For gods have delicate substance, far removed
from human sense, scarce visible to our minds.
It slips from under the thrust and touch of hands,   150
hence can't own anything that could reach and touch us.
For nothing can touch that can't itself be touched.
Yes, even the homes of gods must be unlike
these homes of ours—delicate, like their bodies
(this I'll demonstrate later, at some length).   155
To say further that it was for man's sake
gods meant to build this beautiful world, and hence
we're bound to praise their wonderful handiwork
and deem it deathless, endless, everlasting,
that what gods planned and founded, ages past,   160
for man, world without end, their law forbids
ever by any force to be dislodged,
or troubled by talk and turned all upside-down—
such maunderings, Memmius, and all others like them
are nonsense: what, now, for the Blessed Deathless,   165
could gratitude of ours bestow as gain,
that they might tackle a project for our sake?

6. Lines 146–234 explain Epicurean theology in detail. See also 3.18–30 and 6.70–75.

They were at peace! What latter-day novelty
could make them eager to change their way of life?
The new, I think, must bring delight to him   170
who hates the old; but he who in the past
has known no trouble, but led a happy life:
what could fire his passion for something new?
Or if we'd never been born: what harm in that?
Or should I think life lay in grief and darkness   175
until that dawn when everything began?
All that is born, you see, will want to stay
in life, while pleasure happily holds it here.
For him who never tasted the love of life
nor joined our ranks, what harm to have been not-born?   180
And whence were first implanted in gods' minds,
patterns, ideas for things, for man himself,
so they could know and picture what to make;
or how was the power of atoms ever known
(what they could do by change of place and order)   185
if nature herself had not provided models?[7]
For myriad atoms sped such myriad ways
from the All forever, pounded, pushed, propelled
by weight of their own, launched and speeding along,
joining all possible ways, trying all forms,   190
whatever their meeting in congress could create,
that it's no wonder if they all tumbled
into such patterns and entered on such orbits
as those that govern our cosmos and its changes.

   For though I were ignorant of the basic stuff,   195
still, just from heaven's behavior I would dare
affirm, and assert on many other grounds,
that gods most certainly never made the world
for you and me: it stands too full of flaws.
To begin: of all that heaven's vast sweep protects,   200
mountain, forest, and beast have rudely seized
a share; part, rocks and endless swamp possess,
and oceans, that hold our countries widely sundered.
Two-thirds besides are stolen from us mortals
by scorching heat and everlasting cold.   205
There's good land left, but nature's native force
would choke it with weeds if man did not fight back,
for very life grown strong to heave the hoe
and curse and push the plow and slash the earth.
The clod is fertile, but the share must turn it;   210
our hand must harass and goad the soil to life;

7. Lucretius seems unwilling to grant to the gods the *anticipatio* he grants to man (see Introduction, p. xviii). This would presumably have allowed them to devise a *man* without the necessity of a pre-existing model from which to work.

on its own, it can't rise up to clear, bright air.
And sometimes, even when we've toiled and strained
and the world is all in leaf and full of flowers,
the sun in heaven burns it with fires too high,   215
or sudden rains destroy it, or icy frosts,
or winds with a whistle and wail whirl all away.
Besides, those terrible animals, wild and deadly
to man by land and sea: why now must nature
feed and increase them? Why do the seasons bring   220
disease? Why must untimely death roam free?
And then the infant, like some sailor tossed
from savage seas, lies naked, speechless, helpless
to keep alive, when nature first has heaved
and spilled him into the light from mother's womb;   225
he fills the world with wails—and well he might,
such pain awaits his passage through this life!
But all the animals grow—sheep, cattle, wild;
they need no rattles, either, nor need hear
the lisping, lallying sweet-talk of the wet-nurse;   230
they don't need different clothing for each season.
Lastly, they need no weapons nor high walls
to guard their goods: for all, their every need
pours from the lap of earth and magic nature.

   Now to begin:[8] since physical earth, and water,   235
light-wafting winds, and searing exhalations,
the stuff of which we see our world consists,
are all of substance that is born and dies,
our whole world must be deemed so constituted.
For things whose members and whose parts we see   240
are shaped of substance that is born and dies,
we usually conclude are likewise mortal
and born, they too. Thus when I see the world's
huge parts and members wasted and reborn,
I know that heaven and likewise earth had once   245
their time of beginning, and that they too must crash.

   You must not think, now, that I just snatched up
this concept, claiming earth and fire were mortal,
never doubting that water and air would die,
and claiming they'd all be born and grow again.   250
To begin: no trivial part of earth, when baked
by endless suns and beaten by countless feet,
breathes forth a fog of dust and flying clouds
which strong winds scatter abroad through all the air.
Part of the soil as well is claimed for floods   255

8. Lucretius asserts that our world is made up of earth, air, fire, and water, but contends that these are not primal matter, but compounds of atoms and void. The building blocks of our world are therefore mortal and destructible, as is the world itself.

by rains, and rivers rasp and gnaw their banks.
Besides, all food and increase are repaid
in proper part; and since beyond all doubt
earth the all-mother is also our common tomb,
she gives, but takes away, and grows again.   260
   Further, new water keeps ocean, rivers, springs,
ever brimfull, and brooks run on forever.
This needs no proof: the deep down-flow of waters
everywhere makes it clear. But all top-water
is taken away and fluids don't flood over   265
partly because wild winds, sweeping the waves,
and the raveling rays of heavenly sun reduce them;
partly because they ooze away through earth.
For brine seeps through, and water-substance trickles
back to the source where rivers rise, and there   270
foregathers, to send sweet streams across the world,
where beds, once cut, guide water's bright , clear foot.
   Now let me speak of air: its total substance
is altered, hour by hour, in countless ways.
For all the bits that things slough off float always   275
out into air's wide sea, which must restore them
to things, rebuilding weakened substance, else
everything would dissolve to air-borne dust.
It never stops: things come from things, and drop
back into things; the world's in endless flux.   280
   That well-spring of bright light, the heavenly sun,
endlessly floods the sky with newborn rays
as it supplants light speedily with new light.
For that first bit of brightness dies away
wherever it falls. Here is your proof for this: 285
the minute that clouds start passing underneath
the sun, we'd say they break the light-rays off,
at once their lower parts all die away
and earth is shadowed wherever clouds float by.
Thus you may know things always need new light   290
and those first jets of brightness all are lost;
nor can we see things in the sun, unless
that fount of light gives endless new supply.
Suspended chandeliers, and torches, bright   295
with flickering flames and wrapped in thick, rich smoke,
in similar fashion hasten, with help of heat,
to furnish fresh light; their shimmering fires press,
press on: no beams are broken, no gaps left.
So speedily, by all those bits of fire   300
quick to be born, is death of flame concealed.
Thus we must think that sun and moon and stars

cast light from one new wellspring, then another,
and always lose each first-discharge of flame;
never believe these things live on undamaged.   305
    Next: don't you see rocks, too, succumb to time,
tall towers fall to the ground, and stone decay,
the shrines and statues of gods weaken and sag?
Not even godhead can prorogue the day
of death or make the laws of nature yield.   310
Next: don't we see men's monuments collapse[9]

* * *

see boulders, ripped from mountaintops, roll down;
they can't withstand the powered pulse of time,
though finite: they'd not be torn loose nor tumble   315
if through infinite ages they'd endured,
with never a crack, the wring and wrench of years.
    Then, too, behold this sphere that wraps all earth
about and above: if it begets all things
of itself, as some assert, and takes them back   320
when dead, its stuff must all be born and die.
For all things that give food and growth to others
decrease, then when they take things back, recover.
    Further, if earth and sky had no beginning,
no first-becoming, but have always been,   325
why haven't other poets sung other songs
besides their "War at Thebes" and "Death of Troy"?
Where have men's myriad deeds all gone, to bloom
nowhere implanted in fame's eternal records?
No; as I think, our universe is quite new,   330
our world is young; it started not long ago.[1]
Some arts are just now taking final polish
or still developing: daily, our ships gain new
tackle; today, musicians produced sweet sound.
Nature and nature's law have been revealed   335
just now, and I've been found the first of all
able to tell them in our native tongue.
If you believe all this has been before,
but that those tribes of men were scorched to death,
or that vast earthquakes shook their cities down,   340
or that it rained for days on end, and rivers,
rampaging over the earth, buried the towns,
so much the more you're beaten, and must admit

---

9. Line 312, as it appears in the MSS, is hopelessly garbled and is therefore omitted.
1. The fact that our world had a beginning, and hence will inevitably have an end, is based on a strange argument *ex silentio*: no poetic or other accounts of the world earlier than the stories about the war at Thebes and the destruction of Troy are extant; therefore the world must have come into being not too long before those events took place.

that heaven and earth as well some day must die.
For things that are attacked by such diseases   345
and such disasters, if some grimmer blow
should fall, would tumble in one huge jumbled ruin.
And nothing else so proves our mortal nature
as that we suffer from the same diseases
as did those men whom nature took from life.   350
    Further, things lasting and eternal must
either, because they're solid, repel all blows
and allow nothing to enter them that, once in,
could ravel their tight-knit structure, like the atoms
of matter, whose nature we've already shown;   355
or have the power to last throughout all time
because immune to impact, like the void,
which stays untouched, and suffers never a blow;
or else because there is no space around them
where things might escape, so to speak, or break away,   360
like the Sum of Sums Eternal: outside this
there is no room for escape, nor are there bodies
that could collide and strike and crack its fabric.
But, as I've shown, our world is not just solid
atoms: its substance is combined with void.   365
Nor is it like void, for there's no dearth of atoms
which out of endless space might chance to spring
and in wild whirlwind wreck this world of ours
or bring upon it some other risk of ruin;
nor is there lack of space: vast, deep, and wide   370
it stretches, where a world might lose its walls
or see them pounded and scattered to clouds of dust.
Death's door, I say, has not been locked to sky
or sun or earth or to the sea's deep waves,
but gapes and stares, wide open, monstrous, vast.   375
And so you must admit that all these things
were born, and since they are of mortal substance,
they could not, all the way through endless ages,
have scorned the powered pulse of boundless time.
    Now since the great components of the world   380
so battle each other in useless holy war,
you'll see, I think, that some day their long quarrel
must find an end, if sun, let's say, and heat
should drink up all the water and subdue it—
they try to, but thus far have not succeeded,   385
so much the rivers supply, and even threaten
to drain the ocean's deeps and drown us all.
They can't, of course: the winds that sweep the sea
shrink it, and rays of the sun in heaven undo it;

they know that they could drain the whole thing dry   390
before the waters could reach the goal they seek,
so equal the contest twixt these two war-breathers,
as each seeks victory in their deadly duel;
and one time fire gained the upper hand,
and once, so we hear, the waters reigned on land.   395
For fire won out, licked at a world, and scorched it
that time the horses of the Sun, gone wild,
dragged Phaethon² over the face of heaven and earth.
But then the Father Omnipotent, stung to anger,
with a flash of lightning flung fool Phaethon down   400
from his team toward earth; as he fell, the Sun swooped in
and met him, seized our world's eternal lamp,
gathered and yoked the plunging, trembling horses,
reined them, regained his course, and saved the world.
At least, so the old Greek poets tell the tale,   405
which we reject as far, far from the truth.
For fire can conquer when from the Infinite
come streaming myriad atoms of its substance;
and then its power fails, somehow defeated,
or fuel gives out, consumed by torrid blasts.   410
The waters, too, once rose and near prevailed
when, so we hear, waves washed man's life away.
But when those waters ebbed and turned aside,
all that out of the Infinite streamed against us,
the rains stopped and the force of rivers waned.   415
    But in what ways matter was flung together
to build the earth, the sky, and ocean's deeps,
the courses of sun and moon, I'll neatly tell.
For surely not by planning did prime bodies
find rank and place, nor by intelligence,   420
nor did they regulate movement by sworn pact,
but myriad atoms sped such myriad ways
from the All forever, pounded, pushed, propelled,
by weight of their own launched and speeding along,
joining all possible ways, trying all forms,   425
whatever their meeting in congress could create;
and thus it happens that, widespread down the ages,
attempting junctures and movements of all kinds,
they at last formed patterns which, when joined together,
became at once the origin of great things,   430
earth, sea, and sky, and life in all its forms.

---

2. Phaethon persuaded his father, the sun god Helios, to let him drive the sun chariot across the sky, but he was unable to control the horses, who swung wildly off course. When it appeared that the earth was in danger of being burned to a cinder, Zeus (called, 399, "the Father Omnipotent") intervened and hurled Phaethon from the chariot. For the story, see Ovid, *Metamorphoses* 1.747–2.332.

No sun-wheel flooded with light could then be seen
high-flying here, nor the stars of this great world,
nor sea, nor heavens, nor even earth, nor air,
no single thing that looked like things we know,   435
but rather a weird, chaotic, swirling mass
sprung of all sorts of atoms, whose rude conflict,
spacing, direction, texture, weight, and impact,
force, and speed, linked them in wild war-dance,
because of their shifting shapes and unlike forms;   440
none of them, joined as they were, could stay in union
or move into orbits congruent with each other.
Then pieces began to fly away, and likes
to join with likes, sequestering a world
with members and gross parts discrete and ordered;   445
high heaven, that is, was set apart from earth,
the sea from both, with its wide waters sundered,
and sundered from all, the pure ethereal fires.
   To begin, then, all the particles of earth,
since they were heavy and tangled, moved to join   450
at center, and all sank down to the lowest zone.
The more they moved to join in one great tangle,
the more they squeezed out those that made the sea,
stars, sun, and moon, and the walls of this great world.
For these are all made of atoms smoother far   455
and elements rounder and smaller than are those
of earth. Thus through occasional holes between
earth-particles, ether first broke out and rose
fire-freighted and fleeting, bearing off countless fires,
in ways not differing much from what we see   460
when over dew-gemmed grass the morning sun
sends out its rays of light, first gold, then red,
while lakes and eternal rivers breathe out mist
so that earth herself sometimes appears to smoke.
These vapors rise and gather, then on high   465
they mass in a body, and clouds curtain the sky.
Just so then ether, light and unsubstantial,
hemmed in by mass in a body, turned and twisted,
and scattering wide, here, there, and everywhere,
thus walled all else within its avid arms.   470
Next came the starting up of sun and moon,
whose globes turn midrange in the atmosphere.
Earth laid no claim to them, nor did vast ether:
they were not heavy enough to sink and settle,
nor light enough to course the topmost zones.   475
Yet there they are in midrange, things alive
in motion, forming part of our total world.

Just as, in us, though some parts may remain
fixed in place, yet others there are that move.
Then with these parts withdrawn, the earth at once,   480
where now the broad blue band of sea extends,
fell back and filled its channels with salt brine.
Time passed; each day, the more the tides of ether
and rays of the sun pressed in all round the earth,
out at its edges they whipped and lashed it inward,   485
pushing, propelling, compressing it at the center,
so much the more salt sweat, squeezed from its body,
seeped out to enlarge the sea and floating fields,
and so much more atoms of heat and air
slipped out by thousands and flew away to crowd   490
heaven's high shining precincts, far from earth.
Flat fields sank down; the slope of lofty mountains
grew steeper, for not all rocks, you see, could settle
together, nor every region sink alike.
    Thus, with body compressed, the earth stood weighty   495
and firm; the muck of a universe, so to speak,
sank heavily down to the bottom, like settling dregs.
Then sea, then air, then ether, mother of fire,
were all left pure, with substance clarified,
some lighter than others; and ether, clearest of all,   500
and lightest, too, flowed over the moving air.
Its substance never mingled with the roil
of moving air, but left all else to spin
wild and stormy, confounded and confused,
while, freighted with its own fires, it glided on.   505
That ether could flow at constant, steady speed
in shown by the Black Sea, with its constant tide
that glides on, ever preserving a single course.
    Now let me tell the cause that moves the stars.
First, of the sky: if its great circle turns,   510
we'll say that an air, both top and bottom, presses
its poles, and holds it firmly locked in place;
above it, another flows, in that direction
in which the eternal world's bright stars revolve;
or another beneath, that pushes against the circle,   515
as we see rivers make wheels and buckets turn.
It could be, too, that all of heaven stays fixed
in place, while still the shining stars ride on,
either because ether's swift tides are diked
and move in circles, seeking a channel, and roll   520
fires at random across heaven's vaulted zones;
or else air, flowing from some outside source,
drives fires around; or they themselves can creep

wherever food calls them and invites them in
to graze flame-atoms scattered across the sky.   525
To say for sure, now, which cause fits our world
is hard; but what may be and occur throughout
the All, in various worlds built various ways,
this I will teach, explaining the many causes
which, in the All, might make for stellar movement.   530
Now one of these must be the cause, here too,
for the movement of stars, but which particular one
can scarce be taught when one must move so slowly.

That Earth may rest in the center of the world
its weight must lessen, and bit by bit disperse,   535
and its under-side must have another nature,
since time began joined neatly to make union
with the world's aerial parts on which it rests.
Thus it's no burden, and won't weigh down the air;
as, for a man, his limbs possess no weight: 540
to the neck, the head's no burden, nor do we feel
the total weight of the body upon our feet.
But every outside weight, all that is thrust
against us, is painful—sometimes the very small.
So much does it matter, what power things may possess.   545
Earth is no foreign body, then, brought in
from somewhere, suddenly dropped on alien air;
it had its beginning just when the world began,
and is part of it, as our limbs are part of us.
Besides, when the earth is struck by a thunderclap,   550
its movement sets all things above it shaking,
and this it could no wise do, were it not bound
fast to the aerial parts of the world, and heaven.
For roots common to both hold them enlaced,
since time began joined neatly to make union.[3]   555
Look at the body, too, how much it weighs;
and yet the soul—how tenuous!—holds it up,
because they are joined so neatly to make union.
Besides, what makes the body able to leap
nimbly up, but the soul that rules our limbs?   560
You see what power a tenuous substance has
when joined with something weighty, as the air
is joined to the earth; and the soul is joined to us.

And the burning wheel of the sun can't be much larger
or smaller than our senses show it to us.   565
For from whatever distance fires can throw
their light, and waft their vaporous warmth to us,

---

3. Lucretius here shares the ancient idea that thunder actually causes the earth and the heavenly
bodies to shake.

over that distance they don't lose in mass
of flame, nor does our vision judge them smaller.
Hence, since the heat and light the sun pours out   570
reach to our senses here, and warm the world,
it must be that we judge the size and shape
of the sun correctly, give or take not much.
The moon, too, whether it sheds a bastard glow   575
or throws off light of its own from its own substance,
whichever it is, we say it is no larger
than, with our eyes, we see that it must be.
For all things we observe at far remove
through layers of air will lose their clarity   580
before their size. And therefore, since the moon
affords us a shining face and clear-cut form
(along its edges we always mark it so)
its size is the size we see it in the sky.
Finally, take the stars we see in heaven: 585
since all the fires that we observe on earth,
so long as their flame and flicker are clear to see,
are normally seen to suffer little change
in size either way, for being more remote,
we know the stars are only the slightest bit   590
smaller, or larger, in some least dimension.[4]
    Now it must not surprise us that the sun,
small as it is, can send forth so much light
that it washes and fills the seas and all the earth
and sky, and floods them all with vaporous warmth.[5]   595

✳   ✳   ✳

For this, the whole world's single flowing fount
and open spring, can pour forth floods of light
because, out of all the world, atoms of heat
foregather there, leaping and flowing together,   600
so that their heat pours out from this one source.
Haven't you seen a little spring sometimes
water wide fields and even flood the land?
It could be, too, that from no vast sun-flame
heat raises the air up to the kindling point,   605
if at the right time suitable air is present
to catch on fire when struck by a little heat;
sometimes we see a field of grain or stubble
burst into flame this way from one lone spark.

4. Lucretius here betrays the great central weakness of Epicureanism, its total lack of mathematics, and hence of such simple con- cepts as perspective—to say nothing of astronomy.
5. Line 596 = 584, and is omitted by editors.

Perhaps, high in the sky, the sun's red lamp   610
possesses about it a vast reserve of fire
that can't be seen, because no bright light marks it,
and this brings heat to strengthen the sun's bright rays.
    Nor is the reason simple, clear, and plain,
how, from the summer regions of the Ram,   615
the sun moves toward the winter's turn, then circles
back toward Cancer and the solstice-mark,
and the moon, in a month, covers a distance equal
to that which the sun takes a year's time to run.
No simple reason is offered for this, I say.   620
This explanation comes at once to mind
(Democritus, saintly man, thought it correct):
the closer a given star may be to earth,
the less can the swirl of heaven bear it along.
For on its under side its speed and force   625
and power weaken and fade; hence, then, the sun
along with the tardier stars drops slowly back,
for it is much lower than the fiery stars.
And even more so, the moon: its humbler course,
farther from heaven and closer still to earth,   630
has even less power to race the coursing stars.
The weaker the current that bears it circling on
under the sun, the more all other bodies
catch up with it, pass round it, and move ahead.
It seems to pass from star to star more nimbly,   635
because in fact the stars are moving toward it.
It may be, too, that air from transverse zones
of heaven at definite times flows this way, that way;
the one could drive the sun from summer stars
up to the cold and icy turn of winter,   640
and the other force it from cold and ice and dark
back to the summer zones and fiery stars.
Let us think in similar wise of moon and planets,
that circling widely mark the long, long years:
they may be moved by airs from zone to zone.   645
Don't you see, too, how different winds blow clouds,
the higher in different direction from the lower?
Why should the stars high in the sphere of ether
be less disposed to travel on different tides?
    But night blankets the earth with monstrous murk   650
when from his day-long course the sun attains
heaven's end, and wearily breathes his fires out,
battered and weakened by passage through miles of air,
or because forces that vaulted him over the earth

now force him to take his course beneath the earth.[6]   655

At fixed times, too, Matuta[7] brings the dawn
and spread her rosy light along the heavens,
because the sun, returning from under earth,
reaches for heaven, to fire it with his rays,
or because fires and myriad seeds of heat   660
unfailing stream together at fixed times,
thus always bringing the sun's light to new birth.
Just so, we're told, on Ida's lofty peaks,
when daylight comes, men see wide-scattered fires
that flow then into a sort of ball or sphere.[8]   665
Yet, in all this, it should not seem surprising
that at such definite times these seeds of fire
should gather and build the sun's bright gleam anew.
For we see many phenomena everywhere
that take place at fixed times. The orchards bloom   670
just at fixed times, at fixed times drop their flowers.
No less at definite times life bids the teeth
drop out, and smooth-skinned boys put on soft down
and let the soft beard, too, grow from their cheeks.
Finally, lightning, snow, rain, clouds, and wind   675
occur at times of the year not too uncertain.
Since causes are as they were when things began,
and the world still acts as it did at the very start,
it follows that things recur now in fixed order.

The days, too, lengthen and the nights diminish,   680
and days grow shorter when nights take on increase,
because one sun, that runs both under and over
the earth, marks off unmatching arcs in heaven
and cuts it into unequal hemispheres,
and what it subtracts from one side it replaces   685
on the other, adding just so much to that side,
till it reaches the sign in heaven where the node
of the year makes dark nights equal to the days.
For in the middle, where North and South Wind meet,
the boundary marks of heaven stand equidistant   690
because of the posture of signs all round the circuit
in which the laggard sun marks off the seasons,
flooding both earth and sky with slanting light,
as shown by the science of those who mark the zones

6. This theory of the sun's movement happens to approximate the truth, provided we accept a geocentric universe. As always, Lucretius offers this only as one of a number of possible theories, any one of which may be true, if not in our world, then in some other. See *Introduction*, p. x.
7. Usually called *Mater* ("Mother") *Matuta*, she appears here in her original guise as goddess of the dawn. Later, she was considered goddess of childbirth. For Lucretius, of course, she is, like Venus at the opening of Bk. I, simply a poetic symbol.
8. The reference is to Mt. Ida in the Troad. It is uncertain where this strange bit of meteorology originated, and exactly what it was intended to describe.

of heaven each with a handsome constellation.[9]   695
Or because air in certain parts is thicker,
and under earth this checks bright, flickering fire,
which can't pierce through with ease and reach a dawning.
This is why nights in winter-time are long:
they wait for the rays whose coming marks the day.   700
Or else because, in alternating seasons,
there is faster or slower confluence of the fire
that causes the sun to rise at stated points,
and this is why they seem to tell the truth[1]

* * *

The moon may shine because the sun's rays strike her,   705
and day by day she turns that light the more
to face us, the farther she draws back from the sun,
till, opposite him, she shines with full, bright light,
and rising high in the sky she sees him setting.
Then little by little she's bound to bury her light,   710
so to speak, the closer she glides in toward the sun
and circles away from other star-marked zones;
so will they have it who think the moon is like
a ball that holds its course beneath the sun.
It may be too that she revolves with light   715
of her own to show her various shining shapes.
For there may be a second body that rides
with her and blocks and checks her every way,
yet can't be seen because it's void of light.
And she may turn like a spherical ball, perhaps,   720
painted on half her surface with shining light,
and her sphere, revolving, produces varied shapes
until the side that is possessed of fires
turns to face us and our staring eyes;
then little by little turns back and takes away   725
the side of the ball and sphere that bears the light.
So claims Chaldean science[2] in Babylon,
purporting to prove the astrologers all wrong;
as if what both support could not be true,
or one than the other might be less boldly chosen.   730
Lastly, why couldn't all moons be new-created,
in order always fixed, and in fixed shapes,
then with each day each new creation die
and in its place a different moon take form?

9. Once again, as at 654–55, we have the correct theory of the sun's movement, but offered only as one of a number of possible explanations.
1. After this line, at least one line has been lost.

2. The reference is probably to Berosus, an astronomer and historian of the third century B.C. He wrote a history of Babylon, and is supposed to have introduced the science of astronomy to the Greek world.

It's hard, in reason, to prove this theory wrong,   735
since many things are created in fixed order.
Spring comes, and Venus, and Venus' messenger
walks winged before her, close on Zephyr's footprints,
where Mother Flora[3] has strewn the path before him
and filled the world with color and fresh perfumes.   740
Next in order come heat and drought, and with them
dusty Ceres[4] and seasonal summer winds,
Then Autumn; Bacchus the Bellower walks beside him.
Then with the change of season come more winds,
here, thunder in heaven, and there, the lightning flash.   745
Last, the short days bring snow; all stiff and numb,
Winter returns, trailed by tooth-chattering chill.
Less wonder, then, if at fixed times a moon
is born, and at fixed times destroyed again,
when all these things can happen at such fixed times.   750
    Eclipses, too, when sun and moon are hidden,
can occur, you know, for many different reasons.
For why could Moon deprive Earth of the light
of Sun, and high above Earth run straight at him,
with lightless sphere damming his shining rays,   755
and some other body, at that same time, could not
do this—some body that floats lightless forever?
And why couldn't Sun grow weaker, and at fixed times
dismiss his fires, then fashion light anew,
passing in heaven through spots not fit for flames,   760
where fire must flicker out and be destroyed?
Again, why couldn't Earth deprive the moon
of light, and keep the sun blocked off above her
as she moves each month through that cold cone of shades?
And at that same time couldn't another body   765
catch up with the moon, or float above the sun
to cut off his rays and stop his flood of light?
Then, too, if the moon shines with her own bright gleam,
why couldn't she grow weaker in some fixed zone,
passing through spots not meet for light like hers?[5]   770
    For the rest, since I've explained how everything   772
all through the wide blue world may come to be,
that we may know what force, what cause compels
the sun to change his course, the moon, to wander,   775
or how they may disappear, with light blocked off,
and veil the unsuspecting world in darkness,
like eyes that shut, then open, alight once more,

---

3. As her name suggests, she was goddess of
flowering plants.
4. See 5.14. Bacchus the Bellower: so called
from the cries of his devotees, the Bacchantes.
5. Line 771=764, and is omitted by editors.

to visit all countries with their bright, clear gleam,
now I return to the world's birthday, when earth 780
was soft: what did her young fields first bring forth
to the coasts of light, and trust to the fickle winds?
    First came the race of grasses: earth spread green
bright shining over the fields and every plain,
and flowers burst into color across green fields; 785
then rains were dropped, the race was on, with trees—
all kinds—vast vying to grow up toward the sky.
As feathers and fur first grow, and bristles, too,
on quadruped limbs and bodies of wing-borne birds,
so then young earth first put forth grass and brush, 790
then second in order created mortal kinds,
sprung in their thousands in thousand ways and forms.
For living things could not have dropped from heaven
nor earthbound creatures have come from salty pools.
Rightly the earth is left then with the name 795
of mother, since of the earth all things are born.
And even now from earth rise many creatures
molded by rain and by the sun's hot breath;
small wonder if in those days far more came forth,
and larger, granted an earth and sky both new. 800
Wing-creatures, first, and varicolored birds
abandoned their eggs, hatched out in time of spring,
as now cicadas leave the chrysalis
in summer to seek a living on their own.
Then only did earth first bear your mortal creatures, 805
for water and warmth were flooding over the fields;
whenever the land fell into proper pattern,
there wombs would grow with roots that gripped the earth.
And when at the proper time the full-formed infants
opened them, fleeing from water and seeking air, 810
nature channeled the earth in their direction,
and out of her opened veins made flow a liquid
very like milk, as now, when a woman bears
a child, sweet milk fills her, because her powers
of nourishment all converge upon her breasts.[6] 815
For the babes, earth furnished flood, heat gave them clothes,
and grass, a billowing bed, deep, downy-soft.
But a fresh, young world blew up no ice or snow
or suffocating heat or rough wild winds.
For growth in strength is the law for all alike. 820

6. This weird, surrealistic picture seems to be the invention of Epicurus. It suggests nothing so much as a painting by Salvador Dali. The important point is that all life comes from the earth, by a process that must seem to resemble spontaneous generation, but is rather, to the Epicurean, the result of a fortuitous combination of the appropriate atoms under appropriate conditons. See Bk. II, 886–906.

Meet and properly then, earth won and keeps
the name of mother, since she herself created
mankind, and at its proper season birthed
every wild beast that roams the cordillera,
and every shape and color of bird that flies.   825
But since there must be an end to giving birth,
she stopped, like a wife grown old and tired with years.
For time changes the nature of all the world;
all things must pass from one state to another.
No thing stays like itself: all things change place;   830
nature makes everything turn into something else.
For one thing rots, grows weary and weak with time,
then out of its rubbish another thing grows up.
So, then, time changes the nature of all the world,
and earth takes one condition, then another,   835
can't bear what it could, and can, what it could not bear.

Then, too, earth tried creating hosts of strange
creatures, fantastic things in face and form,[7]
androgynes—twixt and tween, not one, not t'other—
some without feet, and again some lacking hands,   840
some mute and mouthless; eyeless, some, and blind,
some with body and limbs all in adhesion,
unable to act, unable even to move
to avoid danger and take what life requires.
Still more such marvels and miracles she created,
all to no end, since nature deterred their growth;
they longed for the flower of life but could not reach it,
or even find food or join in the act of love.
For many things, we see, must work together
that creatures may procreate and forge their kind: 850
first must be food, then paths in the flesh, through which,
when muscles relax, the genital seed may pass,
that male and female may couple, and have some way
to share and exchange delight, each with the other.

Many kinds of creatures, too, must then have died   855
and been unable to reproduce their kind.
For all you see now breathing the breath of life
had either cunning or courage or nimbleness
to guard and preserve their kind since time began.
And many proved useful to us and, thus commended,   860
survived because we took them as our wards.
Brave lions and predatory beasts kept safe
by valor; by cunning, the fox; by speed, the deer.
But dogs (light-sleeping hearts and loyal souls),

7. Lucretius' theory of the origin of life (see 805–15) leads to a statement that bears startling resemblance to the modern biological theories of the "sport" and "natural selection".

all creatures sprung of the seed of burden-bearers, 865
yes, and the wool-clad flocks, and cow-horned kind,
all have become, dear Memmius, wards of man.
For they were eager to flee predators, and find
peace, and their fill of food, got without pain,
reward from us, paid for their usefulness. 870
But those whom nature had given no powers, either
to live on their own or to supply to us
advantages that would make us let their kind
find food in our protection and keep safe,
these, of course, fell profit and prey to others, 875
all caught in their own death-dealing limitations,
till nature at last rendered their kind extinct.

But there were no Centaurs,[8] nor at any time
could creatures of double nature and two bodies
be built out of unrelated parts, yet equal 880
enough in powers and substance on both sides.
And here is proof for even the dull of mind.
First: at about three years, the horse has reached
his prime; not so, the child: for often still
in sleep he'll seek his mother's milky breasts. 885
Later, when horses are aging, and their strength
and muscle are failing, as life runs toward its close,
then, for the boy the bloom of youth is just
beginning, just starting to clothe his cheeks with down.
Don't then imagine that from the seed of man 890
and horse, Centaurs could be confected and exist,
or Scyllas with bodies half-fish, girt round the waist
with rabid dogs, or other things of this sort,
whose parts we see in conflict with each other,
who reach their prime and grow in strength of body 895
at different speeds, and then grow old and weak,
whose sexual drives and manner of coition
differ, whose physical pleasures aren't the same.
You see how the bearded goat commonly thrives
on hemlock, which to man is deadly poison. 900
Flame, too, will always scorch and sear the flesh
of tawny lions, just as it will all creatures
of guts and blood that live here on the earth:
how, then, could one of these, with triple body
(front, lion; behind, a snake; between, a goat) 905
breathe out of body and mouth a fiery flame?
Thus he who imagines that when the earth was new

---

8. These creatures, half-man, half-horse, are familiar figures from Greek folktales and mythology. Lucretius correctly assesses their complete impossibility as forms of animate life. For Lucretius' explanation of how the *idea* of such creatures as Centaurs, Scyllas, and the like, came into being, see Bk. IV. 722–47.

and heaven fresh-formed, such animals might have been,
(taking his stand on the vain premise of newness)
might utter much other nonsense on like grounds,   910
might say that rivers of gold flowed everywhere
on earth, that hundreds of trees bore gems for flowers,
or that men lived of stature so gigantic
that they could broad-jump over the deep blue sea,
and with their hands make heaven revolve around them.   915
Just because thousands of atoms were in the world
in the days when earth first brought forth living creatures,
this is no sign that groups could have been mixed,
and limbs of one kind of life lapped with another.
For even today all kinds of grasses grow   920
out of the ground, and fruits and shining corn,
yet they cannot be made to intertwine,
but each has its own growth-habit, and all the kinds
by nature's law maintain their differences.
      Man lived in the open then,[9] a harsher breed   925
by far, of course, for a harsh earth gave him birth.
The bones of his frame were heavier far, and longer;
the muscles, fast to his inner parts, were strong.
He didn't succumb with ease to heat or cold
or to strange foods or physical weaknesses.   930
Through many a cycle the sun made through the heavens,
he lived like a wild beast, wandering far and wide.
There was no sturdy guider of the plow,
and no one knew to soften the soil with steel,
or to plant young saplings in the earth, or cut   935
dead branches from the trees with pruning hooks.
What sun and rain produced, what earth created
naturally, man took, to his heart's content.
With oak and acorn he cared for creature needs,
mostly; the arbutes[1] that in wintertime   940
we now see ripen and turn bright scarlet red,
the earth then bore abundantly, and larger.
Besides, the world, then fresh and green, produced
much coarse foodstuffs, ample for sorry souls.
But springs and rivers bade men slake their thirst,   945
as now bright waters, racing down the mountains,
call clear and far to the thirsting animal-kinds.
And men in their ramblings found the sylvan haunts
of nymphs, from which they learned that streams of water

---

9. Epicurean atnthropology. Lucretius' picture of primitive man is surprisingly accurate, but like the ancients in general, he tends to idealize it. His account might be styled the Epicurean version of the mythical Golden Age.

All of its phenomena, of course, are explained in terms of Epicurean atomic theory.
1. This is the strawberry-like fruit of *arbutus unedo*, a shrub or tree of southern Europe.

flowed smooth and abundant, with cool, wet stones awash   950
(cool, wet stones, green-curtained with dripping moss)
learned, too, where they bubbled and burst from open fields.
They'd not yet learned to manage fire, or use
hides—the stripping of beasts to clothe their bodies.
They lived in the woods, in trees or hillside caves;   955
unkempt and dirty, they burrowed in thicket and thorn
to flee the lash of the wind and driving rain.
For the common good, they had no eye, nor knew
of the mutual uses of custom or of law.
Whatever goods luck brought their way, they took,   960
for nature had taught them nothing but survival.
In the woods, Venus linked lovers, flesh to flesh,
for mutual lust would bring the two together,
or else the man's raw force and wild desire,
or a bribe: acorns, arbutes, or fresh-picked pears.   965
With nothing but wonderful strength of arm and leg,
they hunted wild animals in their woodland lairs,
with throwing-stones and heavy clubs for weapons;
many, they killed; a few, they escaped by hiding.
Like bristled boars of the woods, they threw their bodies   970
naked on earth, wherever nightfall caught them,
making themselves a nest of twigs and leaves.
They never wept and wailed, in frantic fright
searching the shadows of night for sun and daylight,
but waited without a word, entombed in slumber,   975
until the sun's red torch brought light to heaven.
For since, from childhood, they'd been used to seeing
darkness and daylight alternately occur,
it could not be that they should ever wonder
or doubt for fear eternal night might grip   980
the earth forever, and sunlight be withdrawn.
No, they were more concerned because wild beasts
often, for them, turned sleep to death and terror.
Driven from home, they fled their stony halls
at charge of a slavering boar or valiant lion,   985
and though it were dead of might, in panic yielded
their leaf-strewn beds to these ferocious guests.
    In those days, too, the human race left life
and its sweet light with scarce more tears than now.
For then more individuals were caught   990
and made live food, fang-torn and bloody, for beasts;
they filled the forest, the hills and vales, with screams
as they watched a live grave bury their living flesh.
But some got away and lived, all lacerated.
Later, they cupped foul sores with trembling hands   995

and with blood-curdling yells begged death to come,
till savage wrenching agony took their lives,
poor, helpless souls, unknowing what wounds might need.
But then no thousands on a single day
followed a flag to death; no howling storms   1000
at sea dashed ships and crews against a reef.
Vain, aimless, foolish, was ocean's endless raging,
and useless his laying aside of empty threats:
the teasing of a tranquil sea could trick
no man to trouble in those grinning waves.   1005
Seafaring—sinful art!—lay then in darkness.
Then, shortage of food brought men to weariness
and death; now, overabundance kills them off.
Through ignorance, they often served themselves
poison; grown wiser, they serve it now to others.   1010
    Then,[2] after they got them houses, hides, and fire,
and woman yielded to man and joined in one[3]

                            *   *   *

were known, and saw their own begotten children,
then first the human race began to soften.
For fire saw to it that shivering flesh could now   1015
not bear the cold beneath a tented sky;
and Venus took toll of strength, and children's smiles
easily tamed their parents' prideful hearts.
Then neighbors began to join in friendship, vowing
to do each other no hurt nor injury.   1020
They made great point of children and womankind,
with childlike cry and gesture signifying
that all men must show kindness to the weak.
Still, not always could they win agreement,
but much the best part honored their covenants;   1025
else all mankind had been destroyed right then
and the race could not have continued to this day.
    Now nature prompted the tongue to utter varied
sounds, and convenience coined the names of things,
much as we see that children now are drawn   1030
to gesture by simple speechlessness of tongue:
they point the finger at everything they see.
All creatures sense their powers and how to use them.
Before horns swell and grow on the bull-calf's brow

2. This final section of Bk. V is concerned with the beginnings and development of human civilization and institutions. It is based in part on ancient tradition (Lucretius' account, for example, of the beginnings of government, 1105–12, resembles Herodotus, *Hist.* I. 96–102) and in part on Roman history (his account of the termination of royal power, 1136–40, resembles the standard account of the expulsion and assassination of Tarquin the Proud: Livy, *Hist.* I. 58–60).
3. After this line, at least one line has been lost.

he rushes, butts, and attacks with them in anger.   1035
The lion's kittens and the panther's cubs
battle away with paw and claw and fang
when tooth and claw have scarce so much as grown.
Birds too, all kinds, we see have confidence
in wings, and flutter their feathers to find support.   1040
And to think that, then, some man invented names
and parceled them out to things, and thence we learned them,
is nonsense: how could one man have known the names
to give things, and utter the changing sounds of speech,
but nobody else at the same time have such powers?   1045
Besides, if other men, too, had not exchanged
words, how could the idea of their usefulness
have burgeoned? Whence came to *him* that primal power
to see with the mind, and know what he wished to do?
Besides, how could one single man browbeat   1050
the rest, to make them learn *his* names for things?
No lesson or argument can teach those who won't listen
what they must do, for they would not give in,
and there's no reason could make their ears submit
to endless drumming of vain, outlandish sounds.   1055
Lastly, in this regard what is so strange
if human beings, efficient in voice and tongue,
should give things different names, each as he views them?
Why! Voiceless cattle, yes, even savage beasts
commonly utter distinctive, different sounds   1060
in fear or pain or in the glow of pleasure.
For this, there are patent proofs, as well you know.
Tease a Molossian hound: at once, soft lips
draw back in a snarl that bares his savage teeth,
a mad and menacing sound, and different far   1065
from when, giving tongue, they fill the world with baying.
And when in gentle play they lick their pups,
bat at them with their paws, rush them, and nip them,
snapping, but softly, with jaws that never close,
far different their little yelps and loving growls   1070
from when they bark in an empty house, or when
they whine and crouch and shrink to avoid the lash.
And doesn't a whinny, again, sound different, too,
when a stallion, young and in his prime, spurred on
by feathery love, runs wild among the mares   1075
(his nostril gapes; he squeals his call to arms)
from other times, when he stands trembling and neighs?
Lastly, the winged kind, the different birds,
eagle and osprey, and the seagull seeking
food and a life out on the salt sea waves,   1080

at other times will utter far different cries
from when they fight over food or battle their prey.
Part of them, with a change of weather change
their raucous tune, as when the ancient tribe
of ravens and flocks of crows call down the rain   1085
and the flood, or sometimes plead for wind and breezes.
If varied feelings, then, force animals,
dumb though they are, to utter varied cries,
how much more likely that in those days men could
use one and another term for different things.   1090

   Lest an unspoken question plague you here,
lightning brought fire to earth to mortal men
first, and from this has spread all flame and heat.
We still see things, kindled by heavenly fire,
burst into flame, the gift of heaven's hot bolt.   1095
To be sure, when branching trees, tossed by the wind,
lean one on the other, and shudder and shake and saw,
by force of pressure they grind and squeeze out fire,
sometimes with a heat that flares to spark and flame,
while trunks and branches rasp against each other.[4]   1100
Either cause could have given fire to man.
Now, cooking and mellowing food by heat and flame
men learned from the sun: they saw so much stuff soften
and rot in the fields with the hot rays beating down.

   With every day man's earlier life and habits   1105
changed with the learning of new ways* * *[4a]
taught by the great of mind and strong of heart.
Then came the earliest cities with their forts
built by the kings as castle, keep, and stronghold;
kings, too, shared out the animals and lands   1110
to each in accord with intellect, strength, and beauty,
for beauty and physical strength were highly prized.
Later men learned of property, and found gold,
which stripped the strong and the handsome of their power;
for people flocked to join wealth's entourage,   1115
even those blessed at birth with strength and beauty.
But if we governed our lives by truth and reason,
great wealth, to man, would be the frugal life
and peace of mind, for there's no lack of little.
But men were agog to win high place and power,   1120
to give their gains long-lasting firm foundation,
that they might live the rich man's carefree life—
all to no end, for, struggling to reach the top,

4. This explanation for the cause of fire sounds
fanciful at first blush, but I am assured by forest
conservationists that it is possible and in fact not
at all uncommon.

4a. The last two words (*et ipni*) are nonsense
and are here omitted.

they made the rivals' road a path of death.
Then from the top sometimes the lightning bolt   1125
of envy hurls then to Hell, disgraced, dishonored;
for envy, like lightning, often vaporizes
the highest and anything loftier than its neighbors.
Better by far be subject, and at peace,
than will to govern the world and hold a throne!   1130
Well, let them go on, exhaust themselves, sweat blood,
as they struggle along the strait road of ambition.
Their wisdom is second-hand, and they attack
problems by hearsay more than by observation,
no sounder today or tomorrow than yesterday.   1135
    Then kings were killed; the ancient majesty
and pride of sceptre and throne fell, overturned;
the bright ensign of royalty lay bloodied
under the feet of the mob, mourning lost glory:
men lustily trampled what they had vastly feared.   1140
Life sank to the depths, the dregs, back to confusion,
with everyone wanting top rank and highest power.
Then, here and there, men learned to choose officials,
establish constitutions, and live by law.
For man grew weary: the life of violence   1145
and hatred left him sick, and more disposed
freely to choose the yoke of law and statute.
For angered men kept calling for revenge
more savage than just law will now permit;
this made man sicken of life by violence.   1150
Thereafter, the fear of consequence stained the prize:
for violence and lawlessness are snares
that often entrap the man from whom they sprang,
and there's no easy life of calm and quiet
for him who breaks the peace, man's common law.   1155
For though he deceived all godhead and mankind,
yet must he doubt that he'll lie hid forever:
yes, many a man has babbled in sleep, we're told,
or, fevered and delirious, has dragged out
in public a tale of sins long, long concealed.   1160
    Now for the cause that spread the almighty gods
through all mankind, and filled our towns with temples,
and set up our calendar of solemn rites
(rites that still flourish where men are great and rich)
cause, too, of the terror in man still deep implanted   1165
that builds new altars to gods all over the world,
and forces our people to hallow the festal days—
it's no great task to give account of this.
Why! Even in those days our mortal kind
when wide awake saw many a gorgeous god,   1170

and even more in dreams—huge, awesome creatures.
They endowed them then with senses, since they seemed
to move their bodies and utter arrogant words
quite fitting their shining beauty and great strength.
They gave them eternal life because their shapes   1175
kept reappearing, and in form unchanged;
yet still, creatures so powerful, they thought,
could not be overcome by casual force.
They thought them, too, more blest by far than men,
because no fear of death could ever vex them;   1180
besides, in dreams they saw them do so much—
such wonders—with never a symptom of fatigue.
Further, they noted the fixed and ordered ways
of heaven, and how the seasons changed each year,
but couldn't discover what caused all this to happen.   1185
They had recourse to handing all these things
to gods: their nod made all the world go round!
They placed the native heath of gods in heaven,
since night and the moon they saw roll through the skies,
moon, day, and night, and night's unsmiling signs,   1190
torches that whip through the darkness, flying flames,
the clouds, the sun, rain, snow, wind, lightning, hail,
the rapid crackling, the rumble, tumble, and roar.
    O luckless human kind, to grant the gods
such powers, and top them off with bitter fury!   1195
What moans for themselves that day, what ghastly wounds
for us, what wails they got our children's children!
Piety isn't to come in humble access,
on view and vested, daily to stone and altar,
to fall prostrate on earth and spread the hands   1200
in hallowed halls, to flood the temple floors
with animal blood, and string prayer onto prayer,
but the power to view a world without dismay.
For when we look up to the vast and ordered regions
of sky, and ether studded with sparkling stars,   1205
and chance to think of the travels of sun and moon,
then into our hearts, distraught by other troubles,
that worry as well is roused to raise its head:
Are there, then, gods whose power, beyond our measure,
sets the bright stars to wheeling, each in its course?   1210
For want of knowledge troubles a mind in doubt:
Did our world have begetting and beginning?
And is there a limit, too, to how much stress
and strain and shaking the walls of the world can stand?
Or are they, by gift of god, forever hale,   1215
and glide down endless tracts of time with power

to scorn the bludgeon and blow of boundless time?
Besides, whose heart does not contract with fear
of gods, whose vitals do not crawl in terror
when lightning's frightful flash sets earth ablaze   1220
and trembling, and thunder rolls across broad heaven?
Don't people and nations tremble, and proud kings
pull themselves up, hard hit by fear of gods?
Has the dread hour of retribution struck
for acts of iniquity, or for words of pride?   1225
Then, too, when a wind in all its wildness sweeps
an admiral of the fleet across the waves
with all his forces, soldiers, elephants,
does he not beg god's peace, and plead and pray
in terror for peace of winds and following breezes,   1230
vainly, for often the hurricane nonetheless
whirls him away to the Waters of the Dead.
To such degree some hidden force grinds down
the life of man, and tramples the savage splendor
of rod and axe, like some vast joke, it seems.   1235
Further, when under our feet the whole earth shakes,
and stricken cities threaten, totter, and fall,
what wonder if mortal kinds rate themselves low
and leave room in the world for gods with vast
wonderful strength and power to rule all things?   1240
   Further, men came upon bronze and gold and iron
and heavy silver, too, and useful lead,
when fire had scorched and burned huge woods to ashes
high in the hills, if lightning fell from heaven,
or people, waging woodland war between them,   1245
in panic set fire against their enemies,
or if, because the soil was good, they meant
to clear rich fields and open grazing land,
or to kill off animals for the wealth they'd bring.
For men had hunted with pit and fire before   1250
they blocked a valley with nets and set on the dogs.
Whatever the reason or cause why fiery flame
with crackle and roar had eaten the woods away
deep into the roots, and baked and fired the earth,
from boiling veins out into hollow spots   1255
in earth came trickling streams of gold and silver,
copper[5], and lead. Later, when they had cooled,
men saw the bright lumps shining in the ground
and, caught by the glitter and smoothness, picked them up:

---

5. The Latin word is *aes*, which means either copper or bronze. Since copper occurs in nature, and bronze (an alloy of copper and tin) does not, it would appear that copper is meant here.

they saw that they were formed and shaped just like   1260
the empty hollows they had left behind.
Then came the thought: these could be melted down
and run to the shape of anything they liked,
and then be drawn by forging into points
and blades as sharp and slender as they wished.   1265
They could make weapons; they could cut down trees,
and hew out boards, and plane their lumber smooth,
and make holes, too, with awl and punch and drill.
They tried this first no less with gold and silver
than with the wild and rugged strength of copper—   1270
uselessly, since their power fell back defeated,
nor could all metals alike endure hard toil.
Yes, copper was valued more, and gold discarded,
because its bent and blunted blade proved useless.
Now copper is scorned; gold has won highest place: 1275
such the changes the wheel of time has wrought!
What once was valued ends in deep despite,
then another moves up and out of low esteem.
The search for it grows each day; men find and praise it,
extol it, grant it honor beyond belief.   1280
    Now, how the nature of iron was discovered,
you may learn easily, Memmius, for yourself.
In ancient times, weapons were teeth and nails
and stones and branches broken from the trees,
flame, too, and fire, once men had come to know them.   1285
Later, men learned the power of iron and bronze.
And bronze they learned to use sooner than iron,
for bronze is simpler to work and more abundant.
With bronze they tilled the soil, with bronze they roiled
the waters of war, and harrowed a waste of wounds,   1290
and seized both herds and lands: no task for them,
thus armed, to conquer the naked and unarmed.
Then little by little the iron sword came in,
and brazen tools became a mockery;
with iron alone men started to plow the soil   1295
and balance the ever uncertain clash of battle.
An armed man climbed a horse's back, with reins
to guide him, and right hand kept in fighting trim,
before he risked battle with team and chariot.
And two-horse teams came before two-and-two,   1300
and before men rode in chariots armed with scythes.
Then elephants with their towered backs, foul beasts,
"snake-hands,"[6] by Carthage taught to bear the wounds

6. See note on 2.537.

of war, sent fighting regiments reeling back.
Thus grim Discord bore one thing, then another,   1305
to terrorize the nations of men in arms,
and each day gave to war some added horror.
　　Men even tested bulls as weapons of war,
and tried attacking the enemy with wild boars.
Some people dispatched strong lions ahead of them,   1310
with trainers in arms and savage animal-men
to manage the beasts and hold them under leash—
a mistake, for the blood-drenched mêlée drove them mad;
gone wild, they tore at the troops, both sides alike,
everywhere shaking their terrible heads and manes;   1315
not even the rider could calm his screaming horse
or temper his terror and rein him against the foe.
She-lions everywhere hurled their goaded bodies
leaped, and flew in the faces of all they met,
and ripped the unwary to ribbons from behind;   1320
they bent men double, slashed them, threw them down
gripping them with great fangs and long, curved claws.
Bulls kept tossing their friends and trampling them;
with horns they gutted the horses, belly and flank,
from beneath, and threatening danger, pawed the earth.   1325
Boars, with their powerful tusks, slashed at their friends,
broke spears, and drenched them with their own wild blood,[7]
and among horse and foot alike spread havoc.   1329
For the mounts shied to escape the savage thrust   1330
of tusks, reared, and with hooves flailed at the winds
vainly: one would have seen their sinews slashed;
they'd crash to the ground and drag themselves across it.
Even those that people had thought were tame as house pets
they saw turn rabid on the field of action,   1335
midst bloodshed, shouts, flight, panic, and dismay,
and couldn't round up one single part of them;
for the wild beasts, every kind, scattered and ran,
as elephants often now, when slashed by sword,
scatter, but savagely maul their own men first.   1340
If men really did this! But I scarce believe
they couldn't have known—predicted what would happen
before they plunged both sides in pain and shame.
We'd better contend this happened in the All,
the myriad worlds created myriad ways,   1345
rather than on some one specific sphere.
But their intent, their hope, was not to win,
but to make the enemy suffer, then die themselves,
a force outnumbered, unnerved, and weaponless.

7. Line 1328 is almost identical with 1327, and is omitted by editors.

Clothes tied together came before textile cloth.   1350
Cloth is post-iron, since iron fashions the loom:
in no other way could we produce such smooth
heddles and spindles, shuttles and rattling scapes.
And nature drove males to work with wool before
the female sex (for in the arts all males   1355
are more ingenious and more skilled by far)
till farmers, strait-laced men, judged this immoral
and voted to pass such tasks to women's hands,
while they, all men alike, endured hard toil
and in hard labor toughened hand and sinew.   1360
But pattern for planting, and seeding's earliest form
were nature herself: she first created things;
for berries and acorns falling from the trees
in time produced a swarm of sprouts beneath them.
At whim thereafter, men set shoots in branches   1365
and buried fresh cuttings in earth about their fields.
They tried to grow first one thing, then another
on their loved lands, and saw wild plants turn tame
in the soil with coddling and gentle, coaxing care.
And with each day they made the woods shrink farther   1370
up-mountain, yielding room for farms below,
for pastures, ponds and streams, grain-land, lush vineyards,
their holdings on hill and plain, for olive groves
to run their blue-grey bands like boundary lines
flowing across the hummocks, dales, and fields,   1375
as now you see lands everywhere picked out
with beauty, lined and adorned with apple trees;
and fruitful orchards wall them all about.
    But imitating the liquid notes of birds
came long before men learned to polish verses   1380
and set them to music, with power to please the ear.
And breezes across a hollow reed first taught
farmers to blow on hollow stems that whistled.
Then little by little men learned the sweet sad tones
that pour from a flute stopped by a player's fingers—   1385
the flute, invented in forest, copse, and field,
those sun-filled spots where shepherds rest alone.[8]
Such music soothed their souls and gave them joy   1390
when filled with food, for then the world looks bright.
Yes, often men lay on soft turf, side by side,
under a tall tree's branches near a stream,
and easily, pleasantly cared for creature needs,
especially when the sun shone, and the year   1395

8. Lines 1388–89 = 1454–55, and are omitted by editors.

in season painted the fresh green grass with flowers.
Those were the times when jest and talk and laughter
were sweet, for then the rustic Muse held sway;
then came impulse to wreathe the head and shoulders
with flowers and leaves, for gaiety and joy,   1400
and, all off-beat, to prance and flail the arms
boldly, and beat bold feet on Mother Earth.
Then came amusement, happiness, and smiles;
it was all so exciting then, so fresh, alive!
Hence came solace for sleep to the wakeful, too;   1405
they spun all sorts of tunes and sang new songs,
and puckered the lip and ran it across the pipes,
and passed on the songs poor sleepers now memorize.
Men learned to observe the rules of music, too,
and all the while gained not one bit more pleasure   1410
than did that woodland tribe, the Sons of Earth.
For what's on hand, if we've learned nothing sweeter
so far, we like the best and deem superb;
then, often, some later and better discovery
destroys the old and alters our feeling toward it.   1415
Thus, men lost taste for acorns; thus, they left
those beds piled deep with grasses and with leaves.
They threw away, too, the animal hides they'd worn—
hides, I suspect, whose finding roused such envy
that their first wearer was ambushed and met death.   1420
Then there was pulling and hauling, much blood was shed;
the hides were ruined and couldn't be put to use.
Then, it was hides; now, gold and purple trouble
and fret men's lives, and wear them out in wars;
and this, I think, makes us the more to blame.   1425
For cold would have killed the naked Sons of Earth
but for those hides; for us, what harm to lack
our gold, our purples stiff with rich brocade,
while we have plain, coarse cloth to keep us warm?
Yes, all for nothing we wretched men toil on   1430
forever, and waste our lives on foolishness;
clearly, because we never learned the limits
of having, and where true pleasure's growth must end.
And little by little this launched life toward the depths
and up from the bottom stirred war's wasteful waves.   1435
    These watchmen, the Sun and Moon, with their own lamps
beating the bounds of earth's wide sphere about,
taught men the cycle of the months and years,
an orderly system, governed by clear-cut laws.
    Soon men were living their lives behind strong walls,   1440
and land was divided in private plots for farming.

The sea then blossomed with sails   *   *   *⁹
men made treaties of mutual aid and friendship,
and poets began verse records of history;
letters had been invented not long before.   1445
And hence our age can't contemplate its past
except where reason shows the path we trod.
  Navigation, agriculture, cities, laws,
war, travel, clothing, and all such things else,
money, and life's delights, from top to bottom,   1450
poetry, painting, the cunning sculptor's art,
the searching, the trial and error of nimble minds
have taught us, inching forward, step by step.
Thus, step by step, time lays each fact before us,
and reason lifts it to the coasts of light;   1455
for men saw one thing clarify another
till civilization reached its highest peak.

9. The last part of this line is nonsense, and at least one line seems to have been lost between 1442 and 1443.

Book VI

First, long ago, to scatter for starving men
seed that bore again, was Athens—glorious name!
She gave new strength, new life; she drew up laws;
she too first brought sweet comfort to mankind
when she begot that man, revealed so great   5
of mind: truth, only truth, poured from his lips!
Though he is dead, his godlike revelations,
known everywhere now, have carried his fame to heaven.
For when he observed that life's demands and needs
were mostly ready at hand for men to take,   10
and life was about as secure as it could be,
that men had wealth and power, distinction, praise
in abundance, and sons whose fame increased their own,
yet for all this they housed hearts no less fearful,
and troubled their minds with profitless complaints   15
forever, and dangerous thoughts that drove them mad,
he concluded the fault must lie within the vessel,
that everything in it was spoiled by its defects—
all those good things men gathered and garnered there.
Partly, he saw it was shoddy and full of holes   20
and thus could never be filled in any fashion;
partly, he noticed that everything it took in
was fouled, so to speak, by its vile effluvia.
And so, by the truths he spoke, he cleansed our souls:
he set due limit upon desire and fear,   25
revealed the Highest Good, what it is we all
pursue, and showed the Way, the modest path
by which to reach it down the true, straight road;
showed evil, too, widespread in human life,
those wing-swift, various products of pure chance   30
or natural law (for nature so ordained),
and from what sally-ports to attack each one.
He proved that humankind mostly through folly
set rolling through their hearts grim waves of care.
For as in the dead of night, children are prey   35
to hosts of terrors, so we sometimes by day
are fearful of things that should no more concern us
than bogeys that frighten children in the dark.
This fright, this night of the mind must be dispelled
not by the rays of the sun, nor day's bright spears, 40
but by the face of nature and her laws.
Then onward, to clothe my great emprise in words!

147

And since I've proved our world a mortal province,
and heaven a fabric built of stuff that's born,
and all things in it that are and have to be,   45
subject to break-up, hear now what remains.
Since we've once mounted into our splendid car[1]

*   *   *

they come, the winds die down, and everything
that had been, reins in its rage and turns to peace.
Besides, men see in heaven and here on earth   50
things happen, that often fill their minds with fear,
and humble their hearts with terror of the gods.
They're crushed; they crawl on earth, because, perforce
through ignorance of causes they confer
on gods all power and kingdom over the world.[2]   55
If people have learned that gods live carefree lives,   58
and still, for all that, wonder by what means
phenomena may occur, especially those   60
they see in heavenly zones above their heads,
then they will slip back into their old beliefs
and take on heartless masters, whom they deem
almighty; poor fools, they don't know what can be
and what cannot; yes, and what law defines   65
the power of things, what deep-set boundary stone;
thus with reason blinded, they err and err.
Reject such thoughts! Far from your mind remove them,
unworthy of gods and alien to their peace!
Else power divine, belittled by you, will often   70
harm you—not that gods' power can be so damaged
that anger would drive them panting for fierce revenge,
but that you'll picture these placid, peaceful, harmless
creatures aboil with billows of rolling wrath,
and then won't enter their temples with peace at heart.[3] 75
Those images, too, that float from sacred flesh
into men's minds to report the shape of gods—
you'll never see them, and keep your peace of mind.
You see what a life is then in store for you.
Though true philosophy make this far removed   80
from us, though I have uttered so many truths,
yet there is still much to be clothed in polished
verses: we must map heaven and learn its laws,
tell of the thunderstorm and lightning flash,

1. After this line an unknown number of lines
has been lost.
2. 50–57 = 90–91, and are omitted by editors.
3. These lines sum up the Epicurean attitude
toward the gods: they have no power either for
good or for evil, but their totally untroubled
lives give us a pattern for the inner peace that is
the essence of Epicurean pleasure. We must
never allow wrongheaded ideas about the gods
to damage this pattern. See 3.18–30,
5.146–234.

what their effects, what cause may bring them on. 85
Don't mark off squares in heaven,[4] and in mad panic
check from which zone the flame flew down, or toward
which quarter it turned, how it could thread its way
into walled places, win through them, and come out.
Lacking a reason and cause for these events, 90
men think gods use their power to make them happen.
The mark of my final goal shines white before me
as I run on: show me the course, bright Muse,
Calliope,[5] peace of man and joy of gods!
Lead me to win my crown, my sign of glory! 95
   To begin: blue heaven is shaken by the thunder
because high over us, up in the air, clouds rush
head-on together, blown by two battling winds.
For no noise comes from parts where skies are clear,
but whenever clouds are gathered in closer files, 100
so much more loud and often come rumble and roar.
Besides, in substance, clouds could never be
as dense as wood is, or as stone, nor yet
as delicate as are fog and floating smoke.
For either, pressed by brute weight, they'd have to fall 105
like stones, or else, like smoke, not hold together
with strength to contain cold snows and sleet and rain.
Yes, they make sounds above our wide, flat world,
as canvas, sometimes, stretched over great arenas,
sends a loud rumble across the props and ridge-poles; 110
again, when winds go wild, it screams and rips,
and practices rustling and crackling, like papyrus[6]
(this sort of thing, too, can be observed in thunder
or as when clothes hung out, or loose papyri
are whirled and whipped through the air by howling winds). 115
Sometimes it happens, too, that clouds can't meet
so much head-on as sideways, passing by
toward different points, catching and scraping each other;
from this, that "dry" sound floods the ear, and rolls
along, until the clouds have lost close contact. 120
   In another way, too, sometimes, I think the world,
hammered by thunder, shakes, and all at once
the walls that enclose its hugeness seem to shatter:
when, without warning, a whirlwind gathers strength,
bores into clouds, and then, imprisoned there, 125

4. Lucretius refers here to the quadrants into
which astrologers, augurs, and other types of
diviners marked off the heavens.
5. Chief of the Muses, her name is associated
with nearly every form of poetry. For Lucretius,
like all such divine figures, she is simply a
symbol of the poetic art.
6. The ancient equivalent of paper, not unlike
it in appearance and texture. It was made from
the pith of a reed that grew abundantly along the
Nile.

spins faster and faster, making the cloud mass hollow
and pressing its substance into a dense-walled sphere.
Later, the force and speed of the wind break through,
and the cloud, with a frightful crash, bursts into shreds.
No wonder, when little bladders, full of air,   130
so often, when suddenly burst, give out small pops!

   There's also a way that winds, blowing through clouds,
might make a noise, for often we see the clouds
floating along branched and with rough projections:
just so, when a northwest wind blows through dense woods,   135
the leaves make noise, and the branches break and splinter.
And sometimes, too, a strong wind takes on speed,
and, head-on, shatters and rips a cloud to shreds.
For plain fact shows us the power that winds possess;
here on earth, where they're gentler, still they pull   140
tall trees up by the roots and blow them over.
There are waves, too, in the clouds, that by sheer weight
(we might say) crash with a roar; this same thing happens
when on deep rivers or on the sea, surf breaks.
It thunders, too, when lightning flares from cloud   145
to cloud: if the one that catches the fire is full
of water, it kills the flame with one loud roar,
as iron, white-hot from a fiery furnace, screams
when we take it and plunge it quickly in ice-cold water.
Besides, if a very dry cloud catches the fire   150
it fairly explodes in flame, with a monstrous crash;
as when fire sweeps a mountain thick with laurels
and, whipped by a whirlwind, turns them straight to ashes;
for, than Apollo's Delphic laurel,[7] nothing
burns with more fearful flash and crackle and roar.   155

   Great ice sheets shattering, too, and crumbling hail
often make noises high in a huge cloud mass.
For when wind crams them together, the clouds compressed
to solid mountains of rain and hail are shattered.

   There's lightning, again, when clouds have run together   160
and struck off atoms of fire, as when a stone
strikes on stone or steel, for then, too, light
leaps out and sheds a shower of fiery sparks.
But the ear hears thunder after the eye has seen
the lightning, because what stimulates the ear   165
always comes slower than things that rouse our vision.
In other ways, too, we learn this: watch a man
at a distance using an axe to fell a tree;

---

7. The laurel, or bay-tree, was sacred to
Apollo. Its leaves, when dry, burn rapidly and
with a loud crackling sound. For the story of
Apollo and the laurel, see Ovid, *Meta-
morphoses*, 1.452 ff.

you'll see the stroke before the blow dispatches
sound to the ear. So, we see lightning first,   170
then hear thunder, though both start off together
from similar cause, produced by one collision.
    In this way, too, with fleeting light, clouds color
the world, and jagged bolts light up the storm:
when wind has entered a cloud, spun round inside it,   175
and hollowed it, as I showed, to a dense-walled sphere,
the motion makes heat; you see all things, by movement,
are heated to incandescence; even lead pellets,
sent spinning for any distance, soften and melt.[8]
Thus when this heated wind splits the black cloud,   180
it throws off seeds of heat in violent bursts,
and these create the jagged flames of lightning.
Sound follows this; it reaches the ears more slowly
than things that come to the windows of our eyes.
This happens, of course, with dense and high-piled clouds,   185
one heaped on top of another, an eerie mass;
be never deceived because, down here, we see
how wide they are more than how high they reach.
For stand and watch when winds will carry clouds,
shaped like mountains, athwart the streams of air,   190
or see them gathered around great mountain peaks,
one cloud piled and pressing upon another,
placed and posted, with every wind entombed.
Then you will come to know how huge they are,
and see their caves, built as with beetling boulders.   195
Now when a storm has risen, these caves are filled
with winds, which, locked in the clouds, turn furious,
and grumble and gowl like wild beasts in their cages;
they send roars through the clouds, now here, now there,
and move in circles, seeking a channel, and roll   200
fire-atoms together, forcing them from the clouds
by millions, and spinning flame in a hollow furnace
till the cloud rips open and bright light flashes out.
    And here is another reason why that swift
clear golden fire may flash down here to earth: 205
the clouds themselves must have uncounted seeds
of fire, for when they're wholly free of water
they often possess a shining tint of flame.
Surely from sunlight they must pick up many
atoms, and hence turn red and pour out fire.   210
Well then, when wind has driven, pounded, and forced these

---

8. This strange and patently impossible idea is
frequently mentioned in ancient literature.
How it got started and why it persisted remain
unexplained. It reappears, 6.306–7. The best
known parallel for Lucretius' lines is Vergil,
Aeneid 9.588.

into one space, they pour out under pressure
atoms that make the color of flame shine bright.
There's lightning, too, when sky-borne clouds thin out.
For when wind gently pulls them apart in passing   215
and breaks them up, those atoms perforce must fall
that make the flash. Then, without ugly terror
and rumble, the lightning comes, and there's no panic.

Finally, what the substance of the lightning
may be is clear from the strokes and from the marks   220
of burning, and signs, the choking smell of sulphur.
For fire, not wind or rain, leaves signs like these.
Besides, they often set fire to roofs of homes;
flames race through the house and soon engulf it all.
This fire, you see, is finest of finest fires;   225
nature has build it of bodies microscopic
and mobile, which nothing at all has power to stop.
The lightning of heaven goes through walls of houses
like shouts and speech; it goes through stone, through bronze,
and in a second turns bronze and gold to liquid.   230
It makes wine, too, evaporate instantly
from flawless jars, because with ease it stretches
and opens the pores of pottery all around.
Then comes the heat; it penetrates the wine
nimbly, breaks up and dissipates its atoms,   235
something we see the sun's heat cannot do
in years, for all its force and heat and speed.
So much more mobile and masterful is the lightning.

Lightning, now—how it comes to be, and have
such force that its stroke can tear a tower apart,   240
demolish houses, scatter their beams and planks,
dislodge and tumble the monuments of men,
kill people, slaughter farm animals everywhere,
what gives it power to do all things like these,
I'll tell you, and stop no more for promises.   245

Consider lightning the product of thick, dark clouds
piled high; it never occurs at all when skies
are clear or when the clouds are light and thin.
And obvious fact proves this beyond all doubt,
for then clouds mass so deep all over heaven,   250
we'd think Hell's barren shadows all escaped
and filling the caverned vastness of the sky;
for in that filthy night of clouds there hang,
hosted above us, faces of black fear,
when storms begin to build the lightning bolt.   255
Often, besides, at sea, a black cloud mass,
like a river of pitch poured down from heaven, falls

far out on the waves, so packed with shadows, and big
with a dead-black freight of lightning and hurricane,
so filled to the full—none more—with fire and wind,   260
that even on land men shiver and run for home.
Consider, then, that over our heads the storm
is towering tall, for never could it black out
the world with murk if cloud weren't piled on cloud
like masonry, heavy and high, cutting off the sun.   265
Nor could rains come and fall so heavily
that rivers flow over their banks and flood the fields,
if heaven were not piled high with towering clouds.
Here, then, the whole extent is full of wind
and fire; hence, here and there, come roars and flashes.   270
I showed above, you know, that hollow clouds
must hold unnumbered seeds of heat, and draw
still more from the rays of the sun and from their glow.
Thus, when the wind that blows them to one spot
(no matter where) has forced out many seeds   275
of heat, and joined to mingle with that fire,
it slips inside; confined, it whirls and spins
and with furnace-heat sharpens the lightning bolt.
For two things make it glow: from its own movement
it turns red-hot, and from the touch of fire.   280
When wind then grows white-hot, and fire has gained
full force and speed, then lightning, as if ripe,
rips through the cloud, bursts out, and speeds away,
filling the world with flashes of light and flame.
A loud noise follows, as if the zones of heaven,   285
blown suddenly to bits, were dropping on us.
Then tremors trouble and try the world, and thunder
rumbles across high heaven, for then the whole
storm front is shattered and shaken; it rolls and roars.
After that crash the rains fall fast and heavy: 290
you'd think all heaven was turning into rain,
and pouring as if to call up the Flood again,
so heavy the fall, as clouds rip open and storm winds
blow, while flashes and roars explode and fly.
Sometimes a powerful wind from outside swoops   295
into a cloud hot with ripe thunderbolts
and tears it apart; at once, out drops that swirl
of fire, for which our native name is "lightning."
(This happens, here, there, wherever the strong wind blows.)
Sometimes, besides, a strong wind free of fire   300
may still, as it wanders miles of space, catch fire,
and rushing along its course, lose certain bodies
which, being coarse, can't pass through air so fast;

others it scrapes from the air and takes along;
small, but blown into compounds, they make fire;   305
in fashion much as a ball of lead,[9] that often
turns hot in its course, when, losing many atoms
of cold, it picks up fire from moving air.
It happens, too, that impact alone wakes fire,
when cold strong wind, though fireless, has struck hard;   310
for when it strikes, you see, with all its force,
atoms of heat may gather and pour from it
and from the thing as well that took the blow;
just so sparks fly when we cut stone with steel.
Nor, because steel is cold, are atoms of heat   315
and light too slow to gather at point of contact.
Thus, too, must things be set afire by lightning
if time and substance are suitable for combustion.
Nor can wind be so plainly, utterly cold,
so hopelessly, as it roars down out of heaven,   320
that if in passage it failed to catch afire
it might not still come warm and mixed with heat.
   Now lightning moves so fast and strikes so hard
and almost races across so swift and smooth,
because, to begin, it gathers force inside   325
the clouds, and builds up pressure as it moves;
then when the clouds can't prison its heightened power,
it bursts out with incredible force and speed,
like a missile hurled from a powerful catapult.
Add, that it's made of smooth and tiny atoms,   330
and nothing can easily stop such substances,
for they disappear and pass down devious paths.
Endless collisions, then, can't slow it down
or halt it; for this, it flies with smooth, swift speed.
Besides, since all things having weight press downward   335
by nature, when impact supplements that weight,
their speed is doubled and their force augmented;
hence, faster and more violently, they strike
and shatter whatever blocks them and fly on.
Lastly, things that come far and fast must gain   340
velocity all the time: it grows with movement,
increases power and force, and heightens impact.
For it makes all atoms whatever of that sort
gather in conclave, so to speak, from Space,
then hurls them together, spinning down that track.   345
Perhaps, in passage, it draws from air itself
atoms that strike and kindle it as it moves.
It passes unharmed through things, and many it leaves

9. See note 8, above.

undamaged: its fluid flame whips through their pores.
And many it fixes fast, when atoms of lightning   350
fall twixt the particles where two fabrics join.
It melts bronze easily, too, and gold it sets
seething at once, for lightning's power is built
on particles—atoms—so smooth and so minute
they slip in easily; and, slipped in, at once   355
they break each contact and loosen every bond.
In autumn the sky-vault tricked with shining stars
and the whole wide world are oftener set to shaking,
and again when springtime opens flowers in bloom.
On cold days, fires are gone, and winds are short   360
of heat, and clouds are not so densely packed.
And so, when weather and season stand midway,
then many causes of lightning happen at once:
these "narrows" of the year mix cold and heat,
and a cloud needs both of these for forging lightning, 365
to set two stuffs in discord and confusion,
and drive air mad with surging wind and fire.
You see, where heat begins, there cold leaves off,
and that's your springtime; thus the two must fight,
unlike as they are, and mixed, cause wild confusion.   370
Again, when the last of heat rolls round, to mix
with the start of cold, the season we call autumn,
here, too, harsh winter days conflict with summer.
That's why we call it the "narrows" of the year;
no wonder if at that season there's so much   375
lightning, and storms race murky across the sky,
since two are at war, wild war, one here, one there,
on this side, flame, on that, wind mixed with water.

It's thus we understand the nature of lightning,
bearer of fire, and see what powers its acts,   380
not by foolish research on Tuscan song,[1]
looking for hints of the hidden intent of god:
"From which zone may the flame fly down, or toward
which quarter turn? How could it thread its way
into walled places, win through them, and come out?   385
What harm might a lightning bolt from heaven do?"
But see! If Jove and the other gods make heaven
shake in her shining zones with fearful sound,
and hurl the fire, each where his will directs,
why don't they strike the heedless sinner, guilty   390
of filthy crime, and make him breathe bright flame

1. The Etruscans had written treatises in which
they ascribed the lightning to deliberate action
on the part of the gods, and asserted that it was
this divine intervention that gave the lightning
its remarkable power. Lucretius of course de-
nies this, as he does all supposed instances of
divine intervention.

through transfixed lungs, harsh lesson to mortal men?
Instead, one conscious of never a shameful act
is wrapped in flames and writhes all innocent,
caught unawares by spiraled fire from heaven.   395
Why, too, do they hurl at deserts—waste of effort!
Or is this throwing-drill and muscle-training?
Why do they let Jove's bolt be dulled on dirt?
Why does *he* let it, nor save it for enemies?
Lastly, when skies are clear, why does Jove never   400
throw lightning to earth and pour out floods of noise?
Or, as the clouds pass by, does he climb down
onto them, that he may aim his bolt close-range?
Why does he hurl at the sea? What charge has he
against the waves, the waters, the brimming plains?   405
And if he'd have us avoid the lightning bolt,
why won't he make us able to see it coming?
If he meant to burn us to death all unawares,
why thunder up there, to warn us out of the way?
Why send in darkness first, and rumble and roar?   410
And could you believe he'd throw in many directions
at once? Or venture to say it never occurs
that more than one bolt falls at a given time?
But it happens again and again, and must be so:
just as it rains and rains in many places,   415
so, many thunderbolts fall at a given time.
And why does he shatter the holy shrines of gods
with his deadly lightning—even his own great temples?
Why break up the gods' fine idols, and deface
great works of art, his images, with mad wounds?   420
Why hit high spots so often? Why do we find
countless signs of his fire on mountaintops?

These facts, now, make it easy to understand
what the Greeks call, simply, "presters" (water spouts)—
how from above they drop down onto the sea.   425
For it happens sometimes that, like a descending column,
one drops from sky to sea; the waters around
seethe madly, stirred by wildly circling winds,
and any vessel that may then be caught
in that mêlée is troubled and in great danger.   430
This happens whenever a strong wind, moving fast,
can't quite break through a cloud, but thrusts it down
from sky to sea, just like a descending column,
slowly, as if a fist and arm up there
were punching, pressing, stretching it toward the waves.   435
When it bursts, the full force of that wind breaks out
over the water and makes weird, seething waves.

For a spinning spiral of wind descends and stretches
the cloud, an elastic substance, out with it;
once it has pressed this cloud mass down to the surface,   440
that wind swoops onto the water, and stirs the sea
into a maelstrom of roaring, raging waters.
And sometimes, too, a whirlwind wraps itself
in clouds by gleaning atoms of cloud from air,
and then drops out of the sky just like a "prester."   445
When this has dropped to the earth and broken up,
it vomits a mass of spiraling, high-speed wind.
As a rule this happens rarely, for on land
mountains are bound to block it; hence, it's viewed
more often where sea and sky stretch wide and clear.   450
    Clouds grow when many atoms, flying high
in the reaches of heaven, all at once form union—
rougher atoms, which, though by smallest barbs
entangled, still may catch and hold each other.
At first, they build the fabric of small clouds;   455
later these catch each other and form groups
and with their joining, grow, and ride the winds,
until at last a savage storm is born.
It happens too with mountaintops: the nearer
they are to the sky, the more their peaks will always   460
be shrouded in a coarse, dark wrack of cloud.
This is because, when clouds first start to form,
too thin as yet for eye to see, the winds
carry and force them against the mountaintops.
Once there, they join to form a greater mass   465
and denser; now they are visible, and we seem
to see them surging from mountain peak toward heaven.
For that upper air is windy and wide, we learn
from fact and experience when we climb high mountains.
Further, that Nature lifts atoms from all the sea   470
by thousands is clear from clothes hung out on shore:
moisture clings to them and they soak it up.
Hence, still clearer, may countless atoms rise
from the salt and restless sea to augment the clouds:
all water is kin, and follows a kindred pattern.   475
Further, from every river and from earth
itself we see warm vapors and clouds arise:
they float from here upward like breath expelled,
and with their darkness curtain the sky, and build,
little by little conjoined, tall towering clouds.   480
There's pressure, too, from the tides of star-clad ether,
compressing clouds to a curtain under the sky.
The atoms that build our clouds and floating fogs

could also come to our sky from outer space.
For I've proved their number numberless, and the Sum   485
of Deeps unbounded; and with what great speed
the atoms fly, I've shown, and how they pass
in a flick of the eye through space beyond the telling.
Small wonder, then, if often in little time,
with such huge clouds, the tempest and dark night,   490
like high-hung curtains, cover land and sea,
since everywhere through every hole in heaven,
and through, as it were, the Great World's pores all round,
there's exit and entrance made for the elements.
     Now hear: how water droplets high in clouds   495
gather and grow into rain, are freed, and fall
to earth, I'll explain. And first I'll prove that many
atoms of water at once rise to the clouds
from everything, and the two increase alike
(the clouds, that is, and the water that's in the clouds)   500
as in us, flesh and blood increase alike,
sweat, too, and other such humors in our bodies.
Besides, they often pick up lots of moisture
out of the sea, like hung-out hanks of wool,
when clouds are carried by winds above the ocean.   505
In similar wise, from every river, moisture
is borne to the clouds. When atoms of water there
have gathered and grown by thousands from every source,
the clouds, enlarged, are doubly driven to drop
their moisture: for winds press hard, and as the clouds   510
pile higher and higher and start to churn, they cause
downward pressure, which forces rain to fall.
Besides, when clouds are thinned out, too, by winds,
or hammered to bits by heat of the sun above,
they drop their moisture and drip with rain, as wax   515
over hot fire melts to a liquid puddle.
But wild rains fall when clouds piled high are wildly
crushed by both heat and water and driving wind.
But rains have often gone on for days, and lasted
long, when seeds of water race in by thousands   520
when saturated clouds, one on another,
gather in high-piled masses from every zone,
and all the earth exhales a steamy breath.
Then, when the storm is darkest, and the sun
shines with his rays across the dripping wrack,   525
a painted bow stands out against black clouds.
     All else that grows up there, up there created,
and all that grows along with clouds, yes, all,
from start to finish: snow, wind, hail, cold frost,

ice—mighty force, great hardener of waters,   530
durance that commonly curbs our eager streams—
it's easy to search them out and see in mind
how they all happen, and why they come to be,
once you have learned what powers the atoms have.
     Come now and learn what causes set the earth   535
to quaking. First, you'll realize that the earth,
under as well as over, is largely filled
with windy caves, and carries countless lakes,
chasms, and cliffs and tumbled rocks inside it,
and under its surface countless hidden rivers,   540
we know, must roll vast waves and sunken rocks,
for facts prove things are like themselves throughout.
Because of the things that lie subjoined below,
the earth above is shaken and tumbled to ruins
when time makes those vast caves down there collapse.   545
All at once, you see, whole mountains fall; their huge
crash sends temblors creeping in all directions—
naturally, since wagons of no great weight
set whole houses to shaking along a street;
they're jostled, too, whenever   *   *   *2   550
has bumped both iron-rimmed wheels from underneath.
Besides, when into a deep, wide body of water,
with passage of time, huge masses of earth roll down,
the earth, still trembling, quakes in the wash of waves,
as a jug can never stand still unless the liquid   555
inside it has stopped its aimless ripple and toss.
     Besides, when wind, gathered in hollow spots
under the earth, leans to one side, exerting
huge force and pressure against those high-roofed caves,
the earth bends in to the sideways thrust of wind,   560
then all the buildings on earth above that spot,
the farther each one reaches toward the sky,
they lean, buckle, and bend in the same direction,
while beams pull loose and dangle, ready to fall.
And men don't like to believe a time will come   565
of ruin and death for this great world of ours,
when they see the earth, so massive, buckle and sway!
If those winds never died down, there'd be no power
could hold things back from death or curb their fall.
Since they blow harder and die down by turns,   570
regroup, so to speak, for attack, but yield to force,
the earth more often threatens us with disaster
than causes it; it bends, but then recoils
and drops slipped masses back in their proper slots.

2. The latter part of this line is unintelligible.

That's why our buildings tremble: top floors more   575
than middle, middle than ground, ground scarce at all.
  Here's something else can cause great quakes like that:
when wind and a huge fast-moving mass of air,
whether external or risen within our world,
breaks into hollow spots in earth, and there   580
inside those giant caves first howls and roars,
setting itself to spinning; then with force
and speed built up, it bursts right out, and splits
the earth deep down and makes a gaping hole.
This happened at Syrian Sidon, and at Aegis   585
of Peloponnese, cities which this discharge
of air and the following earthquake laid in ruins.[3]
And many a town besides has tumbled here
on land in earthquakes; many a city, too,
has sunk, with all its people, in the sea.   590
And if the wind does not burst out, yet still
its speed and force through myriad pores in earth
spread like a chill, and thence produce a shiver,
just as when cold gets deep inside our bodies,
it hits and shakes us, makes us start and shiver.   595
Yes, people in cities tremble in twofold terror;
above, they fear the roofs; beneath, they wonder
how soon old earth will rend her caves to ruin,
or split, to reveal a vast, wide-gaping chasm,
then crumble and fill it with her own debris.   600
And so, though men believe that earth and sky,
in trust to Eternal Weal, will last forever,
sometimes they see disaster, and its force
sinks in, and puts the goad to covert fears
that, under their feet, the earth might suddenly drop   605
into the Pit, and a helpless world behind it,
a Cosmos all collapsed to tangled ruins.
  To begin, men wonder why the sea grows never
larger, with all the water that pours in,
and rivers flowing into it everywhere.   610
Add restless rains and flying thunderstorms,
all dripping their showers and streams on land and sea;
add its own springs; yet all of these won't make
the sum of ocean larger by one lone drop;
small wonder, then, that ocean grows no larger.   615
The heat of the sun draws off a large part, too.
We see, of course, how clothes hung dripping wet
dry out in the natural radiance of the sun,

---

3. The reference is to two famous earthquakes of antiquity, the first of uncertain date, the second of 372 B.C.

but we see the seas are many, and widely spread.
Hence, though the sun, at any single spot,   620
may draw from ocean only the smallest part,
over stretches of water so wide, it must take floods.
Besides, winds too must pick up large amounts
of moisture, sweeping the seas, since many a time
we see our streets dried up in a single night   625
by winds, and the soft mud harden and crust over.
Then, too, I've shown that clouds pick up a lot
of moisture gathered from ocean's broad expanse
and scatter it hither and yon all over the world
when it rains on land and winds bring in the clouds.   630
Lastly, since earth is porous in its structure,
and touches and girds the sea's edge all around,
water, just as it flows from land to sea,
must also seep from the salt sea into earth.
For brine seeps through, and water-substance trickles   635
back to the source where rivers rise, and there
converges, to send sweet streams across the world
where beds, once cut, guide water's bright, clear foot.
   Now, how it happens that mountain-throats like Aetna's[4]
breathe fire sometimes, great swirling exhalations,   640
I will explain. No small disaster struck
when fire-storms sweeping through Sicilian lands
attracted the gaze of people on nearby shores;
seeing the vaults of heaven all smoke and flame,
they felt their hearts fill with cold fear, at thought   645
of what strange new things nature designed to do.
   In this respect, you must look deep and far
and spend long hours in search and observation,
to keep in mind how vast the Sum of Things
and see how tiny a part of the Total Sum   650
one heaven may be, how infinitesimal:
the whole thing less than a man to our whole world.
Lay this all out; examine it carefully;
carefully check it; you'll leave off wondering.
Does anyone wonder, if he has caught a fever   655
and his body begins to burn up with its heat,
or if some other infection racks his flesh?
All at once, a foot swells up: a sharp pain often
seizes a tooth or attacks our very eyes;
a rash begins and spreads a burning itch   660
all over the body, and even creeps inside—
of course, because there are atoms of many kinds,
and earth has plague, and heaven evil enough

4. See 1.722.

to give diseases power and boundless growth.
We must realize then, that for all heaven and earth   665
Infinity always supplies resource enough
to strike the sudden blow that shakes the world,
and send tornadoes racing by land and sea,
make Aetna boil over, and set the heavens aflame.
For this too happens: the zones of heaven turn hot,   670
and storms begin, with heavier fall of rain
wherever atoms of water make chance assembly.
"But the heat—the swirling fire—is far too vast."
Of course! And a river, too, seems huge to one
who never saw a larger; a man, a tree   675
seem huge, and all things else of every kind;
the biggest a man has seen, these he thinks huge.
Yet all put together, plus earth and sky and sea,
are nothing beside the Total Sum of Things.

Yet still, how are the flames roused all at once   680
to blast their way out of Aetna's caverned vastness?
I will explain: to begin, the entire mountain
is hollow, propped, for the most, on granite vaults:
next, all those caverns are full of wind and air—
for wind is air, stirred up and set in motion.   685
This wind blows wild, turns hot, and heats the rock
all round, wherever they touch—earth, too—and strikes
hot fire from them, while flames burst out and spread;
then, straight up the mountain's throat, the wind escapes.
It carries the fire for miles; for miles, it scatters   690
sparks, and rolls a billow of thick black smoke,
and throws out rocks too, heavy beyond belief.
Don't doubt the destructive power of this wind.
Besides, in large part, round the base of Aetna,
the ocean breaks his waves and sucks his tides,   695
and from the ocean's edge, tunnels run deep
down to the mountain's throat. This way must pass[5]

* * *

facts prove that it sinks deep in from the open sea,
and then blows out with a blast, ejecting flame,
hurling up rocks and raising clouds of grit.   700
For up at the top are "punch bowls"[6] so Sicilians
themselves call them; we speak of "throats" and "mouths."
For a number of things, it's not enough to state
one cause, but many, of which one would be true.

5. After this line an unknown number of lines
have been lost.
6. Greek *krateres* (our "craters"), strictly speak-
ing, the large bowls in which wine and water
were mixed for drinking.

As if, far off, you spied the lifeless corpse   705
of a man stretched out, you'd best tell over all
the causes of death, to tell the one that's his.
For you can't convince us that he died of cold,
or by the sword, or by disease, or poison,
and yet, that something of this kind befell him,   710
we know. We'll have to put it this way often.[7]
   The Nile, unique in the world, rises in summer
and floods the fields, all Egypt's only stream.
It waters Egypt often when days are hottest,
either because in summer the North Winds (called   715
from the time of year "etesian") block its mouths
and, blowing against the river, dam it, forcing
its water upstream, to fill it and stop its flow.
For there's no doubt these storm-winds blow against
the current: they blow straight from the cold North Star.   720
The river flows from the south, the Torrid Zone,
where the races of man are black, kiln-burned in color;
it rises deep in the land of midday sun.
It's also possible that great bars of sand
pile up at the river's mouth against the current   725
when seas, stirred up by winds, wash sand in there;
this tends to obstruct the outflow of the river
and make the current run more sluggishly.
It's possible, too, that more rain falls in summer
at head of the Nile, because the "etesian" winds—   730
"Northers"—blow all the rain clouds toward those parts.
You see, when forced to the land of midday sun
they've gathered there, the clouds are packed together
and pressed with force against high mountain peaks.
Perhaps from deep in Ethiopian highlands   735
the floods begin, when the all-pervading sun
sends melted snows cascading to the plains.
   Hear now: the spots called "Birdless"[8] and the pools—
I'll tell you with what nature they're endowed.
First, for the name "Birdless": they're so called   740
from the fact that they are hostile to all birds;
because, when birds fly out across those places
they lose their skill at wing-stroke, furl their sails,
and fall headlong, fluttering, necks gone limp,
down to the ground, if it happens to be dry land,   745
or into the water, if "Birdless Lake" lies there.
At Cumae[9] is such a place, where mountains filled

7. The principle of plurality of causes: see Introduction p. x.
8. Latin *loca Averna*, possibly from Greek *aornos*, "birdless." We do not know how to explain the phenomenon here described by Lucretius.
9. A city on the Italian seacoast, not far from Naples.

with acrid sulphur and boiling springs spout steam.
There's one in Athens, on the Acropolis, too,
right by the Temple of Pallas, Lady of Triton,[1]   750
a spot where cawing crows never direct
their flight, not even when altars smoke with gifts.
Why do they shun it? Not with a watchful eye
for the wrath of Pallas, as Greek poets tell us;
no, it's the nature of the place that does it.   755
In Syria, too, men tell of a spot, it seems,
where horses, too, the minute they set foot there,
collapse, by natural forces overcome,
as if swift hands from heaven had cut them down.
All of these things take place through natural causes,   760
and how those causes begin is clear to see.
We mustn't believe that at these spots are doors
to Hell, and imagine that ghost-gods down below
draw souls from thence to the coasts of Acheron,
as, with their nostrils, wing-foot stags (men think)[2]   765
draw forth the serpent-kind from wild-beast lairs.
How far this is disjoined from truth and reason,
learn, for now I'll explain this very matter.

    To begin, I state, as I've often done before,
that in earth are things of every shape and form: 770
many for food, life-giving, many with power
to infect us with disease and hasten death.
And that some are better for some, others for other
creatures to maintain life, I've shown before,
because of their different substances and different   775
textures, one from another, and outward shapes.
Harmful substances often pass through the ears
or slip up the nose, rough-textured, deadly stuff.
And none too rare are things we should not touch,
things best not seen, things nauseous to taste.   780

    Besides you see how much, to human sense,
is sharply destructive, hard to bear, repulsive.
To begin, we're told the shade of certain trees
is so oppressive it often causes headaches
if people lie benath them on the grass.   785
There's also, on Helicon peaks, a tree with flowers
of odor so foul it commonly kills a man.[3]
These things, you see, all rise up from the soil

---

1. The goddess Athena, called Tritogeneia, "child of Triton," by the Greeks. Triton was a sea god, the reason for Athena's association with him is unknown.
2. This bit of zoological nonsense is on a par with the physical nonsense about lead pellets (see 6.178–79, and note). Lucretius here evinces a healthy skepticism ("men think") about the idea.
3. Another bit of nonsense, quite parallel to that about stags and snakes (see 765). What tree was meant is unknown.

because many atoms of many things, all mixed,
are held in earth, which yields them separately.   790
At night, a fresh-doused lamp offends our nose
with an acrid stench, yet, next us, puts to sleep
a man subject to fainting and mouth-foaming.
Musk smells rank, yet a woman drops to sleep
(and pretty embroidery slips from dainty hands)   795
if she has sniffed it during her menstrual flow.[4]
Countless other things too unstring the joints
of weary bodies, and trouble us, heart and soul.
Besides if you should linger in hot baths
after eating too much, how easily it can happen   800
that in midpool you'll crumple, time and again.
How easily, too, will deadly fumes of charcoal
slip to the brain if we've not first drunk water![5]
And when high fever grips the human frame,
a whiff of wine is like a knock-out blow.   805
See too how earth herself produces sulphur,
how asphalt gathers, with its fetid stench.
Besides, when men trace veins of gold and silver,
scratching with tools at earth's deep hidingholes,
what odors float upward from Scaptensula![6]   810
What evil exhalations goldmines breathe!
What do they do to a man's face and complexion!
Haven't you seen or heard in what short time
men commonly die, how soon their life gives out—
those who constrained by force must do such work?   815
All these miasmas earth wafts up in waves
and breathes them out to the open under the sky.

   Thus "birdless" places must send up a force
deadly to birds, that rises from earth to air,
and in some sections poisons a zone of heaven;   820
and soon as a bird flies into such a zone
she's caught by invisible poison there and, crippled,
falls from that zone down where the miasma guides her.
There she collapses, and this same miasma
takes what remains of life from all her body.   825
First, one might say, it causes a sort of faintness;
then, when they've fallen into the very source
of poison, the birds must there gasp out their lives
because the foul stuff then is all around them.

---

4. A strange bit of gynecological lore. It prob-
ably belongs in the same class with the
phenomena mentioned 6.178–179 and 6.765.
5. Lucretius appears to be referring to carbon
monoxide poisoning, about which, of course,
the ancients knew nothing. His suggested
prophylaxis—a drink of water—seems singu-
larly ineffective.
6. A Latinization of *Skapte Hyle*, a mining
center in Thrace. It would be interesting if the
reference really were to "fire-damp," the
poisonous and explosive gas that has so often
been responsible for mine disasters.

Sometimes, too, "Birdless," with its strong miasma,   830
may dissipate air that lies between the birds
and earth, and leave the place there nearly void.
Then, when birds come flying above that spot
their wings are crippled, beating on empty space,
and at once all power of flight is stripped away.   835
Here, since their wings can't bolster or propel them,
they're naturally compelled by weight to fall
to earth; near-felled in passing through empty space,
they let life trickle from every body-pore. [7]

                        *   *   *

Now water in wells is colder in summertime   840
because heat turns earth porous, making it lose
to the winds all atoms of native heat it owns.
And so, the more the earth is draïned of heat,
the colder the water that's hidden in the earth.
Then when all earth, compressed by cold, congeals   845
and, so to speak, contracts, by that contraction
it squeezes into the wells what heat it has.
At Ammon's shrine, men say, there is a spring,
by daylight cold, warm in the hours of night.
Men too much marvel at this spring, and think   850
a hot sun under the earth speedily heats it
when night with frightening darkness clothes the world.
But this is far removed from truth and reason.
Why! When the sun, in its course above, caressing
water's bare body, could still not make it warm   855
for all the force of heavenly light and heat,
how could it, under earth, that great, coarse body,
heat water through and fill it with steamy warmth?
Especially since it scarce can slip its heat
through walls of houses, for all its fiery rays!   860
How, then, explain it? Just that around the spring
the earth is porous, and warmer than most soil,
and close to the water are many atoms of fire.
Soon as night smothers earth in dewy darkness,
the earth, deep down, turns colder and contracts,   865
and thus, as if compressed by hand, it squeezes
all atoms of fire it has into the spring;
these turn the water's touch and vapors warm.
When the sun rises, its rays make earth expand
and loosen its fabric, as vapor and heat increase;   870
then back to their ancient homes go atoms of heat,
and all the water's warmth withdraws to earth.

---

7. After this line an indeterminate number of lines have been lost.

This is the reason the spring turns cold in daytime.
Besides, the sun's rays trouble the fluid structure
of water: by day, the heat-waves weaken its fabric,   875
and hence it throws off all the atoms it has
of fire, as commonly it lets go the cold
it contains and melts the ice and breaks its bonds.[8]

    There's a cold spring,[9] too, over which when tow is held
it picks up fire at once, and starts to blaze,   880
and in like manner a torch ignites and, floating,
shines on the waves wherever breezes blow it.
Why? Simply that in the water are many atoms
of fire; these particles must rise up from earth
itself at the bottom, then up through all the spring   885
and bubble straight out and pass to the open air,
yet not so many that they can heat the water.
Besides, they're scattered; some sudden force propels them
out of the water, then makes them group above it.
As in midsea Fount Aradus sends up   890
fresh water, displacing the salt waves all around;
and Ocean, in many other regions, too,
brings timely help to thirsting mariners
by making sweet waves rise amid the salt.
Just so the atoms may bubble up through that spring   895
and then burst out of it toward the tow, and join
together or cling to the substance of the torch.
They'll blaze up then with ease, for tow and torch
hold also many atoms of fire concealed.
Don't you see too, how, when you move a wick   900
just snuffed toward lamps at night, it will catch fire
before it touches the flame, and a torch likewise?
Other things, too, once touched by actual heat,
flame up at a space, before the fire engulfs them.
This we conclude, then, happens with that spring, too.   905

    To continue: I'll explain what natural law
gives this stone, here, the power to pull on iron
(Greeks call it a "magnet," a patronynic name,

---

8. These labored explanations of an entirely illusory phenomenon vividly illustrate one of the most serious gaps in ancient science, the nearly total lack of empirical and experimental data. The supposed differences in water temperatures were simply the result of contrast with the temperature of the surrounding air: as it grew warmer, the water seemed colder, and *vice versa*. The shrine of Ammon, an Egyptian god identified by the Greeks with Zeus, and by the Romans with Jupiter, was in an oasis in Libya.
9. The reference seems to be to a spring at Dodona, in the mountains of Epirus, where there was a famous oracle of Zeus. The anomalous powers here ascribed to the spring by Lucretius are mentioned elsewhere in ancient literature (esp. in Pliny's *Natural History*), but no convincing explanation for them has yet been forthcoming. Lucretius' argument, based as it is on analogy with another anomalous phenomenon, the supposed freshwater spring that bubbles up through the salt waters of the Mediterranean, is far from convincing. See note 8 above. The spring called *Aradus* was either on the island of that name or—as Lucretius implies—in the sea between the island and the coast of Phoenicia.

because it comes from the fatherland of Magnetes.)
Men find this stone amazing. Why? Sometimes   910
it makes a chain of rings depending from it;
from time to time one sees five rings or more,
in order descending, tossed by gentle breezes;
one clings to another from its under side,
as each from the other learns the stone's firm grip,   915
so strongly does its force flow through them all.

   In matters like this, much must be clarified
before the thing itself can be explained;
I must approach it by ways long roundabout,
hence you must listen with care and pay close heed.   920

   To begin: each thing we see must be releasing
an endless stream of particles, that disperse
to strike our eyes and stimulate our vision.
From certain things, too, odors ever flow,
as cold from rivers, heat from sun, and tides   925
from sea that eat away the longshore dikes,
and ceaseless varied sounds pass through the ear.
Besides, to the lips comes often a damp, salt taste
when we walk beside the sea; and when we watch
wormwood stirred and dissolved, bitterness hits us.   930
To such degree from every thing things stream
away, and are released in all directions
with never a halt or rest allowed their flowing;
for sentience in us is constant: all the time
we are seeing, smelling, and hearing the sounds of things.   935

   Now let me repeat how porous all things are
in substance: my opening lines made that quite clear.
Yes, though for many things one needs to know this,
yet first and foremost, for this very thing
that I'm about to discuss, we must assert   940
that nothing conforncs us but matter mixed with void.
First: it is fact that in caves the rocky roofs
are sweating with moisture and beaded with trickling drops.
All over our bodies, too, sweat trickles out;
beards grow, and hair on every limb and joint.   945
Food spreads into every vein, increasing, feeding
the body's extremities; fingernails, toenails, all.
When cold, likewise, passes through bronze, or heat,
we feel it, likewise feel it pass through gold
and silver when we grasp a brimming cup.   950
Besides, words fly through curtain walls of stone
in houscs; odors seep through, and cold, and heat
of fire, which commonly pierces strong, cold steel.

Besides, the corselet of the sky draws round[1]

* * *

when serious illness slip in from outside   955

* * *

and storms that take their start by land or sea

* * *

displaced over land and sea they rightly cause

* * *

since there's no substance not of porous structure.
    Further, not every single particle
that's cast from things will cause the same sensation   960
or match all things alike in just one way.
To begin: sun dries out earth and bakes it hard,
but softens ice, and shining on high mountains
causes the high-piled drifts of snow to melt;
wax, too, set in its heat is liquified.   965
Fire, too, turns bronze to liquid and softens gold,
but shrivels hides and flesh and makes them shrink.
Then water hardens steel fresh from the fire
but softens hides and flesh made hard by heat.
Wild olive as much delights the bearded goat   970
as if dipped in nectar and dripping with ambrosia,
and yet, for man, no tree bears bitterer fruit.
Take marjoram, too: pigs shun it, and all kinds
of perfume: to bristly pigs, that's caustic poison;
for us, sometimes, it almost brings new life.   975
To us, again, mud may be filthy stuff—
pure foulness—yet to pigs it seems delightful;
they roll in it over and over, insatiably.
    One topic clearly remains to be discussed
before I attempt to explain my basic problem.   980
Since things are varied, their many passageways
are bound to be endowed with different structure,
each having distinctive nature and direction.
The senses vary in living creatures, too;
each has the special things it gathers in.   985
Sounds come one way, we see, and by another,
tastes and flavors, and odors by still one more.

1. Although most editors accept these lines as they stand, they seem to me to be quite incoherent, and to have no logical connection either to what precedes or to what follows. A connective thought between 953 and 958 certainly seems to be missing.

Besides, one thing, we see, will seep through stone,[2]   990
another through wood, another pass through gold,
another trickle out through glass and silver.
For this way images pass, and that way, heat,
and down one path one thing outstrips another.
The nature of paths, of course, makes this occur   995
by endless varying, as I showed before,
because things differ in substance and in texture.
    Now since these things have all been clearly proved
and settled by way of preface for us here,
for the rest, it will be easy to explain   1000
and show what cause it is that pulls hard iron.
First: from this stone, atoms must stream by thousands,
or ebb and flow to hammer and shatter the air
that lies in place between the stone and iron.
Then when that place is emptied, and clear space   1005
lies open between, at once the atoms of iron
fall forward into the void, but since they're linked,
they cause the ring as a whole to move and follow.
And there's no thing more tightly intertwined,
confined, and coherent in its basic atoms   1010
than iron—that thing so strong, cold, frightening.
And since atoms are pulling, it's no wonder
if numerous particles drawn from iron can't move
into space without the whole ring coming, too;
and this it does: it follows, till it arrives   1015
at the stone, and there it's held by unseen bonds.
This happens in all directions, where there's space
made empty: atoms next to void will move
right into it, whether crosswise or straight up.
They're driven, of course, by outside blows; alone   1020
and of themselves they couldn't rise in air.
That this may happen more readily, one force
likewise comes as a help and aids their movement:
soon as the air in front of the ring turns rarer
and the space is made more nearly void and empty,   1025
at once it happens that all the air that lies
behind exerts a forward thrust and push.
For air surrounding things pounds on them always,
but just this time propels the iron, because
on one side space is empty and takes it in.   1030
This air I mention, slipping subtly through
iron's countless pores, down to its smallest parts,
strikes and propels them, as wind and sail a ship.
Besides, all things have air in them—they must,

2. Lines 988–989 = 995–996, and are omitted by editors.

since things are porous in substance, and the air   1035
lies all around and up against them all.
This air, then, hidden deep inside the iron,
is ever tossing in restless motion; thus
it doubtless pounds and pushes the ring inside.
Well! Off goes the ring where it's already tumbling   1040
and trying to go—that is, toward empty space.
    Sometimes it happens too that iron draws back
from the stone, by turns attracted and repelled.
Samothracian rings[3] will even jump—I saw them,
and iron filings going wild inside   1045
bronze cups, when magnet-stones were passed beneath them;
so eager they seem to be to escape the stone.
When bronze intervenes, such vast discord results
because, you see, the "tide" of bronze comes first
and occupies the iron's wide-open channels;   1050
then when the stone's "tide" comes, it finds the iron
all full, and can't seep through, as formerly.
Thus it must strike and hammer the iron fabric
with its current; in this way, it repels and tumbles
through bronze, what *without* bronze it will attract.   1055
    Don't wonder why the "tide" now, from our stone
can't have a like effect on other things.
Partly, weight holds them fast: such kind is gold;
their substance, partly, is porous: here, the "tide"
flows through untouched, and nowhere makes an impact.   1060
Ligneous matter, it seems, is of this kind.
Between these two, then, lie our ferrous metals;
once they've absorbed some particles of bronze,
they can be pushed by the "stream" from magnet-stones.
    Still, these are not so different from other things   1065
that all too few of the sort may come to hand
for me to report—things suited for single union.
First: mortar alone makes stones grow fast together,
and neat's-foot glue holds wood in such close bond
that faults in the boards cause cracks more frequently   1070
than slackening of the grip of neat's-foot glue.
Juice of the grape will boldly mate with springs
of water, while heavy pitch and light oil can't.
The purple dye of the murex joins in union
with woolen yarn, and never can be removed,   1075
not if you scrub it with all of Neptune's floods,
not if you wash it with Ocean's every wave.
Besides, doesn't just one thing link gold to gold,

---

3. Why "Samothracian"? No one knows. They must have been of some ferrous metal to behave as
Lucretius says they did.

and isn't bronze joined to bronze by pale-grey lead?
How many others, now, could be found? What, then?   1080
You don't really need these long and complex proofs,
and I don't need to expend all this vast effort;
it's better to tell much briefly, in few words.
Things whose fabrics show opposites that match,
one concave where the other is convex,   1085
and *vice versa*, will form the closest union.
Others, too, could be coupled and held fast
by a system of interlocking hooks and eyes;
this is most probably true of iron and magnet.

Now, what is the cause of disease, or, whence arising   1090
can violent illness suddenly blow up death
and disaster for humankind and hordes of beasts?
Let me explain: to begin, I showed above
that atoms of many things give life to us;
their opposites, too, cause of disease and death,   1095
must fly by thousands. When they chance to rise
and trouble the sky, the air becomes diseased.[4]
And all this mass of pestilence and disease
comes either from elsewhere, floating like clouds and fogs
through skies above us, or rises many times   1100
from earth itself, when it turns damp and putrid,
assaulted out of season by sun and rain.
Don't you see too how people, traveling far
from home and country, suffer from change of climate
and water, because things are so new and strange?   1105
How do we think that British climate differs
from Egypt's, where the world's wheel limps along;
how different the climate of Pontus from Cadiz,
and on, where men are black, kiln-burned in color.
When we remark that all these four are different,   1110
with their four winds and their four heavenly zones,
we note that men, too, widely differ in build
and color and suffer diseases tribe by tribe.
There's elephantiasis: this occurs in Egypt
along the Nile, midway, and nowhere else.   1115
Attica suffers from gout; there's eye-disease
in the Argolid[5]; one place attacks one part
and one, another: the cause is different air.
Thus when an atmosphere not native to us
shifts, and a dangerous air mass starts advancing,   1120
as clouds creep over slowly and compel
all heaven to darkness and change where they move in,

4. The idea that diseases, especially those of (miasma) was common in antiquity.
epidemic character, were caused by foul air 5. The northeast section of the Peloponnesus.

so, when that atmosphere comes into ours,
it spoils and renders it alien like itself.
Well then, this fresh disaster and disease   1125
drops on our waters or settles on our grain,
or other fodder of beasts and food of man,
or even remains suspended in the air,
and when we inhale these now commingled airs,
our bodies perforce absorb disease as well.   1130
In similar fashion, too, sometimes distemper
strikes cattles, or "wind"[6] the sluggish, bleating sheep.
Nor does it matter whether we come to spots
unhealthy for us and change the air that clothes us,
or nature herself brings pestilent atmosphere   1135
to us, or something we never used to have,
that, coming new upon us, may do us harm.

Disease like this, one time, a tide of death,
poisoned the very fields in Cecrops-land,[7]
emptied the streets, drained Athens of her people.   1140
Starting deep within Egypt's bounds, it came
by stages across large air and open sea
to settle at last on all Pandion's people.[8]
Then in their thousands men fell sick and died.
They first showed symptoms of headache and of fever,   1145
with both eyes bloodshot, watering, and bright.
The lining of the throat exuded dark
blood, and the larynx was blocked and closed by ulcers;
blood trickled from the tongue, voice of the soul;
it was weak and painful, sluggish, rough to touch.   1150
The infection then pushed down the throat and filled
the chest, and flowed on into the patient's heart;
at that point, all his hold on life gave way.
When he exhaled, his breath came out foul-smelling,
with a stench like carrion flesh tossed out to rot.   1155
Next, all his mental powers failed, and all
his body grew weak, for death was close at hand.
The pains were unbearable; agonizing fears
went ever with them; the patient moaned and groaned.
A cough that often persisted day and night,   1160
endlessly racking and wrenching limb and sinew,
left the exhausted sufferer drained of strength.
And yet one could not observe excessive heat
or feverishness on any body-surface;

6. This is a guess at the meaning of *aegror*, a word that occurs only here. The Latin itself means only "pain" or "illness." Bailey translates "distemper." "Wind" is listed in Webster as a disease of sheep.
7. Attica.

8. The Athenians. Pandion was a mythical king of Athens. The description here is of the famous plague that struck Athens in 430 B.C.. Lucretius with amazing accuracy renders into Latin verse the description given by Thucydides, 2.47–52.

rather, the patient's skin was cool to touch.   1165
Still his whole body was red and deeply ulcered,
as when erysipelas spreads over all the limbs.
But the inner parts were inflamed, clear to the bone;
the stomach within burned like a flaming furnace.
Nothing was light or thin enough to bring   1170
relief to the patient: "just cool and fan him always."
Some, burning with fever, hurled their naked bodies
into the ice-cold waters of rivers and drowned.
Many fell head-first into the depths of wells,
and as they reached the water, their mouths gaped open.   1175
An endless, parching thirst engulfed their flesh,
and made a cloudburst seem a mere light shower.
Their sufferings knew no rest; their bodies lay
exhausted. Doctors muttered, shook, fell dumb,
as over and over those staring eyes turned toward them,   1180
infected, burning with fever, never asleep.
Men showed many other fatal symptoms, too:
a mind deranged by agony and by fear,
a grim expression, the madman's piercing stare,
the hearing impaired, ears full of roaring sound,   1185
the breathing rapid, or slow to come, and labored,
the neck all wet and shiny with streaming sweat,
the spittle in tiny droplets, saffron-colored,
and salty, hawked from the throat with hard, hoarse coughs.
In the hands, the tendons cramped, the fingers trembled;   1190
at the feet, a chill began, and bit by bit,
soon spread. Then as the final moment came,
the nose was pinched, the tip of the nose was sharp,
eyes hollow, temples sunk, skin cold and taut,
lips in a snarling grin, brow tight and swollen;   1195
not long thereafter they lay still and dead.
In general, when the sun's eighth lamp grew warm,
sometimes the ninth, they rendered up their lives.
If any, as men say, "escaped dark death",
they also later wasted away and died   1200
with suppurating ulcers and black feces;
or chronic headaches followed by a rush
of noxious blood that passed through blocked-up nostrils:
this way, men's life and substance all flowed out.
If any escaped this hemorrhage of foul blood,   1205
still the disease would pass on into muscle
and organ, down to the genitals themselves.
Some, burdened by terror of the doors of death,
lived by excision of the virile organ;
some with the loss of hand or foot remained   1210

alive, and some by sacrificing eyes:
so bitter a fear of death had come upon them.
Some even suffered total amnesia,
and couldn't even remember who they were.
And though on the ground unburied bodies lay   1215
one on another, yet bird and animal-kind
would all shy off, to avoid the nauseous stench,
or if they'd eaten, at once fell sick and died.
In general, though, no bird was rash enough
to appear, those days, no grim wild animal   1220
came out of the woods: they, too, were largely sick
and dying. First of all, the faithful dogs,
collapsing on every street, lay gasping, panting:
the deadly disease racked them and took their lives.
By thousands, the dead were rushed to the grave, unmourned.   1225
No therapy was proposed that worked for all.
For what gave one the right to roll the air
of life on his lips, and gaze on heavenly zones,
to others was fatal and brought a prompt demise.
Pathetic here, and bound to rouse profound   1230
compassion, was this· when anyone observed
himself infected, as though condemned to die,
he lost his courage and, full of grief, lay down
to wait for death: right there, he lost his life.
You see, the infection never flagged: contagious,   1235
greedy, it passed from one man to another,
as if twixt wool-clad flocks and cow-horned kind.
And this above all else piled death on death.
Yes, all who shrank from visiting their sick
from too great lust for life and fear of death   1240
were later punished: they died disgraced, forgotten,
with none to help them, victims of neglect.
But those who stayed on hand died by contagion
and of the labors forced on them by conscience ·
and the sufferers' wistful and heart-rending pleas.   1245
This way all truly good men met their death.[9]

*   *   *

one here, one there, all vying to entomb
their own, they came home tear-stained, sick at heart;
thereafter, many took to their beds in grief.
Such were the times, no man could be discovered   1250
untroubled by death or sorrow or disease.
    Further, every shepherd and herdsman now,
likewise the brawny hand, guide of the plow,

9. After this line, an indeterminate number of lines have been lost.

fell sick, and in dark huts their bodies lay
huddled, ragged, diseased, consigned to death.   1255
Over dead babies one might well have seen
the lifeless bodies of parents, and again
on mother and father the child yield up his life.
In no small part the affliction flowed from farm
to city; infected farmers brought it there,   1260
coming in sickly hosts from every quarter.
They filled the squares and houses; packed together,
they died in windrows as the press grew worse.
Many, prostrate by thirst, crawled through the streets
and lay where they fell, close by the water fountains,   1265
dead, cut off from the waters that seemed so sweet.
And everywhere through the public parks and streets
people lay sick and dying; one could see
their tattered, rotting flesh, bandaged with rags,
wasting away, their bodies skin and bones,   1270
already half-buried in pus-filled sores and filth.
And death besides had filled each holy shrine
of the gods with lifeless bodies; the sacred precincts
were everywhere loaded with corpses unremoved
where temple guards had packed the grounds with strangers.   1275
For now, to scruple and fear of god, men paid
small heed; their present agonies prevailed.
Nor was the mode of burial maintained
that people of Athens hereto had always practiced,
for every man was shaken and filled with fear;   1280
each mourned and buried his own as best he could.
Shortage of time and means called forth much horror;
people would lay their kindred atop the pyres
others had put together, and with loud cries
would thrust in the torch; often much blood was shed   1285
as men fought rather than leave their dead unguarded.

A Brief Bibliography

Bailey, Cyril. *Epicurus, the Extant Remains*, etc. Oxford, Clarendon, 1926.

———. *Epicurus and the Greek Atomists*. New York, Russell and Russell, 1964.

———. *Lucretius, De Rerum Natura, Text, Translation, and Commentary*, 3 vols. Oxford, University Press, 1947.

———. *Lucretius, on the Nature of Things* (translation). Oxford, University Press, 1926.

De Witt, N. W. *Epicurus and His Philosophy*. University of Minnesota Press, 1964.

Geer, R. M. *Lucretius* (translation). New York, Bobbs-Merrill, 1965.

Gordon, C. A. *A Bibliography of Lucretius*. London, Hart-Davis, 1962.

Hadzsitts, G. D. *Lucretius and His Influence*. New York, Cooper Square, 1963.

Humphries, R. *Lucretius: The Way Things Are* (translation). Indiana University Press, 1968.

Leonard, W. E. *Lucretius, Of the Nature of Things* (translation). New York, Everyman, 1950.

Minadeo, R. *The Lyre of Science*. Wayne State University Press, 1969.

Santayana, G. *Three Philosophical Poets: Lucretius, Dante, and Goethe*. Garden City, New York, Doubleday, 1953.

Sikes, E. E. *Lucretius, Poet, and Philosopher*. Cambridge, University Press, 1936.

Winspear, A. D. *Lucretius and Scientific Thought*. Montreal, Harvest House, 1963.